I0760121

Byzantine Emperor Constantine V, 'the Dung-named'

Byzantine Emperor Constantine V, 'the Dung-named'

General, Patriarch, Iconoclast, Reformer

Leslie Ivings

Pen & Sword
MILITARY

First published in Great Britain in 2025 by
Pen & Sword Military
An imprint of Pen & Sword Books Limited
Yorkshire – Philadelphia

ISBN 978 1 03611 482 4

A CIP catalogue record for this book is available from the British Library.

Typeset by Mac Style
Printed in the UK by CPI Group (UK) Ltd, Croydon, CR0 4YY.

The Publisher's authorised representative in the EU for product safety is Authorised Rep Compliance Ltd., Ground Floor, 71 Lower Baggot Street, Dublin D02 P593, Ireland.
www.arccompliance.com

For a complete list of Pen & Sword titles please contact

PEN & SWORD BOOKS LIMITED
47 Church Street, Barnsley, South Yorkshire, S70 2AS, England
E-mail: enquiries@pen-and-sword.co.uk
Website: www.pen-and-sword.co.uk
or
PEN AND SWORD BOOKS
1950 Lawrence Road, Havertown, PA 19083, USA
E-mail: uspen-and-sword@casematepublishers.com
Website: www.penandswordbooks.com

Contents

Acknowledgements

This book is dedicated to my parents, for all those long suffering days with me. You remain my guiding force and source of love; nothing would have been possible without you both.

First of all I would like to thank Pen & Sword and my editor Phil Sidnell, who believed in a book proposal enough to give a first time author the chance to write this book. Your guidance and help through this entire process has been of incalculable value.

I would like to thank all the authors and institutions that have been cited and mentioned in this book, without your hard work and inspiration this volume would not have been possible. I hope as a first time author I managed to do you justice.

To Professor Robbie Robinson, for mentoring me in my undergraduate days in Potchefstroom and for all the cups of coffee and tea over the years, and to Professor Martine de Marre, from UNISA, for all the encouraging words and emails over the years.

To Professor Matthew Kramer, Churchill College, Cambridge, Professor Jacob L. Mackey, Occidental College Los Angeles and Professor Tara Welch of the University of Kansas for teaching me how to actually write!

To Professor Steven Hunt, University of Cambridge, and the Journal of Classics Teaching (JCT) for providing me with sound advice and plenty of distractions with many great books to review.

To my dearest love Rachel Marneweck, for pushing me to not give up on this project, you are as always the light of my life. My dear friend, intellectual guide and my first de facto editor, Dr Craig Eisenstein for all the lunches and great conversation, for being a sounding board and a creative force bar none. This book is ultimately your doing!

To my friends Carl Niehaus, Santie Henrey, Nelson and Ritchie Pestana, Nick and Nicola Karageorgiu, Jose and Nicolise Teixera and Mohamed Iqbal Kaloo words cannot accurately describe my thanks to you for the support, love and kindness you showed me during time writing this book. I owe you a huge debt.

To the Classical Association of South Africa (CASA) and the South African Society for Medieval and Renaissance Studies (SASMARS) for the initial inspiration to write this book.

Gratia vobis ago

Dr Leslie Ivings is a former History Teacher and an Alumnus of North West University (Potchefstroom), where he studied History, Law and Politics, and the University of South Africa where he studied Ancient History and Classical Culture. This is his first book.

Foreword

The Byzantine Empire, with its richly woven history, complex political intrigues, and unparalleled contributions to art, theology, and governance, has always captured the imagination of historians and readers alike. This empire, bridging the ancient and medieval worlds, stood as a bastion of Christian civilization while navigating the turbulent waters of internal dissent, external threats, and profound ideological shifts. Few figures embody the challenges and contradictions of Byzantium as compellingly as Emperor Constantine V. Ruling during the tumultuous eighth century, Constantine V was both a soldier and a reformer, a pious man who championed Iconoclasm, and a visionary whose policies left an indelible mark on the empire.

Constantine V's reign was pivotal, spanning decades marked by civil strife, religious controversy, and intense warfare. He pursued a series of reforms that transformed the Byzantine state, reshaping its military, economic, and administrative structures to withstand the fierce challenges of the era. Known as 'the Dung-named' by later Iconophile chroniclers – who sought to malign his legacy by calling him 'Copronymus' (literally, 'the Dung-named') – Constantine V's Iconoclastic policies sparked some of the most intense debates in Byzantine history. These policies aimed to purify the church from what he and his followers saw as idolatrous practices, yet they also led to fractures within Byzantine society and pitted generations of emperors, clergy, and common people against each other in a theological struggle for the soul of Christendom.

The history of Constantine V's reign offers a window into the Byzantine Empire's resilience and adaptability. Constantine's commitment to Iconoclasm, his consolidation of imperial power, his calculated approach to governance, and his unyielding stance against external adversaries helped Byzantium endure and even thrive in an era of geopolitical instability. Moreover, his focus on fiscal reform and rural land management stabilized the economy, laying a foundation that would support the empire long after his death. His military campaigns against both the Umayyad Caliphate and the Bulgars reflected a strategic foresight, strengthening Byzantine defences along critical frontiers and safeguarding its core territories from encroachment.

Yet Constantine's legacy remains as complex as his policies. His efforts to centralize power and impose strict doctrinal uniformity earned him both admirers and detractors. Over centuries, Iconophile chroniclers like Theophanes the Confessor shaped perceptions of his reign, leaving posterity with a polarized view of his achievements and failings. More recent historians, however, have re-evaluated Constantine's contributions, recognizing his role as a statesman who reformed and revitalized the Byzantine Empire during a precarious period. By reassessing Constantine's legacy, this book seeks to provide a balanced perspective, exploring how Constantine's decisions influenced both his contemporaries and generations that followed.

In examining Constantine V's life, policies, and historical significance, this book sheds light on a ruler whose influence can be felt not only in Byzantine history but also in the broader context of medieval Europe. Constantine V's reign underscores the profound impact that one ruler's vision can have on an entire civilization. His story, a tale of resilience, reform, and controversy, reveals both the grandeur and the vulnerabilities of Byzantium.

The following pages offer an in-depth study of Constantine V's life, exploring his administrative genius, military acumen, and theological convictions. Drawing upon both contemporary chronicles and modern interpretations, this book presents a comprehensive view of a man who shaped an empire, divided a society, and left a legacy that historians continue to debate. It is our hope that readers will come to appreciate the depth and complexity of Constantine V's reign and understand why his legacy, though divisive, is integral to the story of Byzantium.

Chronological Tables

List of Patriarchs of Constantinople
St Cyrus (705–711 CE)
John VI (712–715 CE)
St Germanus I (715–730 CE)
Anastasius (730–754 CE)
Constantine II (754–766 CE)
Nicetas I (766–780 CE)

List of Umayyad and Abbasid Caliphs
Al-Walid I (705–715 CE)
Sulayman (715–717 CE)
Umar II (717–720 CE)
Yazid II (720–724 CE)
Hisham (724–743 CE)
Al-Walid II (743–744 CE)
Yazid III (744 CE)
Ibrahim (744 CE)
Marwan II (744–750 CE)
As-Saffah (750–754 CE)
Al-Mansur (754–775 CE)

List of Popes
Constantine (708–715 CE)
St Gregory II (715–731 CE)
St Gregory III (731–741 CE)
St Zachary (741–752 CE)
Stephen II (752–757 CE)
St Paul I (757–767 CE)
Stephen III (768–772 CE)
Hadrian I (772–795 CE)

List of Byzantine Emperors: Time of Crisis – The Isaurian Dynasty

Justinian II (705–711 CE)
Philippicus (711–713 CE)
Anastasius II (713–715 CE)
Theodosius III (715–717 CE)
Leo III 'The Isaurian' (717–741 CE)
Constantine V 'Copronymus' (741–775 CE)
Leo IV 'The Khazar' (775–780 CE)

Timeline of Key Events in the Life and Reign of Constantine V

717–741 CE: Reign of Leo III (Constantine V's father)

717 CE – Leo III becomes Byzantine Emperor. He successfully defends Constantinople against the Second Arab Siege, marking a turning point for the empire's stability.

726 CE – Leo III issues an edict against the veneration of icons, starting the First Iconoclasm and sparking religious controversy across the empire.

730 CE – Leo III intensifies Iconoclastic policies, which will strongly influence his son Constantine V's later reign.

741 CE: Constantine V Ascends to the Throne

18 June 741 CE – Constantine V becomes emperor upon Leo III's death. He inherits a stable but divided empire.

742–743 CE: Civil War with Artabasdos

742 CE – Artabasdos, Constantine's brother-in-law, rebels and declares himself emperor, supported by Iconophile forces. He seizes control of Constantinople.

743 CE – Battle of Amorium. Constantine V defeats Artabasdos and reasserts control over the empire. The rebellion's failure solidifies Constantine's power and his commitment to Iconoclasm.

754 CE: Council of Hieria and Intensified Iconoclasm

754 CE – Constantine V convenes the Council of Hieria, which formally condemns the veneration of icons. This council marks the peak of Iconoclastic policy in Byzantium and reinforces Constantine's authority over the church.

756–775 CE: Military Campaigns and Border Conflicts

756–775 CE – Constantine V leads a series of campaigns against external threats, particularly focusing on:

1. The Bulgars: Constantine leads repeated invasions to protect the northern border. Key battles include the Battle of Marcellae (756 CE) and Battle of Anchialus (763 CE), both of which are bloody but strategically inconclusive.

2. The Umayyad Caliphate: The eastern border sees constant pressure. Constantine fortifies the border and strengthens the empire's eastern defence.

747 CE: Battle of Akroinon

747 CE – Byzantine forces, led by Constantine's generals, decisively defeat the Umayyads at the Battle of Akroinon. This victory temporarily halts Arab incursions and secures Anatolia.

766 CE: Iconophile Persecution Intensifies

766 CE – Constantine V intensifies his persecution of Iconophiles. Many clergy, monks, and nobility are arrested or executed. This year marks one of the most severe phases of Iconoclastic enforcement.

775 CE: Constantine V's Death and Succession

14 September 775 CE – Constantine V dies while on campaign against the Bulgars. His son Leo IV, known as 'Leo the Khazar', succeeds him, initially maintaining Iconoclastic policies.

Posthumous Events and Legacy of Constantine V's Reign

780 CE: Empress Irene and the Rise of Iconophile Influence

780 CE – Constantine V's son, Leo IV, dies, leaving his young son, Constantine VI, as emperor. Irene, Constantine V's daughter-in-law, becomes regent. Although initially an Iconoclast, Irene gradually supports the Iconophile faction.

787 CE: Second Council of Nicaea

787 CE – Under Empress Irene's influence, the Second Council of Nicaea reverses Iconoclasm, restoring the veneration of icons and denouncing Constantine V's policies. This marks the end of the First Iconoclasm.

814–842 CE: The Second Iconoclasm

814–842 CE – Iconoclasm resurges under Emperor Leo V, with Constantine V's legacy partly inspiring this renewal. The Second Iconoclasm officially ends in 843 CE, when the veneration of icons is definitively restored.

Family Tree of Constantine V (718–775 CE)

Emperor Leo III ('the Isaurian') (c. 685–741)
Constantine V's father and predecessor as emperor. Leo III was known for founding the Isaurian Dynasty and initiating the First Iconoclasm in the Byzantine Empire.

Empress Maria of Amnia
Constantine V's mother and wife of Leo III. Little is known about her background, but she was likely a supporter of her husband's policies.

Constantine V ('Copronymus') (718–775, ruled 741–775)

Marriages and Children

First Wife: Tzitzak (later known as Irene)
Daughter of a Khazar Khagan. This marriage was a political alliance that symbolized an alliance between the Byzantine Empire and the Khazars.

Son: Leo IV ('the Khazar') (750–780)
Heir to the throne, known for his relatively moderate stance on Iconoclasm compared to his father.

Leo IV married Irene of Athens, who would later become empress and end the period of Iconoclasm.

Grandson: Constantine VI (771–797)
Became emperor in 780 under his mother Irene's regency. Known for his struggles with his mother's influence and eventual blinding and deposition.

Second Wife: Maria
There are few details about Maria, and it is unclear if they had any surviving children.

Third Wife: Eudokia
They had six children together, though details about each are limited. Known children include:

Christopher (likely a co-emperor or appointed successor, but predeceased his father)
Nikephoros
Niketas
Three unnamed daughters

Succession and Key Descendants

Leo IV (son with Tzitzak/Irene)
Irene of Athens (wife of Leo IV and later empress regent)
Constantine VI (son, co-ruler, later sole emperor)

The Children of Eudokia (half-siblings of Leo IV)
Nikephoros and Niketas, who held lesser titles but were part of the imperial court during Constantine V's reign.

Prologue

The Rise of Constantine V

The first section of the expanded prologue introduces the complex historical and familial context that shaped Constantine V's rise to power. We explore the external and internal threats facing the empire, the political climate of the imperial court, and the Iconoclastic crisis. This background sets the stage for understanding Constantine V's character, the challenges he faced, and the decisive role he played in the future of the Byzantine Empire.

Thematic Overview

This book provides a comprehensive and in-depth examination of Emperor Constantine V, a key but often controversial figure in Byzantine history, focusing on his reign, policies, and lasting legacy. The thematic structure of the work is designed to highlight the various aspects of Constantine V's rule, shedding light on his achievements, the challenges he faced, and his complex reputation in the centuries following his reign. By weaving together political, military, religious, and cultural threads, the book aims to present a nuanced view of Constantine V, moving beyond traditional demonization to evaluate his broader influence on the Byzantine Empire and medieval history.

1. Political and Military Reforms

A central theme of this work is the exploration of Constantine V's political and military strategies, which redefined the structure of the Byzantine Empire during the eighth century. Constantine's reign was marked by significant military and administrative reforms that aimed to strengthen the empire's defences and centralize imperial power. His successful military campaigns against the Arabs, including his pivotal victories at the Battle of Akroinon, cemented his status as a defender of Christendom and solidified Byzantine control over critical border regions.

The book examines Constantine's reorganization of the Byzantine military, focusing on the establishment of the theme system, which became a cornerstone of Byzantine military strategy and governance for centuries. By placing a greater emphasis on the military role of local leaders ('*strategoi*'), Constantine V not only bolstered military readiness but also contributed to a shift in the power dynamics between the central imperial authority and provincial elites. This theme of military centralization and the consequences it had on the Byzantine state is a recurring thread throughout the book.

2. The Iconoclast Controversy

The Iconoclast controversy, which looms large over Constantine V's reign, is another central theme of this work. Constantine's aggressive stance against the veneration of icons sparked fierce opposition, particularly from the church and religious factions within the empire. While many modern scholars have viewed this conflict through a religious lens, this book also examines the political and socio-economic dimensions of Iconoclasm.

Constantine V's Iconoclasm was not only a theological dispute but also a strategy aimed at consolidating imperial control over the church. By challenging the authority of the clergy and reducing the economic power of monasteries, Constantine sought to weaken ecclesiastical influence in the Byzantine state. The book explores how this policy reshaped the relationship between the emperor and the church, presenting Constantine V's Iconoclasm as part of a broader effort to establish the emperor as the ultimate authority in both political and religious matters.

The enduring impact of Constantine's policies on later periods, particularly the Second Iconoclasm and the eventual resolution of the issue in the ninth century, is a major theme. The tension between imperial authority and religious orthodoxy that Constantine instigated is shown to resonate throughout Byzantine history, influencing subsequent rulers and shaping Byzantine religious practice for generations.

3. Legacy and Reputation

The theme of Constantine V's legacy and reputation is a crucial aspect of the book. Historians have long viewed Constantine V in a polarized light, with many sources depicting him as a tyrant, a heretic, and a destroyer of the Byzantine religious tradition. The derogatory nickname 'Copronymus' (meaning 'Dung-named'), bestowed upon Constantine V by later Iconophile historians, reflects the vilification he faced in the post-Iconoclast era.

However, the book seeks to challenge this negative portrayal by examining Constantine's policies and their long-term impact on the Byzantine Empire. Through a detailed analysis of his military, political, and economic reforms, as well as his role in shaping the empire's governance, the book argues that Constantine V should be considered a transformative figure who contributed significantly to the strength and stability of the Byzantine Empire.

The book also highlights the shift in modern scholarly perspectives on Constantine V. By re-evaluating his reign through a more nuanced lens, the work aligns with contemporary historical reassessments that seek to understand the emperor's policies as part of the broader context of Byzantine governance. This theme of reinterpreting Constantine's legacy in light of new scholarship offers a fresh perspective on his place in Byzantine and world history.

4. Social and Economic Impact

Another key theme in this work is the exploration of the social and economic impact of Constantine V's policies, particularly on the peasantry and the nobility. By centralizing the administration and implementing new systems of taxation and land distribution, Constantine sought to bolster the empire's financial stability and military capabilities. His establishment of the theme system, which integrated military service with landholding, created a new class of peasant-soldiers who played a crucial role in defending the empire's borders.

The book examines how these reforms affected different social classes within the empire, particularly the peasants who were tasked with providing the empire's military manpower. While these changes provided greater stability for the empire, they also placed burdens on the lower classes, contributing to social tensions and unrest. In contrast, the aristocracy, which saw its influence curtailed by Constantine's policies, responded with resistance to his reforms. These tensions between the emperor and the elite are explored as part of the broader socio-political landscape of the Byzantine Empire during Constantine V's reign.

5. The Cultural and Religious Dichotomy

A final major theme in the book is the cultural and religious dichotomy that defined Constantine V's reign. While the emperor sought to unite the empire under his vision of a strong, centralized state, his policies often clashed with the deeply ingrained religious traditions of the Byzantine people. The Iconoclast controversy, in particular, exposed the tension between the emperor's desire for control and the church's insistence on religious freedom and autonomy.

The book delves into how these cultural and religious divides played out on both a theological and political level, offering a detailed analysis of the intellectual and cultural consequences of Constantine's policies. The impact of his reign on Byzantine art, church-state relations, and religious practice is explored, particularly in relation to the Iconoclastic movement and the eventual resolution of the controversy.

6. Influence on Successor Emperors

Constantine V's influence on subsequent Byzantine rulers is another recurring theme. His son, Leo IV, and other successors were forced to navigate the legacy of Constantine's Iconoclastic policies, with some continuing his reforms and others seeking to reverse them. The tensions between Iconoclasm and Iconophilism, as well as the broader political, military, and social reforms initiated by Constantine, shaped the governance of the empire for generations to come.

The book traces how the succession of Constantine V's policies, particularly his military and administrative reforms, laid the groundwork for later developments in Byzantine governance, especially during the ninth and tenth centuries.

Conclusion: A Reassessment of Constantine V's Role in History

In conclusion, this book offers a comprehensive and multifaceted view of Constantine V, re-evaluating his reign within the broader context of Byzantine history and world history. By exploring his military, political, and religious policies, as well as his lasting influence on the Byzantine Empire, the work challenges traditional portrayals of Constantine V and presents him as a ruler whose actions had far-reaching effects on the empire's structure and legacy.

Ultimately, the book invites readers to reconsider the complexities of Constantine V's reign, recognizing both the successes and the controversies that marked his rule. Through a balanced and nuanced analysis, it highlights Constantine V's place among the Byzantine emperors and in the broader historical narrative, ensuring that his legacy is understood not only in terms of Iconoclasm but also through his contributions to the empire's military strength, political consolidation, and governance.

Research Approach of the Book on Constantine V

This book on Emperor Constantine V takes a meticulous, multi-faceted approach to analyzing his reign and its long-term implications for the Byzantine Empire. Given the complexity of Constantine V's rule, which was marked by significant military and administrative reforms, as well as his contentious Iconoclastic policies, the research methodology has been designed to be thorough and interdisciplinary. By combining a close reading of primary sources, a critical engagement with secondary literature, and an exploration of broader themes in Byzantine history, the book provides a comprehensive analysis of Constantine V, his policies, and his legacy. The methodology reflects a careful balance between traditional historical analysis and more recent approaches to understanding the Byzantine past, which includes examining the social, cultural, and intellectual contexts of the period.

1. Primary Sources: Direct Evidence from the Eighth Century

The foundation of the research in this book rests on a careful examination of primary sources, many of which come from contemporary or near-contemporary historians, chroniclers, and religious figures who lived during or shortly after Constantine V's reign. These sources form the backbone of the narrative, offering invaluable insights into the political, military, and religious developments of the eighth century.

Theophanes the Confessor's *Chronographia*: One of the central primary sources for the reign of Constantine V, *Chronographia* is a comprehensive chronicle written by Theophanes, a monk who lived during the eighth and early ninth centuries. As an ardent supporter of the Iconophile (pro-icon) movement, Theophanes presents a biased view of Constantine V, often portraying him negatively due to his support of Iconoclasm. Despite this bias, *Chronographia* is an indispensable source for understanding the religious and political conflicts of the period, as well as the broader context of Byzantine society under Constantine V. The book examines Theophanes' portrayal of Constantine, acknowledging his bias while also critically engaging with the content to explore the Iconoclastic controversies, the emperor's military campaigns, and the broader cultural context of the era.

The *Paschal Chronicle*: This anonymous work is another critical source for reconstructing the reign of Constantine V. Written from a somewhat more neutral standpoint compared to Theophanes, the *Paschal Chronicle* chronicles key events in the history of the Byzantine Empire, including Constantine's reign. Its account of military conflicts, administrative reforms, and religious developments offers a different perspective on Constantine V's actions. The book places significant emphasis on comparing the *Paschal Chronicle* to other sources to assess the accuracy and nuance of its portrayal of Constantine, as well as to cross-reference military events and political decisions.

Acts of the Ecumenical Councils: One of the most significant religious events during Constantine V's reign was the Second Council of Nicaea in 787 CE, which reversed the policies of Iconoclasm. The Acts of the council offer direct insight into the religious tensions of the time, particularly the theological debates surrounding the veneration of icons and the role of the emperor in religious matters. The book explores the political and ecclesiastical impact of Constantine V's Iconoclasm by examining these Acts and considering the larger theological debates within the empire.

Letters, Imperial Decrees, and Legal Texts: In addition to chronicles and religious writings, the research draws on various imperial decrees and legal texts issued by Constantine V. These sources reveal the emperor's administrative practices, his military strategies, and the implementation of his policies, particularly regarding the military, the economy, and religious practices. The analysis of Constantine V's laws provides a window into the internal workings of the Byzantine Empire and offers crucial insights into his governance and efforts to consolidate imperial power.

2. Secondary Literature: The Broader Scholarly Context

Secondary literature plays an essential role in contextualizing and interpreting primary sources. Modern scholarship on the Byzantine Empire offers a wealth of material that enables a deeper understanding of the political, military, religious, and social dynamics of Constantine V's reign. The book draws heavily from both traditional Byzantine historiography and recent scholarship to create a balanced and nuanced view of his rule. By engaging with key works from historians, theologians, and scholars of Byzantine art, this book situates Constantine V's reign within the broader development of the empire during the early medieval period.

John Haldon's *The Byzantine Wars* (2002): Haldon's work is essential for understanding the military strategies of the Byzantine Empire during the eighth century. It offers in-depth analyses of Constantine V's military reforms, including his role in defending the empire from Arab invasions and his reorganization of the Byzantine army. The research draws on Haldon's interpretation of Byzantine warfare and military culture, particularly the strategic innovations introduced under Constantine V, which had lasting effects on the empire's military organization.

Warren Treadgold's *A History of the Byzantine State and Society* (1997): Treadgold's comprehensive work on Byzantine political and administrative history is crucial for understanding the political environment in which Constantine V ruled. The book examines the centralization of power under Constantine V, his military reforms, and the structure of Byzantine governance. Treadgold's analyses provide the necessary framework for understanding the emperor's relationship with the aristocracy, the church, and the peasantry, as well as the long-term effects of his reforms on Byzantine statecraft.

Judith Herrin's *Byzantium: The Surprising Life of a Medieval Empire* (2007): Herrin's work provides valuable context for understanding the cultural and religious environment of Constantine V's reign. Her book offers an accessible yet scholarly overview of Byzantine history and highlights the complexity of the relationship between church and state during the eighth century. The research engages with Herrin's work to explore how Constantine V's Iconoclastic policies influenced the cultural identity of the Byzantine Empire and shaped the political climate of the period.

Timothy E. Gregory's *A History of Byzantium* (2005): Gregory's authoritative text offers a broader historical perspective on the development of the Byzantine Empire, making it an important source for understanding the historical significance of Constantine V's reign. The book offers a chronological overview of the empire's political and cultural evolution, placing Constantine V's reign in the context of broader Byzantine history.

Additionally, the book draws on journal articles, edited volumes, and monographs from specialists in specific areas of Byzantine studies, such as religious history, art history, and economic history. This broad base of secondary literature provides the context needed to interpret Constantine V's actions and to evaluate their consequences for the empire.

3. Interdisciplinary Approach: Integrating Art History, Theology, and Social Theory

A distinctive feature of this book's research methodology is its interdisciplinary approach, which draws upon art history, theology, and social theory. These fields provide essential insights into the cultural, religious, and social aspects of Constantine V's reign, which cannot be fully understood through political or military analysis alone.

Art History and Iconography: The Iconoclastic movement led by Constantine V was not only a theological controversy but also a cultural and artistic one. The book incorporates insights from art historians such as Robin Cormack and Leslie Brubaker, who have explored how Byzantine Iconoclasm influenced the production and dissemination of religious art. By analyzing changes in iconography and artistic traditions during Constantine V's reign, the research explores how his policies affected the visual culture of the empire, with a focus on the shifting roles of religious images, monasteries, and the church in shaping Byzantine artistic heritage.

Theology and Religious Debate: The book extensively examines the theological debates that were central to the Iconoclast controversy. Works by John Meyendorff and A.H.M. Jones on Christian Iconoclasm provide insight into the broader theological arguments surrounding the veneration of icons and the role of the emperor in defining religious practice. This analysis helps place Constantine's Iconoclastic policies in a broader theological context, illustrating the complex interaction between imperial authority and ecclesiastical power.

Social Theory and Political Economy: The research applies social theories on governance, state-society relations, and the role of elites to understand the social and political dynamics of Constantine V's reign. Drawing on ideas from scholars such as Peter Brown and Michael McCormick, who have examined the political economy of the Byzantine Empire, the research explores how Constantine V's policies affected the peasantry, the nobility, and the church. His efforts to centralize power and reduce the influence of local elites are analyzed through the lens of social theory, providing a richer understanding of the emperor's place in Byzantine society.

4. Critical Reassessment: Re-evaluating Constantine V's Legacy

One of the primary goals of this research is to reassess Constantine V's legacy in a more balanced and nuanced way. Historically, Constantine has been vilified, especially by later Iconophile sources that portrayed him as a ruthless, despotic ruler. The book challenges this traditional view by critically engaging with both pro- and anti-Constantine sources, seeking to uncover the complexities of his reign and the motivations behind his policies.

By placing Constantine V's actions within the broader context of Byzantine history and considering his strategic decisions from a military, political, and economic perspective, the book presents a more sympathetic interpretation of his reign. It acknowledges his authoritarian tendencies and the controversies he instigated, but it also emphasizes his achievements in military defence, administrative reforms, and efforts to strengthen imperial power. This reassessment is informed by recent scholarly debates about Byzantine Iconoclasm and governance, which have sought to view Constantine V's actions as part of a broader imperial strategy rather than as isolated or driven solely by religious ideology.

Conclusion: A Multifaceted and Holistic Approach

In conclusion, the research approach of this book combines careful analysis of primary sources, engagement with secondary scholarship, and an interdisciplinary methodology to provide a comprehensive and nuanced understanding of Constantine V's reign. This book's aim is not only to re-evaluate his controversial legacy but also to contribute to the broader historiographical conversation on Byzantine history and governance. Through a balanced exploration of his military, political, religious, and cultural policies, the research offers new insights into Constantine V's role in shaping the course of Byzantine history and provides a fresh perspective on the Byzantine Empire's evolution during the eighth century.

The Byzantine Empire at a Crossroads

By the middle of the eighth century, the Byzantine Empire stood at a precipice. What had once been a thriving and expansive civilization was now a mere shadow of its former self. The Byzantine Empire, which had outlasted the fall of the Western Roman Empire in 476, was struggling with both external and internal pressures that threatened its stability.

External Threats: The Arab Conquests and the Rise of Islam

The most immediate and existential threat facing the Byzantine Empire in the eighth century came from the Arab Caliphates, which had emerged in the wake of the Prophet Muhammad's death in 632. The Islamic expansion had spread rapidly across the Middle East, North Africa, and the Iberian Peninsula, and by the time Constantine V was born in 718, the Arab forces were marching toward the Byzantine heartlands.

The Arab siege of Constantinople in 717–718 was a pivotal moment. The city's impregnable walls, reinforced by the Byzantine navy, managed to repel the Muslim forces, marking a significant military victory for the empire. Yet, while the siege had been repelled, the empire was far from secure. The eastern provinces of the empire – particularly Syria, Palestine, and Egypt – had already been lost to the Caliphate. The Byzantine Empire, now hemmed in by Arab forces to the east and south, faced a chronic state of warfare and defence that would dominate its political and military landscape for the foreseeable future.

By the time Constantine V ascended to the throne, the threat of a second siege of Constantinople loomed large. The Arab forces were regrouping and constantly probing the empire's borders. The Byzantines, weakened by years of warfare and internal division, needed a strong, unified leader capable of stemming the tide of the Islamic advance.

The Bulgar Threat to the North

While the Arab forces represented the most direct threat to the Byzantine Empire's survival, the Bulgars to the north were an ever-present danger. In the late-seventh and early-eighth centuries, the Bulgars had consolidated their power in the Balkans, establishing a formidable empire that threatened Byzantine territories in the region.

Though the Bulgars were sometimes allies and sometimes adversaries, their raids and invasions were a constant strain on the empire's resources. By the 730s, the Bulgars were regularly attacking Byzantine provinces in Thrace and along the empire's northern frontier. Constantine V would need to contend with both the Arab and Bulgar threats simultaneously, a challenge that would demand not only military acumen but also strategic diplomacy.

The Fragility of Imperial Power

Internally, the Byzantine Empire was plagued by political instability. The imperial throne, which had once been the symbol of Roman authority, was often the target of intrigue, betrayal, and assassination. Emperors could rise to power through military prowess, but their reigns were rarely secure. Family members, military commanders, and court officials all vied for control of the imperial palace and the empire's resources.

Leo III: Father of the Iconoclast Movement

Constantine V's path to the throne was deeply shaped by the legacy of his father, Leo III, the Isaurian emperor who reigned from 717 to 741. Leo III's policies were transformative, and his Iconoclastic reforms would become the defining issue of Constantine V's reign. To understand Constantine's early life and motivations, it is essential to first understand the broader historical context in which his father operated.

The Iconoclastic Crisis

One of Leo III's most controversial and lasting policies was his stance on religious icons. In 726, Leo issued a decree prohibiting the veneration of religious icons, including images of Christ, the Virgin Mary, and the saints. Leo's reasons for this policy were partly theological and partly political. He believed that the veneration of icons was a form of idolatry, a direct violation of the biblical commandment forbidding the worship of graven images. In addition, Leo saw the veneration of icons as a source of division within the Church and as a potential challenge to imperial authority.

Leo's Iconoclastic edict was not only an attack on religious practices but also a bold assertion of imperial control over religious matters. In the early centuries of Christianity, the Church had grown increasingly powerful, sometimes rivalling the emperor for authority in the Christian world. By targeting the Iconophile movement, Leo sought to weaken the power of the Church and assert imperial supremacy. In the eyes of the emperor, the Church should be subjugated to the will of the state, not the other way around.

However, Leo's Iconoclastic reforms sparked fierce resistance from large segments of the Byzantine population, particularly from the monastic communities and from bishops who relied on the veneration of icons to bolster their authority and influence. The ecclesiastical response to the emperor's decree was violent. Riots erupted in Constantinople, and many church leaders were exiled or imprisoned for defying imperial orders. The religious schism that resulted from the Iconoclastic movement would divide the Byzantine world for centuries.

The Political and Religious Challenges of Leo's Reign

Leo's Iconoclastic policies were not simply a matter of religious reform but also a reflection of the empire's precarious political situation. Leo had come to the throne during a time of crisis. The empire was reeling from the loss of territories to the Arabs and from internal factionalism. Leo needed to consolidate his power, and he saw the Iconoclast movement as a means of asserting imperial control.

Leo's reign was marked by a series of military victories that bolstered his reputation as a strong and capable ruler. His defence of Constantinople against the Arab siege in 717–718 earned him the title of 'the Saviour of the City'. He also led successful campaigns in the east, stabilizing Byzantine territories in Asia Minor. However, his religious reforms alienated many within the empire, particularly the Church and the aristocracy, and these divisions would have profound consequences for his family and his son, Constantine V.

Constantine V: Childhood and Family Dynamics

Constantine V was born in 718, the son of Leo III and his wife, Maria. He grew up in the shadow of his father's military campaigns and religious reforms. The Isaurian Dynasty, which Leo III had founded, was not universally popular, and the family's rise to power was marked by both military strength and political intrigue.

Constantine V's Military Acumen and the Defence of the Empire

With the throne secured, Constantine V had to deal with the multitude of threats facing the empire. The most immediate of these was the ongoing conflict with the Arab Caliphate.

The Battle for the East: Repelling the Arabs

Constantine V's military prowess was soon put to the test. In 746, he launched a campaign to drive the Arabs out of Byzantine-held territories in Syria. His forces were successful in pushing the Arabs back, securing the eastern borders of the empire for the time being. Constantine V's military success in the east was crucial for the survival of the empire, and it solidified his position as a capable and respected leader.

Internal Rebellions and the Iconoclast Struggle

While Constantine V dealt with external threats, he also had to manage the deepening divisions within the empire over his father's Iconoclastic policies. The Church, led by the Patriarch of Constantinople, was deeply resistant to Constantine's edicts. Constantine's efforts to suppress the veneration of icons led to widespread unrest, and many of the empire's most influential religious leaders were exiled or executed.

This struggle between the emperor and the Church would dominate Constantine V's reign. It was a battle for the soul of the empire, one that pitted imperial authority against the religious convictions of a deeply pious population.

The Iconoclastic Crisis and Its Legacy

The religious upheaval that would come to define Constantine V's reign was set in motion by his father, Leo III, but it was Constantine V who would be remembered for taking these policies to their most extreme. The Iconoclastic controversy, though rooted in theological convictions, was also a political struggle that transcended religious lines. It became a battle for control of the empire, its institutions, and its culture.

Leo III's Initial Edict and the Political Context

When Leo III issued his first decree banning the veneration of religious icons in 726, it was clear that this was not merely a theological stand but also a strategic decision. Leo saw the growing power of the Church and its vast wealth as a challenge to imperial authority. The popes, bishops, and monastic communities had become increasingly influential over the years, often exerting more power than the emperor, especially in the religious matters of the state. By targeting the Iconophiles, Leo hoped to restore the emperor's dominance over the Church. His decree was a direct challenge to the clergy, with significant consequences for the relationship between the imperial court and the Church.

Leo's policy alienated much of the population, particularly the rural peasantry, who revered the icons, seeing them as divine protectors and mediators of salvation. To many, the destruction of these sacred objects was not just a doctrinal issue – it was an attack on their faith itself. In urban centres like Constantinople, the resistance was more political, as factions aligned with monasticism and icon veneration clashed with supporters of the emperor.

This initial clash between state and Church foreshadowed the deepening divide that would unfold under Constantine V. While his father's reforms had been controversial, Leo III had not gone as far as to engage in the wholesale destruction of icons. Constantine V, on the other hand, would take a more ruthless approach to the Iconoclastic movement.

Constantine V's Iconoclastic Zeal

Upon his ascension to the throne in 743, Constantine V inherited a Byzantine Empire deeply divided over the issue of Iconoclasm. While Leo III had introduced the reforms, Constantine would take them to extremes. Constantine V was determined to carry out his father's vision and put an end to the widespread veneration of icons once and for all.

Constantine's enforcement of Iconoclasm was brutal. He exiled or executed bishops and abbots who resisted his policies. He seized and destroyed countless religious images, and monasteries that were caught continuing the veneration of icons were purged. By the late-740s, monasticism itself, which had once been a major force in Byzantine religious life, was severely weakened under Constantine's rule. Monks who had once enjoyed autonomy were now under constant threat of exile or execution.

The most significant aspect of Constantine's Iconoclastic policies was not just his crackdown on religious dissent but his vision of a centralized, imperial Church that was under the direct control of the emperor. In Constantine V's view, the emperor was not only the secular ruler of the empire but also the ultimate arbiter of religious matters. His policies sought to eliminate the political power of the Church, weakening its influence over the lives of Byzantines and increasing the emperor's control over both state and religion.

The religious factions within the empire were not idle during these years. Iconophile resistance did not disappear – on the contrary, the resistance became more organized. The Church, particularly the papacy, would oppose Constantine's policies, leading to deep divisions that would affect not just the eastern empire, but also its relationship with Rome. The Western Church, though often at odds with the Byzantine emperors, was united in its defence of icons, and this ideological divide would lead to the formal rupture between East and West in later centuries.

The Iconoclasts and the Monastic Communities

The rise of monasticism in the Byzantine Empire was one of the most powerful forces in Byzantine society and culture. Monasteries were centres not only of religious life but also of scholarship, education, and wealth. The monastic communities were often deeply conservative and traditional in their religious practices, and the veneration of icons was at the heart of their liturgy.

Constantine's war against the monasteries was a direct attack on this powerful institution. By removing the icons and dismantling the religious image-cult that had been central to monastic spirituality, he challenged the very identity of the monastic movement. The persecution of monks and the destruction of their monasteries were among the most controversial aspects of his reign. These measures were, in part, an attempt to control the masses – religious life was deeply entwined with social life in the Byzantine world, and Constantine V understood that to control the Church was to control the people.

For many, the persecution of monks was a cultural tragedy. The monasteries had been key to preserving the intellectual and religious heritage of the Roman world, and their destruction represented the erosion of a centuries-old tradition. Yet for Constantine V, the battle against monasticism and icon veneration was a battle for the soul of the empire itself. It was, in his eyes, an imperial victory over religious power, ensuring that the emperor alone held authority over all matters, spiritual and secular.

The Military Campaigns of Constantine V: Consolidating Power

While religious disputes dominated much of Constantine's reign, his military campaigns were equally critical to his rise to power and his ability to maintain control of the empire.

The Defence of the Eastern Frontier

Constantine V's most pressing concern upon ascending to the throne was the threat of the Arab Caliphate. The Arabs had already made significant inroads into Byzantine territory, capturing Syria, Palestine, and Egypt. By the 740s, the Umayyad Caliphate, though in decline, was still a powerful force that posed a serious threat to the Byzantine heartland.

Constantine's father, Leo III, had famously repelled the Arab siege of Constantinople in 717–718, but that victory did not put an end to the Arab threat. By the time Constantine V took the throne, the empire was still in a state of near-constant warfare. The Arabs, under various caliphs, had been making incursions into Asia Minor and the southern Balkans, and Constantine V would need to strengthen the empire's defences.

Constantine's response was swift and decisive. He launched a series of military campaigns against the Arabs in the east, with a particular focus on securing the borders of Anatolia, where Byzantine forces were vulnerable to Arab raids. In 746, Constantine V led a major offensive against the Umayyads, pushing their forces back and securing the Byzantine frontier for the time being. His victories were critical in maintaining the empire's territorial integrity.

By the end of the 740s, Constantine V had not only repelled the Arabs but had also launched retaliatory campaigns into Arab-held territory, securing several victories. The defence of Asia Minor and the reconquest of key border fortresses were critical in ensuring the survival of the Byzantine Empire, solidifying Constantine's reputation as a military leader capable of defending the empire from external threats.

The Bulgar Threat and the Battle for the Balkans

While Constantine V faced threats in the east, he was also forced to contend with the growing power of the Bulgars in the Balkans. The Bulgars, led by Khan Tervel, had been a constant thorn in the side of the Byzantine Empire since the early seventh century. They had at times allied with the Byzantines, but at other times, they had raided Byzantine territory and threatened the empire's northern frontier.

In the 740s, the Bulgars had become increasingly aggressive, raiding Byzantine provinces and attacking the empire's vulnerable borders. Constantine V, determined not to allow the Bulgars to encroach on Byzantine territory, launched several successful campaigns into the Balkans. His military strategy relied on both offensive and defensive measures, securing key fortresses and cutting off Bulgar supply lines. By 756, Constantine V had secured a major victory over the Bulgars, forcing their khan to accept Byzantine terms and retreat from the empire's borders.

These military victories, both in the east against the Arabs and in the north against the Bulgars, were crucial to Constantine's consolidation of power. His military successes allowed him to strengthen his authority within the empire and ensure that his reign would not be undermined by external threats.

The Lasting Legacy of Constantine V

Constantine V's reign, though marked by controversy, was one of significant transformation for the Byzantine Empire. His policies shaped the empire's future trajectory, especially in relation to its military and religious institutions.

The Long-Term Effects of Iconoclasm

Though Constantine V's aggressive stance on Iconoclasm left a bitter legacy, it also had long-term effects on the structure of the Byzantine state. By centralizing control over the Church and asserting imperial dominance over religious matters, Constantine V set a precedent for the future relationship between the emperor and the Church. His Iconoclastic policies would continue to affect the empire long after his death, with the issue remaining unresolved until the end of the eighth century.

A Stronger, Militarily-Competent Empire

Through his military reforms and successful campaigns, Constantine V ensured that the Byzantine Empire was capable of defending itself from external threats. His leadership in repelling the Arabs and Bulgars was a testament to his ability as a military commander and his determination to safeguard the empire's territorial integrity.

The Inheritance of a Divided Empire

While Constantine V succeeded in consolidating power and defending the empire, he left behind a legacy of division. The Church was deeply divided over Iconoclasm, and this schism would eventually contribute to the rift between the Eastern and Western Churches. Additionally, his persecution of monasticism and religious dissent created long-standing tensions within the Byzantine population, tensions that would outlast his reign.

In the end, Constantine V's reign was one of both triumph and tragedy. He left the empire stronger militarily but deeply divided religiously, and his policies would reverberate throughout Byzantine history for centuries to come.

This prologue has outlined the major factors that shaped Constantine V's early life, his rise to power, and the legacy of his reign. By delving into the political, military, and religious struggles that marked his rise, we see the complexities of his rule – his determination to centralize imperial power, the controversy of his Iconoclastic policies, and the military prowess that ensured the empire's survival in a time of grave threats.

Chapter 1

The Byzantine Empire

Section 1: The Byzantine Empire in the Eighth Century

The Byzantine Empire that Constantine V inherited was a shadow of its former glory but remained a formidable and complex civilization. Its territories, once sprawling across the Mediterranean, had shrunk considerably due to relentless external invasions and internal discord. By the early eighth century, the empire was faced with not only existential threats from its neighbours but also significant challenges from within, as ideological, economic, and political struggles pulled at the fabric of the state. To understand Constantine V's life and rule, it is essential to examine the empire's precarious situation and the reforms undertaken by his predecessors to restore its strength.

The History of the Byzantine Empire: 711 to 717 CE – The Emperors and Their Challenges

The Byzantine Empire, after enduring a series of profound transformations throughout the seventh century, entered the eighth century in a state of flux. The Umayyad Caliphate's rise as a major power in the eastern Mediterranean, combined with internal political instability, posed serious challenges for the empire. Between 711 and 717 CE, the empire saw a sequence of emperors who grappled with both external threats and internal factions. The period began with a fragile military and political structure, weakened by the loss of key provinces like Syria, Egypt, and North Africa, and it culminated in the Siege of Constantinople (717–718 CE), one of the most critical events in Byzantine history.

The emperors who ruled during these years were tasked with not only defending the empire's remaining territories but also dealing with significant political strife, religious conflict, and the tensions of an empire on the brink of collapse. The reigns of Anastasius II, Philippicus, Theodosius III, and Leo III the Isaurian would provide a fascinating, complex narrative of struggle, military manoeuvring, and strategic decision-making, ultimately leading to a pivotal moment in Byzantine history.

Emperor Anastasius II (711–713 CE): Weak Leadership in Troubling Times

The Assassination of Philippicus Bardanes: A Turning Point in Byzantine Politics

The assassination of Philippicus Bardanes in 713 CE stands as one of the most dramatic and consequential events in the early eighth century Byzantine Empire. Philippicus was emperor for a mere two years, from 711 to 713, but his reign, marked by significant internal strife and external threats, ended in a bloody coup. His death was not only a result of his unpopular policies and ineffective rule but also a symbol of the broader political instability that plagued the empire during this period.

Background to Philippicus' Ascension

Philippicus Bardanes, before his rise to power, was a military leader with experience in the Byzantine army. His ascent to the throne in 711 CE came after the assassination of Emperor Anastasius II, who was overthrown by a coup led by the Byzantine military elite, disillusioned with his failure to respond effectively to both external and internal threats.

Philippicus, a military officer and a Patrician by birth, was selected as the emperor by the factions within the Byzantine army who were dissatisfied with Anastasius' weak rule. Though he was a seasoned military commander, Philippicus' reign was beset with problems from the outset. His policies, especially his Iconoclast leanings, alienated key segments of the Byzantine aristocracy and the Church, which would play a pivotal role in the events leading to his demise.

The Political and Religious Context

One of the most significant issues that Philippicus faced was the Iconoclast controversy, which emerged in full force during his reign. Iconoclasm, or the rejection of religious icons, had been a polarizing issue within the Byzantine Empire. The Iconoclast movement, although formally launched by Emperor Leo III in 726 CE, found its earliest seeds during the reign of Philippicus.

Philippicus' own Iconoclast stance, which supported the removal and destruction of religious images, was not universally accepted. The powerful monastic communities and the clergy were staunch defenders of icon veneration, and Philippicus' policies alienated these important sectors of Byzantine society. While his actions were not as overt or systematic as those of his successor, Leo III, the seeds of religious division were planted during Philippicus' reign.

In addition to his religious policies, Philippicus struggled with several other challenges. The Byzantine military was stretched thin, particularly on the eastern frontier, where the Umayyad Caliphate posed a persistent threat. The Arab invasions of the Byzantine territories in the Eastern Mediterranean had left the empire vulnerable, and Philippicus failed to mount a successful defence. His inability to respond adequately to these military pressures contributed to his unpopularity.

Moreover, Philippicus' reign was marked by administrative disarray, as his failure to unite the Byzantine aristocracy and military commanders alienated many of those who had initially supported his rise to power. His weakness in addressing both religious and military issues set the stage for growing discontent.

The Coup and Assassination

The growing dissatisfaction with Philippicus' rule eventually culminated in a military coup in 713 CE. By this time, the emperor had made several political and military missteps that undermined his authority. One of the key factors was his perceived inability to address the Arab threat, which was rapidly advancing into Byzantine territory, particularly in the east.

The situation was exacerbated by internal divisions within the military, as various factions of the army and the Byzantine elite began to conspire against Philippicus. His failure to secure a decisive victory against the Umayyads, despite his earlier efforts, left the empire's defences in disarray. Philippicus' control over the military was increasingly questioned, and key military leaders began to plot against him.

The coup was led by Anastasius II, a prominent general, who had been one of the chief conspirators in the overthrow of Philippicus. The plotters seized the opportunity during a period of military unrest to strike against the emperor. Philippicus, who had largely been removed from direct military decision-making by this time, was caught off guard by the sudden uprising.

Philippicus was captured, and shortly after being overthrown, he was assassinated. His death occurred in 713 CE, and his body was dumped unceremoniously, symbolizing the complete loss of power and legitimacy. This was not just the fall of an emperor but the collapse of his entire faction and the broader Byzantine political establishment that had supported him.

Aftermath and Political Implications

The assassination of Philippicus was a decisive turning point in the history of the Byzantine Empire. His death marked the end of the short-lived reign of an emperor who had failed to unite the empire in the face of mounting external threats and religious division. His assassination paved the way for the rise of Theodosius III, a more politically neutral figure, who would soon find himself facing many of the same problems that had led to Philippicus' downfall.

The political instability of this period can be traced directly to the division within the empire. The military aristocracy, dissatisfied with the ineffective leadership of Philippicus, turned to Theodosius III as a temporary solution. However, even his reign was marked by weakness and internal factionalism, which would eventually lead to the rise of Leo III the Isaurian, who would go on to play a crucial role in the defence of Constantinople against the Umayyad siege of 717–718 CE.

The Legacy of Philippicus

Philippicus Bardanes' legacy is one of missed opportunity and failure. Despite his military background, which could have made him a strong leader in a period when the Byzantine Empire was facing unprecedented external challenges, he proved unable to handle the internal political strife or deal effectively with the rising tide of Islamic expansion in the east. His reign stands as a symbol of the fragility of Byzantine power during this period and the importance of strong military leadership in an era defined by external invasions and internal power struggles.

Moreover, Philippicus' stance on Iconoclasm, though it did not become fully institutionalized under his rule, foreshadowed the Iconoclastic policies of his successors, especially Leo III. The division he created with the Church and religious institutions would persist long after his death, contributing to one of the most profound religious and political crises in Byzantine history.

In sum, the assassination of Philippicus was not just the fall of one emperor, but a moment that marked the height of Byzantine political instability in the early eighth century. His inability to navigate the complex political and military landscape of the time ultimately led to his violent end and left the empire vulnerable to both internal and external threats. However, his death also paved the way for the rise of stronger emperors, most notably Leo III, who would later steer the empire through one of its most defining moments.

* * *

Anastasius II, the first emperor of this period, was a patrician who was selected to rule in 711 CE following the assassination of Philippicus Bardanes. His reign, lasting only two years, is often viewed as a time of weak leadership during a critical moment in Byzantine history. As a result of internal strife and external pressures, Anastasius II's reign proved to be ineffective in the face of increasing military and political crises.

At the time of his ascension, the Umayyad Caliphate was at its zenith, having recently gained control of vast swathes of land across the Mediterranean, including most of the Byzantine territories in the east. The loss of Syria, Egypt, and North Africa had severely weakened the Byzantine Empire's military capabilities, while the expansion of Islamic rule created an urgent need for defence. Anastasius did not have the charisma or authority to unite the empire in the face of this looming threat.

The empire had a series of border crises during his reign. From 711 to 717, Byzantine forces were pressed by the Umayyad armies, especially along the eastern frontier in Anatolia. While Anastasius did attempt to strengthen the military response by recruiting more soldiers and calling for military campaigns to push back the invaders, his plans faltered due to weak coordination and factionalism within the Byzantine elite.

Anastasius II's reign also witnessed the continuing religious controversy surrounding the Iconoclast movement, as factions within the empire clashed over religious iconography and the use of religious images. Anastasius himself was initially seen as supportive of Iconoclasm (the rejection of religious icons), but he failed to implement effective policy, and his reign became marked by political division, leading to his downfall in 713 CE. Anastasius II was overthrown in a coup led by the military commander Philippicus, who took the throne after Anastasius was exiled, a moment that set the stage for the following turbulent years.

Emperor Philippicus (713–715 CE): Failing Military Leadership and Internal Conflict

The reign of Philippicus marked another brief, tumultuous period for the empire. Coming to power in 713 CE, Philippicus was a military officer and a staunch Iconoclast. His reign, like that of Anastasius, was dominated by significant political instability and external threats. Philippicus, who had risen through the military ranks, was perhaps expected to offer strong leadership in the face of increasing threats from the Umayyad Caliphate. Unfortunately, his leadership did not live up to expectations.

One of Philippicus' first significant challenges came from the Umayyad invasion of Anatolia. Maslama ibn Abd al-Malik, the Umayyad general, led a campaign against the Byzantine territories in Asia Minor and the surrounding areas. Philippicus responded by mobilizing troops, but despite his efforts, the Byzantine forces struggled to counter the well-organized Umayyad army.

The lack of military coordination and effective leadership contributed to the Byzantine losses in the field, leaving much of the empire vulnerable. While Philippicus sought to strengthen the empire's defences, he failed to form a solid military strategy to push back the Umayyad invasion. By 714 CE, the Umayyads had gained further ground, and the threat of conquest loomed large.

In addition to military failures, Philippicus faced growing political dissent from within his own ranks. Like Anastasius II, his leadership was undermined by internal factions within the Byzantine elite, which viewed him as an incompetent ruler. The military aristocracy, frustrated with Philippicus' ineffective defence of the empire, turned against him. After a series of rebellions and conspiracy plots, Philippicus was overthrown in 715 CE, marking the end of his reign and the beginning of the rise of Theodosius III.

Emperor Theodosius III (715–717 CE): Political Weakness and External Threats

The reign of Theodosius III began in 715 CE after the overthrow of Philippicus. A civil administrator by background, Theodosius lacked the military experience necessary to confront the growing external threats. Though his reign began with an attempt to restore order after the chaos of Philippicus' rule, the empire was still in disarray, with little unity within the imperial court and even less coordination between the military and civilian leadership.

The Umayyad threat remained constant and pressing. Under Maslama ibn Abd al-Malik, the Umayyad Caliphate was preparing for a final push to seize Constantinople. The Byzantine Empire was severely weakened, and Theodosius III's failure to unify the empire against the Umayyads and address the ongoing military problems left the empire vulnerable.

One of the most crucial moments during Theodosius III's reign occurred in 717 CE, when the Umayyad Caliphate launched its final assault on Constantinople, the heart of the Byzantine Empire. The Siege of Constantinople was a decisive moment in Byzantine history. Maslama's forces laid siege to the city with both a large army and a naval blockade. The defenders of Constantinople, however, were not only protected by the formidable Theodosian Walls but also by the innovative use of Greek fire, which decimated the Umayyad navy.

Despite the defensive success, Theodosius III's inability to organize a coherent military response and his growing unpopularity among the Byzantine aristocracy contributed to his abdication in 717 CE. As a result, he was forced to step down in favour of Leo III the Isaurian, a general with a proven military track record, who would go on to become one of the most successful Byzantine emperors.

Emperor Leo III the Isaurian (717–741 CE): Turning the Tide

Leo III, who came to power in 717 CE after the abdication of Theodosius III, is undoubtedly one of the most significant figures in Byzantine history. His reign marked the beginning of a new chapter for the empire, one of military resurgence, political stability, and the initiation of the Iconoclast controversy, which would divide the empire for generations.

Leo III's most defining moment came in 717–718 CE, when he successfully defended Constantinople against the Umayyad siege. The Umayyads had amassed a large army and navy to conquer the city, but Leo's leadership and the use of Greek fire led to a significant victory for the Byzantines. The defeat of the Umayyads at the gates of Constantinople marked the end of the Umayyad expansion into Byzantine territory and secured the empire's survival for decades to come.

In addition to his military success, Leo III began to reform the Byzantine army and strengthen its defensive capabilities. He restructured the empire's themes (military districts), placing more control in the hands of local military commanders, which helped to create a more effective and responsive military system.

Leo III also began the Iconoclast movement in 726 CE, declaring that the veneration of icons was a form of idolatry and that they should be destroyed. This sparked significant religious and political controversy within the empire, creating a division between those who supported Leo's reforms and those who opposed them. The Iconoclast controversy would go on to define the empire's religious and political landscape for much of the eighth and ninth centuries.

Conclusion: A Critical Period in Byzantine History

The years from 711 to 717 CE were a time of profound political, military, and religious turmoil for the Byzantine Empire. The reigns of Anastasius II, Philippicus, and Theodosius III highlighted the difficulties faced by the empire during a time of military decline, internal strife, and religious division. However, it was Leo III the Isaurian who emerged as a figure capable of reversing the empire's fortunes, both in terms of military defence and internal stability.

Leo's success in repelling the Umayyad siege of Constantinople in 717–718 CE secured the future of the empire and laid the groundwork for reforms that would define the Byzantine military structure for generations. Although his religious policies would lead to a centuries-long division in the empire, his reign marked a period of recovery and renewal. The legacy of Leo III and the empire's ability to survive this critical moment would have profound implications for the Byzantine Empire's resilience in the centuries that followed.

Decline and Challenges

The Byzantine Empire's glory days of imperial expansion had long passed by the time Constantine was born in 718. The empire's borders had receded dramatically, with the most significant losses occurring during the seventh century. A vast portion of the Eastern Roman Empire was lost to the rapid conquests of the Islamic Caliphates which emerged from Arabia in the early seventh century. By the eighth century, the empire had lost Egypt, Syria, and North Africa, regions that had been essential not only for their agricultural wealth but also due to their strategic importance as buffer zones against invaders. The loss of these provinces deprived the empire of critical resources, manpower, and revenue, making it harder to sustain the military and administrative apparatus that held the state together.

Internally, the empire was also under strain. The late seventh and early eighth centuries had seen a series of short-lived and weak rulers, many of whom were unable to maintain stability in the capital, let alone defend the empire's borders. The Byzantine throne had become a precarious position, as coups, assassinations, and palace intrigues marked the period. Emperors struggled not only against external enemies but also against rivals within their court. As a result, governance was often unpredictable, and confidence in the state was low among the populace. This instability made it difficult to rally the necessary support for sustained military campaigns or economic reforms. By the time Leo III, Constantine's father, took the throne in 717, the empire's administrative apparatus was weakened, and its military was in a constant defensive posture.

Religious Disunity

Religion, one of the empire's strongest unifying forces, was also a source of tension and division. As the Christian faith permeated Byzantine society, the emperor was expected not only to lead as a political figure but also to act as a guardian of orthodoxy. Yet theological divisions had been growing within the empire, as various factions debated the nature of Christ, the role of the Virgin Mary, and the veneration of religious images, or icons. The controversy over Monotheletism, an attempt to reconcile differing views on Christ's nature, had already set the stage for the theological disputes that would embroil Constantine's family and, later, his reign.

Monotheletism emerged as a theological position intended to appease factions within the empire who argued over Christ's nature. It held that Christ had only a single will, a compromise that sought to unite the Monophysites (who believed in a single divine nature) and Chalcedonian Christians (who believed in Christ's dual human and divine natures). Despite these efforts, Monotheletism was ultimately rejected by the Council of Constantinople in 681, which affirmed the two-will doctrine of Christ. This theological defeat, however, did not put an end to religious debate; instead, it created lingering divisions. By Constantine's time, these theological disagreements had laid the foundation for new conflicts, especially over the veneration of icons.

Icons – religious images of Christ, Mary, and the saints – had become a ubiquitous part of Byzantine religious practice. They were used in worship and veneration, considered by many believers to be essential links to the divine. However, a growing faction within the church and the imperial court began to question this practice, fearing it bordered on idolatry. They argued that the veneration of icons detracted from the worship of God and suggested that it was the cause of the empire's ongoing military failures. This belief was reinforced by the empire's defeats against the Muslim Arabs, whose faith eschewed images entirely and who had experienced rapid military success. The seeds of Iconoclasm – opposition to the veneration of icons – were thus planted, foreshadowing a major religious crisis that would dominate Constantine's reign.

The Rise of Islam and External Threats

While the empire struggled with internal discord, a powerful external threat loomed large: the rise of Islam. In the century before Constantine's birth, the Islamic Caliphate had emerged as a formidable force, swiftly conquering large swathes of territory that had once been part of the Roman Empire. The Arab-Byzantine wars, which began in the seventh century, placed constant pressure on Byzantium's eastern frontier. Arab forces launched repeated raids into Anatolia, and they were only barely repelled from the capital itself during two major sieges of Constantinople.

The Umayyad Caliphate, which ruled from Damascus, was a relentless adversary. Following the loss of Syria and Egypt, Byzantium's eastern territories were left highly vulnerable, and the empire was forced into a defensive posture. This era of constant warfare with the Caliphate necessitated a restructuring of the Byzantine military and administrative systems to handle ongoing, large-scale military mobilizations. Under the theme system, the empire organized its military into regional districts, which allowed it to maintain a standing force close to the frontiers and ready to respond to Arab incursions.

The Second Arab Siege of Constantinople in 717–718, launched by the Umayyads, was a pivotal moment for the Byzantine Empire and its new emperor, Leo III. Lasting nearly a year, the siege saw the Arab forces encamped around Constantinople in a seemingly unstoppable push to take the Byzantine capital. However, thanks to a combination of Leo III's strategic brilliance, the use of Greek fire, and the empire's strong fortifications, the Byzantines managed to repel the invaders. The victory was seen as a miracle and galvanized support for Leo's new reign. It also bought the empire time to regroup and reorganize its defences, preventing the Caliphate from launching further large-scale attacks against the capital for decades. Leo's successful defence not only secured his position as emperor but also helped to establish the reputation of his dynasty as capable defenders of Christendom.

Political Fragmentation and Economic Strain

The empire's military efforts were costly, straining an already fragile economy. As a result of constant warfare and territorial loss, the Byzantine state was forced to impose heavy taxes on its remaining lands. This burden often fell on the peasantry, who were the backbone of the empire's agriculture and military. As the traditional landowning aristocracy grew more powerful, small farmers struggled under the tax burden, leading to social unrest and resentment toward the central government. To counter these economic and social issues, Byzantine emperors began implementing reforms aimed at ensuring the empire's survival. Leo III's initiatives, which Constantine would later build upon, sought to create a more sustainable fiscal structure and reduce corruption within the government.

In response to these challenges, the theme system was introduced to address both military and economic needs. The system decentralized military recruitment and support, placing soldiers on land plots within specific regions and allowing them to farm their own land to support themselves. This innovation allowed the state to maintain a military presence in strategic locations without overtaxing the central treasury. Additionally, it created a semi-professional class of soldier-farmers who could respond quickly to threats, an essential adaptation for an empire constantly beset by foreign incursions.

A Precarious Empire on the Edge of Revival

By the time of Constantine's birth, the Byzantine Empire was an embattled state, facing tremendous pressures from all directions. The victories achieved by Leo III brought a measure of stability, but the empire's future remained uncertain. Constant military threats, economic strain, and religious controversies kept Byzantium in a precarious position. However, Leo's successes had shown that strong, determined leadership could stave off defeat and even lay the groundwork for revival.

For Constantine, this was the world he would inherit – a world of dangers, opportunities, and legacies. He would be expected not only to defend the empire but also to restore it to strength. These early years, shaped by his father's victories and reforms, instilled in him a deep awareness of the need for unity, discipline, and strategic foresight. The Byzantine Empire was a state in need of transformation, and Constantine, born into an era of reform and conflict, would rise to meet that challenge.

Section 2: The Isaurian Dynasty's Beginnings and Leo III

When Constantine V was born, he entered a Byzantine Empire still trembling from years of military defeats, internal strife, and the constant threat of conquest. His father, Leo III, rose to power in a volatile and uncertain period, emerging as a leader who brought stability, military success, and sweeping reforms that would shape Constantine's future rule. Leo III's ascension to power was both improbable and remarkable, marking the beginning of the Isaurian Dynasty and setting the stage for a revitalization of the Byzantine Empire. This section delves into Leo III's rise, his military achievements, his crucial reforms, and the start of the Iconoclastic controversy, which would profoundly affect the political and religious landscape Constantine would inherit.

The Rise of Leo III

Leo III's origins were humble and far from the imperial court, making his rise to the throne an improbable one. Born in the region of Isauria, a rugged area in south-eastern Anatolia (present-day Turkey), Leo came from a background that was typical of many Byzantine soldiers: rural, modest, and deeply rooted in the empire's military traditions. This background, however, gave him an invaluable understanding of the empire's social and military structures, as well as a strong connection to the people of Asia Minor, who formed the backbone of the Byzantine military. He was known for his sharp intelligence, his dedication to military discipline, and his grasp of tactical and strategic warfare, all of which helped him advance through the ranks.

By the early 700s, Leo was serving as a military leader in the theme system – a system that organized the empire's territories into military districts. He quickly established a reputation as a competent and capable commander, respected by his soldiers and recognized by his superiors for his ability to manage troops effectively and defend Byzantine territory. Leo's opportunity for leadership came during a period of severe crisis. The Byzantine throne had been the subject of multiple coups and changes, creating a climate of constant instability. Emperors came and went in rapid succession, often unable to secure their rule against both external invaders and internal rivals.

In 717, Leo seized his opportunity. The reigning emperor, Theodosius III, was perceived as weak and unable to defend Constantinople against the ever-present Arab threat. Seeing the empire's need for strong leadership, Leo, supported by the military and political factions within the capital, launched a successful coup and deposed Theodosius III, ascending the throne as Leo III. His rise was not simply a matter of ambition but a response to a dire need for competent leadership that could restore the empire's stability.

The Defence of Constantinople

One of the first tests of Leo's leadership came almost immediately after he assumed power: the Second Arab Siege of Constantinople. In 717, the Umayyad Caliphate launched a massive military campaign aimed at capturing the Byzantine capital. This siege represented one of the most formidable threats the city had faced, as an Arab army surrounded Constantinople, cutting off essential supply lines. If Constantinople fell, it would likely mean the end of the Byzantine Empire.

Leo's response to this existential threat displayed his strategic genius and established his legacy as a protector of the empire. He quickly organized the defence of the city, rallying both soldiers and civilians to prepare for the impending siege. One of the decisive factors in the defence was the Byzantine navy's use of Greek fire, a highly flammable substance that could burn even on water, allowing Byzantine ships to inflict devastating damage on the Arab fleet. The precise composition of Greek fire remains a mystery, but its psychological and military impact was profound, as it effectively repelled the Arab naval forces attempting to breach the city's defences.

The winter of 717–718 proved to be a severe one, further hindering the besieging Arab forces. Leo took advantage of the weather and the attrition it caused among the Arab troops, conducting sorties and using the city's walls to repel assaults. After months of gruelling siege warfare, the Arab forces, depleted by cold, starvation, and disease, were forced to abandon their efforts. The Byzantine victory was nothing short of miraculous. Not only had Leo saved Constantinople, but he had also dealt a major blow to the Umayyad Caliphate's expansion into Europe.

The successful defence of the capital marked a turning point in Byzantine fortunes. Leo's triumph was seen as a divinely-sanctioned victory, boosting his legitimacy as emperor and establishing him as a strong, capable leader. His success instilled a renewed sense of hope and pride within the empire, as many Byzantine citizens came to believe that their emperor had been chosen by God to protect them and preserve the Christian faith against Islamic expansion.

Leo's Policies and Reforms

With the immediate threat to Constantinople dealt with, Leo set about strengthening the empire's internal structures to prevent future crises. He implemented a series of reforms aimed at stabilizing the economy, improving military organization, and restoring the efficiency of the Byzantine administrative system. These reforms would lay the groundwork for the empire's recovery and would have a profound impact on Constantine V's future reign.

Economic Reforms

- Leo III inherited an economy weakened by decades of warfare and loss of territory. To address this, he sought to create a more resilient financial base for the state by streamlining tax collection and reducing corruption within the bureaucracy.

- Leo's policies aimed to balance the state's need for revenue with the need to prevent over taxation, which had previously driven many peasants into poverty and fostered resentment toward the central government.

Military Reforms

- Leo refined the theme system, which divided the empire into military districts where soldiers were settled on land plots and could provide for themselves through farming. This system allowed the empire to maintain a stable military presence without overly burdening the treasury.
- By expanding and strengthening the theme system, Leo increased the number of soldiers available for defence, especially along the eastern frontiers, which were vulnerable to Arab incursions. This semi-professional military class became a cornerstone of Byzantine defence, providing the empire with a quick-response force that could repel raids and invasions.

Legal Reforms

- In an effort to ensure justice and reduce corruption, Leo embarked on legal reforms, revising and updating the legal code to reflect contemporary needs and enforce stability. The *Ecloga*, a revised code of law issued during his reign, sought to make Byzantine law more accessible and fair. It placed a greater emphasis on moral and social values aligned with Christian principles, setting a legal precedent that would shape the Byzantine legal tradition for generations.

Leo's reforms represented a shift toward a more self-reliant and resilient empire, one better equipped to withstand future crises. His emphasis on streamlining bureaucracy and strengthening military and economic foundations were policies that Constantine would later expand upon.

Leo and the Beginnings of Iconoclasm

While Leo III's military and administrative successes garnered him respect, his religious policies became a source of division and controversy. By the time he became emperor, a growing faction within the empire viewed the veneration of icons – images of Christ, the Virgin Mary, and saints – as problematic. Some, influenced by both theological reasoning and the influence of Islamic attitudes toward religious imagery, saw icons as idolatrous and believed their use was contrary to true Christian practice.

Leo began to adopt Iconoclastic (image-smashing) views, perhaps seeing icon veneration as a distraction from proper worship or a cause of divine disfavour. In 726, he issued an edict that condemned the use of icons and ordered their removal from churches and public spaces. This decree marked the beginning of what would come to be known as the Iconoclast controversy – a fierce dispute that would shape Constantine V's reign and plunge Byzantine society into conflict.

The reaction to Leo's Iconoclastic policies was mixed. Some, especially among the military and certain regions in Asia Minor, supported the emperor's stance, viewing it as a necessary return to a purer form of Christianity. However, others, particularly in Constantinople and among monastic communities, saw the policy as an attack on their faith and traditions. Monasteries became centres of resistance, as monks and Iconophiles (icon-lovers) defended the role of images in worship and argued that icons served as important symbols of the divine.

Leo's Iconoclastic policies, though only moderately enforced during his reign, laid the groundwork for what would become a deep societal rift. Theologically, the controversy centred on the nature of divine representation and the proper expression of faith. Politically, it became a means for the emperor to assert control over the church, undermining clerical power and strengthening imperial authority. By initiating Iconoclasm, Leo set in motion a series of events that would have far-reaching consequences for Byzantine society and culture, and would become one of the central issues of Constantine's reign.

Leo's Legacy and the Empire Constantine Would Inherit

Leo III's reign marked the beginning of a transformation for the Byzantine Empire. His military victories, particularly the defence of Constantinople, restored a sense of stability and purpose to an empire long battered by internal and external threats. His administrative and military reforms created a more robust state, one that was better prepared to face the challenges of the eighth century. However, his Iconoclastic policies sowed the seeds of division, leaving behind a controversy that would consume Byzantine society.

For Constantine V, Leo's achievements provided both an inspiration and a framework for his future rule. He would inherit a more stable and militarily resilient empire but also an increasingly polarized society. Leo's legacy was both that of a defender of Byzantium and a controversial religious reformer.

Section 3: The Birth and Early Life of Constantine V

Constantine V was born in 718, the son of Leo III and Maria of Amnia. His birth coincided with a critical moment in Byzantine history, coming during the Second Arab Siege of Constantinople. Leo's remarkable defence of the city against the Umayyad Caliphate and his subsequent ascension to the throne as emperor meant that Constantine's life would be bound up with the fate of an empire in transition. As the only son and heir of Leo III, Constantine was destined to inherit not only the throne but also the burdens of an empire that demanded both political stability and religious coherence. This section delves into Constantine's early years, his education, and the shaping influences of his father's policies, particularly the Iconoclastic stance that would later define his reign.

Birth Amidst Siege and Victory

The year of Constantine's birth, 718, marked a significant turning point for the Byzantine Empire. The capital city of Constantinople had withstood an intense year-long siege by the Umayyad Caliphate, one of the greatest threats Byzantium had ever faced. This miraculous victory over the Muslim forces was not only a strategic and military triumph for Leo III but also a moment that reinvigorated Byzantine morale. Many citizens saw the survival of Constantinople as a divine sign that God still favoured the Byzantine Empire.

For Leo III, the birth of his son Constantine in this context carried profound symbolic weight. Constantine came to embody the promise of continuity for the Isaurian Dynasty, a dynasty Leo was striving to establish. His arrival in a time of victory and renewal tied his destiny to the empire's fortunes, creating an image of the young prince as the heir to a renewed Byzantine state. The narrative of his birth became part of the imperial family's legend, with many later chroniclers interpreting it as a sign of Constantine's divine favour and as a herald of future success.

Early Childhood and Imperial Education

Growing up in the Byzantine imperial palace, Constantine V was immersed in the traditions and responsibilities of Byzantine royalty from a young age. The Great Palace of Constantinople, the heart of Byzantine governance, was not just a royal residence but also a political and cultural centre where Constantine would have been exposed to the complexities of statecraft. The palace housed various officials, soldiers, and religious figures, each representing different aspects of the Byzantine state.

Constantine's education was thorough and carefully planned, reflecting the high expectations his father had for him. Leo III, recognizing the precarious state of the empire, would have emphasized the importance of military prowess and administrative knowledge, traits he himself had demonstrated during his reign. Constantine's early education would have included classical Greek literature, philosophy, and rhetoric, as well as Christian theology. The Byzantine curriculum was influenced by the works of ancient Greek philosophers such as Aristotle and Plato, but it was also steeped in Christian doctrine, reflecting the dual heritage of Greco-Roman and Christian culture that defined Byzantium.

Given Leo's emphasis on military organization and discipline, Constantine was likely introduced to the fundamentals of warfare at an early age. Byzantine princes were often expected to understand the principles of strategy, logistics, and battlefield tactics, and Constantine's upbringing was no exception. From his tutors, he would have learned not only how to lead an army but also the intricacies of the theme system, the military-administrative structure that had been reformed by his father. This education prepared him to govern as both a warrior and an administrator, capable of responding to the constant military threats that Byzantium faced.

Additionally, Constantine was instructed in Christian doctrine and the Bible. However, his religious education was distinctive in that it was shaped by his father's Iconoclastic beliefs. Leo III's opposition to the veneration of icons, which he saw as idolatrous, meant that Constantine's theological training would have emphasized the importance of Iconoclasm – the rejection of religious images – in Christianity. This early exposure to Iconoclastic teachings would shape Constantine's personal convictions and ultimately influence his policies when he became emperor.

Formative Influences and the Shadow of Iconoclasm

One of the most significant influences on young Constantine was his father's controversial stance on Iconoclasm. By the mid-720s, Leo III had publicly condemned the use of icons, initiating a series of edicts that sought to remove religious images from Byzantine worship and public life. The Iconoclastic policy, while only modestly enforced during Leo's reign, created a deep division within Byzantine society. Some, especially in the military and among the administrative elite, supported the emperor's stance, believing it aligned with pure Christian practice and would secure divine favour for the empire. However, many others, particularly among the clergy and monastic communities, saw Iconoclasm as heretical and feared that it undermined the foundations of Christian faith.

Growing up in the imperial palace, Constantine would have been exposed to these ideological conflicts from an early age. The theological arguments surrounding Iconoclasm were complex and deeply emotional, involving questions about the nature of Christ, the role of images in Christian worship, and the authority of the church versus the state. Leo III's Iconoclastic policies placed Constantine in a unique position; as the emperor's son and heir, he was expected to uphold his father's religious reforms, yet he also faced the challenge of reconciling these policies with widespread opposition.

Constantine's early exposure to Iconoclasm shaped his theological views, aligning him with his father's beliefs and instilling in him a sense of duty to continue Leo's work. His education in this environment taught him not only the intellectual justifications for Iconoclasm but also the political necessity of enforcing religious unity. Constantine learned that maintaining imperial authority sometimes required suppressing dissenting views, especially in matters of faith. These lessons would inform his later policies as emperor, as he became one of the most ardent supporters of Iconoclasm, even intensifying its enforcement.

Public Role and Grooming for Leadership

From a young age, Constantine was groomed to fulfil his role as heir to the throne. In Byzantine tradition, imperial heirs were often given public responsibilities early to familiarize them with the demands of leadership and to secure their position in the eyes of the people. Leo III was careful to present Constantine as a capable and legitimate successor, likely involving him in ceremonial events and military inspections. Such events helped Constantine build a public image, establishing him as the future defender of the empire and the guardian of the Isaurian Dynasty.

In 720, when Constantine was just two years old, he was crowned co-emperor by his father. This early coronation was a symbolic act, solidifying his position as Leo's chosen successor and ensuring a smooth transition of power. Co-rulership allowed Constantine to share in the responsibilities of governance, albeit in a limited way during his youth. As co-emperor, Constantine would have been involved in state affairs, even if only ceremonially, learning first-hand the mechanics of imperial governance and the weight of imperial duty.

This early role also reinforced Constantine's sense of dynastic duty and the importance of maintaining the stability that his father had worked so hard to achieve. The act of crowning Constantine as co-emperor highlighted Leo's vision of a continuous and stable line of succession, a vision that would be crucial for a state as fragile as Byzantium. Constantine's position as co-emperor allowed him to observe his father's decision-making processes, providing invaluable insights into the responsibilities he would one day shoulder.

Military Training and Early Campaigns

Military training was an essential part of Constantine's preparation as heir to the throne. Leo III, a seasoned military commander, likely emphasized the importance of martial prowess and strategic acumen. As a young prince, Constantine was instructed in the use of arms, horseback riding, and the tactics of Byzantine warfare, ensuring that he would be able to lead troops in the field when necessary. This military training was not merely symbolic; given

Byzantium's precarious position, the emperor was expected to lead his soldiers personally and defend the empire against external threats.

Constantine's early exposure to military matters included participation in campaigns alongside his father, though his role was likely limited to observation in his younger years. By accompanying Leo on these expeditions, Constantine gained practical experience in the complexities of military logistics, the discipline required to maintain an army, and the challenges of confronting foreign forces. He witnessed the organization of troops, the enforcement of discipline, and the importance of morale, lessons that would later serve him well as a military leader.

Conclusion: A Prince Shaped by Crisis and Reform

Constantine's early life was marked by the challenges and reforms his father implemented to save the Byzantine Empire. His birth in a time of crisis, his education in both classical and Christian thought, and his exposure to Iconoclasm and military affairs all contributed to shaping him into a future emperor. His upbringing emphasized duty, discipline, and loyalty to the empire, while his close relationship with his father instilled in him a commitment to the Isaurian Dynasty's vision of Byzantine strength and religious unity.

By the time Constantine reached adolescence, he was already well-prepared to assume the throne, equipped with a thorough education, a deep understanding of statecraft, and a fervent belief in the principles of Iconoclasm. Constantine's early life was not without its challenges, but the trials he faced served to strengthen his resolve and prepare him for the arduous path ahead. In many ways, Constantine's upbringing foreshadowed the kind of ruler he would become: a fiercely determined, often uncompromising emperor, ready to defend his beliefs and his empire at all costs.

Section 4: Constantine's Ascension to the Throne

Constantine V officially ascended to the Byzantine throne in 741, following the death of his father, Leo III. His journey to power, however, was anything but smooth. Constantine's reign began amid political instability and a brewing religious crisis that he inherited from Leo. The empire was divided by the Iconoclastic controversy, and Constantine's legitimacy as emperor was tested almost immediately. His ascension set the stage for a tumultuous rule characterized by military campaigns, political strife, and religious reform. This section delves into Constantine's initial years on the throne, exploring the obstacles he encountered, the power struggles he faced, and the early policies he implemented to consolidate his authority and secure the empire's future.

The Transition of Power

When Leo III passed away in 741, Constantine, then in his early twenties, took the throne as his designated successor. His father's decision to crown him co-emperor at the age of two had secured Constantine's position in theory, but the reality of governance required more than symbolic authority. Constantine inherited an empire that Leo had strengthened but not fully stabilized, with tensions simmering both domestically and on the frontiers. Leo's death left a vacuum that opportunistic factions and rivals sought to exploit.

One of Constantine's immediate challenges was to gain the loyalty of the military, which had been instrumental in his father's rise to power. While Leo's military successes had won him the support of many soldiers, Constantine needed to prove himself worthy of command. His upbringing had prepared him well; he was familiar with military strategy, had observed his father's campaigns, and had been groomed for leadership. However, Constantine's authority was soon put to the test by a formidable rival: his brother-in-law, Artabasdos.

Artabasdos' Rebellion

Constantine's first significant test as emperor came in the form of Artabasdos' rebellion. Artabasdos, a powerful general and the husband of Constantine's sister, Anna, had held the prestigious title of *Strategos* (military governor) of the Armeniac theme, one of the empire's key military regions. Leo III had carefully placed his allies in positions of power, but Artabasdos saw an opportunity to assert his own claim to the throne. Seizing upon dissatisfaction with Constantine's Iconoclastic policies and the tensions within the empire, Artabasdos launched a rebellion soon after Constantine's ascension.

Artabasdos quickly gained the support of several themes, or military districts, which provided him with a strong base of loyal soldiers. In a calculated move, he declared himself emperor in 742, claiming that Constantine was an illegitimate ruler due to his association with Iconoclasm. Artabasdos positioned himself as the defender of traditional Christian orthodoxy and icon veneration, a stance that resonated with the monastic communities and large segments of the Byzantine populace who opposed Constantine's Iconoclastic policies.

With the backing of the Armeniac and Opsikion themes, Artabasdos marched on Constantinople. Constantine, however, refused to surrender his claim. Instead, he prepared to confront his brother-in-law, determined to defend his right to rule. This internal conflict, known as the civil war of 742–743, became one of the defining events of Constantine's early reign.

The Civil War of 742–743

The civil war that erupted between Constantine V and Artabasdos was a brutal affair, characterized by shifting allegiances, fierce battles, and the clash of two competing visions for the empire. The conflict drew in both military forces and ideological factions, pitting Iconoclasts against Iconophiles. Artabasdos' appeal to the anti-Iconoclast sentiment gave him an edge in winning popular support, particularly among the clergy and the residents of Constantinople. However, Constantine's strategic skills and his resolve to secure his throne proved crucial in the conflict.

Constantine's approach to the war was methodical and decisive. He began by rallying his loyal forces, securing the loyalty of the Anatolic and Thracesian themes, two of the empire's most powerful military regions. Using his understanding of the theme system, Constantine effectively mobilized these soldiers to confront Artabasdos' forces. Despite facing the logistical challenges of fighting within his own empire, Constantine displayed a tenacity and strategic acumen that underscored his preparedness for military leadership.

The pivotal moment of the civil war came in 743 when Constantine's forces decisively defeated Artabasdos in a series of battles near Sardis. The conflict culminated in Constantine's return to Constantinople, where he reasserted control over the capital and took measures to prevent further dissent. Artabasdos and his family were captured, and Constantine ordered severe punishments for the rebels, including blinding and imprisonment. This display of force was intended not only to eliminate his immediate rivals but also to send a clear message about the consequences of defying the emperor. Through this victory, Constantine solidified his position as the legitimate ruler, demonstrating both his military competence and his willingness to defend his authority ruthlessly.

Consolidation of Power and the Strengthening of Iconoclasm

Having secured his throne, Constantine turned his attention to consolidating his power and addressing the ideological rift within the empire. Artabasdos' rebellion had highlighted the strength of the opposition to Iconoclasm, and Constantine recognized that the Iconophile faction posed a continuing threat to his rule. In response, he intensified his commitment to Iconoclasm, determined to root out what he perceived as a corrupting influence within Byzantine Christianity.

Constantine's Iconoclastic policies went beyond those of his father, Leo III. Whereas Leo had taken a relatively cautious approach to Iconoclasm, enforcing the removal of icons in a measured manner, Constantine pursued a more aggressive campaign. He implemented stricter laws against the production and veneration of icons, ordering the destruction of religious images in churches and public spaces. Monasteries, which were hotbeds of Iconophile sentiment, faced particular scrutiny, as Constantine saw them as centres of resistance to imperial authority.

To support his policies, Constantine convened a council in 754, known as the Council of Hieria. This council, held at the palace of Hieria near Constantinople, was composed of bishops sympathetic to Iconoclasm, and it issued a formal condemnation of icons. The council's decrees reinforced the emperor's stance, declaring that the veneration of images was tantamount to idolatry and therefore heretical. This ruling gave Constantine a theological justification for his policies and strengthened his position against his religious opponents.

The intensification of Iconoclasm was not solely a matter of faith for Constantine; it was also a political strategy aimed at consolidating his authority. By aligning the church with his vision of Christianity, Constantine sought to unify the empire under a single ideological framework. His Iconoclastic policies, though deeply divisive, allowed him to assert control over the religious sphere and reduce the influence of the Iconophile clergy, who had often challenged imperial authority. In this way, Constantine's commitment to Iconoclasm became both a personal conviction and a tool of statecraft, helping him to centralize power and reinforce his legitimacy.

Military Campaigns and Defence of the Empire

While Constantine focused on internal consolidation, he also faced significant external threats that required his attention. The Byzantine Empire was surrounded by hostile powers, including the Arab Caliphate in the east and the Bulgar Khanate to the north. The Umayyad and later Abbasid Caliphates posed an ongoing threat to Byzantine Anatolia, periodically launching raids and testing the empire's defences.

In response to these threats, Constantine undertook a series of military campaigns to strengthen the empire's borders and deter foreign incursions. His campaigns against the Arabs focused on securing the eastern frontier, particularly the regions of Cappadocia and Cilicia, which were vulnerable to raids. Constantine implemented a policy of fortified defence, constructing new fortifications and bolstering existing defences along the eastern border. These measures helped to limit the effectiveness of Arab raids and provided a buffer zone that protected the empire's core territories.

In the north, Constantine faced a more immediate and challenging threat from the Bulgars, who posed a direct threat to Constantinople and the Balkan provinces. The Bulgar Khanate had grown in power and frequently raided Byzantine territory, destabilizing the northern frontier. Constantine launched several campaigns against the Bulgars, aiming to weaken their power and secure Byzantium's northern borders. His efforts met with mixed results; while he managed to repel some Bulgar attacks, the conflict remained unresolved, highlighting the ongoing vulnerability of the northern regions.

Constantine's military campaigns underscored his commitment to defending the empire and his understanding of the need for a proactive defence strategy. His focus on fortifications and strategic positioning reflected the principles of Byzantine military doctrine, which emphasized defensive strength and the use of fortified positions to compensate for the empire's limited manpower. Although he faced considerable challenges, Constantine's efforts to secure the empire's borders contributed to a sense of stability that allowed him to focus on internal reform and religious policy.

The Establishment of a Legacy

Constantine's early reign was marked by a series of trials that tested his resilience, strategic acumen, and commitment to his father's legacy. From the civil war with Artabasdos to the intensification of Iconoclasm and the defence of the empire's borders, Constantine navigated each challenge with determination and an unyielding belief in his role as the protector of Byzantium. His policies, though often harsh, were aimed at securing the empire's future and asserting the authority of the Isaurian Dynasty.

By the end of his first decade as emperor, Constantine had established himself as a ruler willing to make difficult decisions to maintain his power and stabilize the empire. His consolidation of Iconoclasm, his military campaigns, and his unrelenting suppression of dissent created a legacy of strength and control that would define his reign. However, his actions also deepened the divisions within Byzantine society, setting the stage for the conflicts that would continue to shape the empire in the years to come.

Chapter 2

Civil War and Consolidation of Power

Section 1: The Rebellion of Artabasdos: The Civil War of 742–743

The civil war of 742–743 marked one of the most critical and tumultuous periods in the early reign of Constantine V. The conflict not only tested Constantine's resolve and military prowess, but also exposed the deep ideological and political divides within the Byzantine Empire. As he struggled to assert his authority against a formidable rival, the civil war had lasting implications for both the stability of the empire and the nature of its religious policies. This section examines the origins of the civil war, the unfolding events of the conflict, and its consequences for Constantine's reign.

Origins of the Conflict

The seeds of the civil war were sown even before Constantine V ascended the throne. Following the death of Leo III in 741, the empire was rife with factions and power struggles. Leo's Iconoclastic policies had polarized society, creating a schism between the supporters of the emperor's religious reforms and those who opposed them, particularly the monastic communities and the clergy. Although Leo had managed to unify the empire under his leadership, the aftermath of his death saw these tensions surface in the form of competing claims to the throne.

Artabasdos, a general of considerable influence and the brother-in-law of Constantine, emerged as a prominent figure opposing the new emperor. With his connections to the military and the support of the Armeniac theme, Artabasdos sought to capitalize on the discontent surrounding Constantine's Iconoclastic policies. He positioned himself as a defender of the traditional Christian faith, appealing to those who viewed the veneration of icons as an essential aspect of their religious practice. Artabasdos declared himself emperor in 742, challenging Constantine's authority and igniting the flames of civil war.

As the conflict began, the loyalty of the military became a critical factor. Many soldiers were drawn to Artabasdos, who presented himself as a champion of orthodoxy. His appeal to the populace and military leaders put Constantine at a disadvantage, forcing him to rally his supporters and demonstrate his ability to lead effectively. The factionalism within the army created a volatile environment that could shift in favour of either side.

The Outbreak of War

The conflict erupted in earnest when Artabasdos gathered his forces and marched on Constantinople. His initial successes were bolstered by the support of several themes that had grown dissatisfied with Constantine's leadership. The operation was well-coordinated, and his forces advanced toward the capital, threatening the imperial authority that Constantine had yet to establish fully.

In response to Artabasdos' advance, Constantine quickly mobilized his loyal troops. He understood that the defence of Constantinople was paramount – not just for the preservation of his reign, but for the integrity of the Byzantine Empire itself. The city had been the heart of the empire for centuries, and losing it to a rival would have severe implications for his legitimacy. Therefore, he prepared for a showdown that would define his rule and the future of Byzantium.

Constantine's strategy focused on consolidating his military strength and forging alliances with loyal themes. He emphasized the need for unity among his supporters and called upon them to defend the empire against what he portrayed as a usurpation of power by Artabasdos. This appeal to loyalty and duty resonated with many soldiers, who understood the stakes involved. The mobilization of these forces showcased Constantine's ability to galvanize support and harness the traditional military ethos of the Byzantine army.

The Battles of 742–743

The civil war came to a head with a series of battles between the forces of Constantine and Artabasdos. The initial encounters were marked by fierce fighting and shifting allegiances. Artabasdos, initially buoyed by his momentum, sought to seize control of key locations within the capital region and to destabilize Constantine's command.

One of the earliest and most significant battles occurred near the city of Amaseia. Here, Constantine's forces, bolstered by reinforcements from the Thracesian theme, clashed with Artabasdos' army. Despite being outnumbered, Constantine demonstrated exceptional tactical acumen. He utilized the terrain to his advantage, employing ambush tactics and flanking manoeuvres that caught Artabasdos off guard. The battle ended with a decisive victory for Constantine, showcasing his ability to inspire and lead his troops even in the face of adversity.

In the months that followed, the conflict escalated, with both sides engaging in a series of skirmishes that resulted in heavy casualties. As the war continued, the situation became increasingly precarious for Artabasdos. His initial support began to dwindle, as the realities of war took a toll on his troops and the populace grew weary of the ongoing conflict. In contrast, Constantine's forces were more cohesive and motivated by a clear objective: to restore imperial authority and preserve the legacy of the Isaurian Dynasty.

As the war progressed, the conflict also took on a personal dimension. Artabasdos, feeling the pressure of defeat, began to employ more ruthless tactics, resorting to scorched-earth strategies to undermine Constantine's resources. This approach alienated some of his former supporters, who were disillusioned by the devastation brought upon their lands.

The Turning Point

The turning point in the civil war came in 743, when Constantine launched a series of offensives aimed at decisively defeating Artabasdos. With the winter months approaching, both sides recognized the importance of securing a favourable position before the onset of adverse weather conditions. Constantine's forces, now more organized and resolute, began a coordinated push against Artabasdos' remaining strongholds.

One of the critical moments occurred during the siege of the fortress at Amorium, a vital strategic location that Artabasdos had fortified. The siege was arduous, marked by intense skirmishing and psychological warfare. Constantine employed a strategy of attrition, cutting off supply lines and surrounding the fortress. As the siege wore on, the morale of Artabasdos' forces began to falter. Reports of dwindling supplies and mounting casualties spread, leading to desertions and defections.

The decisive battle took place on the fields outside Amorium. Constantine's forces launched a full-scale assault on the beleaguered defenders, employing a combination of heavy infantry and cavalry charges to break through Artabasdos' defences. The battle was fierce, but the loyalty and determination of Constantine's troops prevailed. Artabasdos' forces were routed, and the once-mighty rebel general was forced to retreat, marking a significant turning point in the war.

The Battle of Amorium (742 CE): A Detailed Analysis of Military Equipment, Tactics, and Strategy

The Battle of Amorium, fought in 742 CE, was a decisive moment in the Byzantine civil war between Emperor Constantine V and the rebel general Artabasdos. This battle, not only significant for its immediate political consequences, was also a profound illustration of Byzantine military prowess and organization. To fully appreciate the significance of the battle, we must delve deeper into the military equipment and tactics employed by both sides, as well as the strategies that ultimately determined the outcome.

Constantine V's victory over Artabasdos can be attributed to several factors, including his reorganization of the Byzantine army, the effective use of cavalry and infantry, and the coordination of various branches of the military. However, it was the combination of these elements, alongside his personal leadership and military reforms that enabled him to achieve a decisive and enduring victory.

Context of the Battle

The Battle of Amorium was fought between the forces of Constantine V, who had reigned as emperor since 741 CE, and the forces of Artabasdos, a former general and would-be emperor. Artabasdos had risen in rebellion against Constantine V, largely due to disputes over religious policies, especially the ongoing conflict over Iconoclasm. Artabasdos, who was an Iconophile (supporter of the veneration of icons), had gained the support of many elements of the Byzantine military and some segments of the populace. However, Constantine V, a staunch Iconoclast, had implemented sweeping reforms in the military and administration, which played a key role in his ability to defeat Artabasdos.

By the time of the battle, Constantine V's army had been well-organized and well-equipped, with a strong focus on cavalry, discipline, and tactical innovation. In contrast, Artabasdos' army was less cohesive, hindered by internal divisions and ideological motivations that did not translate into a unified military strategy. The battle itself took place near the city of Amorium, located in central Asia Minor (modern-day Turkey), an area strategically important for controlling the region and protecting the eastern frontiers of the Byzantine Empire.

Byzantine Military Structure and Equipment

The Byzantine army under Constantine V had undergone a series of reforms that greatly increased its effectiveness on the battlefield. These reforms were aimed at increasing both the efficiency and flexibility of the military, making it capable of dealing with both internal revolts like Artabasdos' rebellion and external threats from the Arabs. Key to this transformation was the use of combined arms, integrating heavy cavalry, infantry, and siege equipment in ways that maximized their complementary strengths.

Cavalry: The Backbone of Byzantine Power

One of the cornerstones of Constantine V's military reforms was the increased reliance on cavalry, specifically the cataphracts and kavallaroi. These mounted soldiers formed the elite of the Byzantine army and played a central role in the victory at Amorium.

- **Cataphracts:** The cataphracts, heavy cavalry units, were heavily armoured soldiers, both the horse and rider, armed with long spears or lances. These units were a formidable force on the battlefield, designed to break enemy lines and engage in devastating shock charges. The armour of the cataphracts consisted of a combination of chainmail and plate armour, designed to offer protection while allowing the rider to remain mobile. The importance of the cataphracts in Byzantine military strategy cannot be overstated; their ability to charge into enemy lines, disrupt infantry formations, and cause chaos was key to Constantine's success at Amorium.

- **Kavallaroi (Light Cavalry):** Alongside the cataphracts, the kavallaroi or light cavalry played an important role in providing reconnaissance, harassing enemy formations, and securing the flanks of the heavy cavalry. These units were generally less armoured but more mobile, armed with bows or short swords, allowing them to be highly effective in skirmishing and flanking manoeuvres. At Amorium, the light cavalry would have been used to flank Artabasdos' forces, exploiting any weaknesses in his formation while allowing the cataphracts to engage directly with the enemy's centre.

Infantry: A Key Support Force

While the cavalry played a central role, the infantry in the Byzantine army was also crucial in supporting the cavalry and holding the line. Byzantine infantry was typically armed with spears, swords, and shields, and was often organized into tight formations that could defend against both cavalry and infantry charges.

- **Legionaries:** The infantry in the Byzantine army was divided into units of legionaries, who were heavily armoured soldiers armed primarily with spears and spatha (a type of longsword). The heavy infantry was designed to withstand direct attacks from cavalry and provide a stable line of defence for the rest of the army. In battle, these troops would form a solid centre that could absorb attacks while waiting for the cavalry to execute their shock charges. The infantry was also used to support the cavalry by engaging with the enemy when the cavalry forces were tied up in combat.
- **Archers:** The archers, though fewer in number than the other two groups, provided essential ranged support. They used composite bows that were highly effective at long range, harassing the enemy and forcing them into defensive positions. The archers could also be used to create gaps in the enemy's formation by concentrating fire on key areas, thus weakening the enemy's cohesion and making it easier for the cavalry to exploit openings.

Siege Weapons and Artillery: The Backbone of Offensive Power

Although Amorium was not a siege battle, the Byzantine army was equipped with advanced artillery that could be used in any situation. These included:

- **Ballistae:** Large crossbow-like weapons that fired bolts or heavy projectiles at long range. These weapons were useful for targeting infantry formations, disrupting enemy cavalry charges, or damaging fortifications.
- **Catapults:** Smaller siege weapons designed to hurl stones or incendiary devices. While primarily used in sieging fortifications, catapults were also effective in disrupting enemy lines or causing chaos in crowded formations.

Shields and Armour: Defence and Protection

Soldiers in the Byzantine army wore a combination of chainmail and lamellar armour, which provided protection without overly hindering mobility. The shields, typically round or oval, were often reinforced with metal to enhance durability. The armour, in conjunction with the shield, made the Byzantine soldiers resilient to attacks from both enemy archers and cavalry.

Artabasdos' Forces: Weaknesses and Tactical Challenges

While Artabasdos commanded a significant force, his army lacked the cohesion and discipline that characterized Constantine V's troops. Artabasdos' army had several weaknesses that led to its eventual defeat:

- **Lack of Cohesion:** Artabasdos' forces, while sizable, were not as well-organized as Constantine's. They were composed of diverse groups, including rebel soldiers, Iconophile supporters, and defectors from the imperial army. The ideological divisions between these factions resulted in poor coordination on the battlefield. Some of Artabasdos' troops were more loyal to the imperial cause than to the rebel leader, weakening the overall morale and effectiveness of the force.
- **Limited Cavalry:** Although Artabasdos had cavalry, it was not as well-equipped or as numerous as the forces of Constantine V. Artabasdos' cavalry was less organized, lacking the elite cataphracts that were essential to breaking enemy lines and achieving battlefield dominance. This disadvantage became particularly evident during the battle, as Constantine's cataphracts overwhelmed Artabasdos' cavalry.
- **Poor Strategic Deployment:** Artabasdos deployed his forces in a way that made them vulnerable to Constantine's superior tactics. While he attempted to use his infantry to hold a defensive line, Constantine's cavalry proved too powerful to resist. Artabasdos was unable to react

swiftly enough to the threats posed by Constantine's well-coordinated forces, particularly the cavalry's flanking manoeuvres.
- **Underestimating Constantine's Leadership:** Artabasdos failed to anticipate the tactical brilliance of Constantine V. Constantine, an experienced and strategic military leader, had proven himself in previous campaigns, and he used his superior battlefield awareness to outmanoeuvre Artabasdos. The emperor's ability to adapt quickly to changing situations and capitalize on the strengths of his army played a crucial role in the defeat of Artabasdos.

Tactics and Strategy: The Byzantine Victory

Constantine V's tactical brilliance was on full display during the Battle of Amorium. His army used a combination of heavy cavalry charges, disciplined infantry, and effective use of terrain to defeat the forces of Artabasdos.

- **Concentration of Force:** Constantine's primary tactic was the concentration of his forces at the right time and place. By focusing his attention on a key point in the enemy's line, he was able to overwhelm Artabasdos' defensive positions. Once the enemy line was broken, the Byzantine forces pressed the advantage and swiftly pursued the retreating rebels.
- **Use of Cavalry:** The cataphracts played a central role in the battle. Constantine deployed them effectively, using them to charge directly into the heart of Artabasdos' army. This direct assault disrupted the rebel forces' cohesion, forcing them into disarray and weakening their ability to mount a defence.
- **Flanking Manoeuvres:** Constantine's light cavalry, the kavallaroi, were used to execute flanking manoeuvres, hitting the rebel forces from the sides while the cataphracts engaged from the front. This coordination between cavalry and infantry created a pincer effect that rendered Artabasdos' forces unable to respond effectively.
- **Swift Pursuit:** After breaking the enemy's lines, Constantine's forces pursued the retreating rebels relentlessly. This prevented Artabasdos from regrouping or recovering any significant forces, ensuring that the victory was decisive.

Conclusion

The Battle of Amorium was a defining moment in Constantine V's reign, marking the end of a serious challenge to his authority. Through effective use of military reforms, equipment, and tactics, Constantine was able to defeat

Artabasdos decisively and secure his position as emperor. The battle also highlighted the importance of cohesion, discipline, and strategic thinking in Byzantine military success. Constantine V's victory at Amorium would go on to shape the future of the Byzantine Empire, ensuring his reforms would be remembered as a key factor in the empire's continued strength during the eighth century.

Aftermath and Consequences

With the defeat of Artabasdos at Amorium, the momentum of the civil war shifted dramatically in favour of Constantine V. His victory not only reaffirmed his position as emperor but also allowed him to initiate a campaign of retribution against those who had supported his rival. Artabasdos was captured, along with his family, and brought before Constantine, who was faced with the difficult decision of how to deal with his former brother-in-law.

In a demonstration of both power and political acumen, Constantine chose to blind Artabasdos – a punishment that was both a means of incapacitating a rival and a clear signal to potential usurpers. This act of severity was intended to solidify Constantine's position and deter future rebellions. The blind general would no longer pose a threat to the empire, and the brutal nature of the punishment sent ripples of fear through any would-be challengers.

The aftermath of the civil war had profound implications for Byzantine society. The conflict intensified the divide between Iconoclasts and Iconophiles, leaving deep scars in the fabric of the empire. Constantine's harsh measures against the supporters of Artabasdos and the enforcement of his Iconoclastic policies fostered resentment among those who had adhered to the veneration of icons. Monasteries, which had been centres of resistance, faced increased scrutiny and repression under Constantine's rule. The civil war not only secured his throne but also entrenched the ideological divisions that would plague the empire for decades to come.

In the years that followed, Constantine sought to rebuild and stabilize the empire. He understood that the civil war had weakened the Byzantine state, both militarily and socially. His efforts to consolidate power included a series of reforms aimed at unifying the empire under his vision of Iconoclasm. However, the scars of the civil war lingered, and the divisions it created would remain a source of conflict as different factions within the empire continued to vie for influence and power.

Overall Conclusion

The civil war of 742–743 was a defining moment in the early reign of Constantine V. His ability to navigate the political landscape, rally loyal supporters, and emerge victorious against a formidable rival solidified his position as a powerful emperor. Yet, the conflict also revealed the fragility of Byzantine unity and the deep-rooted tensions surrounding Iconoclasm. As Constantine moved forward to govern the empire, he carried with him the lessons learned from the civil war – a reminder that the struggle for power was not only about military might but also about navigating the complex interplay of faith, loyalty, and ideology.

Section 2: Consolidation of Power and Iconoclastic Policies

In the wake of the civil war against Artabasdos, Constantine V faced the monumental task of consolidating his power over the Byzantine Empire. With his rival defeated and the imperial authority temporarily reaffirmed, he set about implementing a series of reforms that would shape the trajectory of his reign. However, his aggressive promotion of Iconoclasm and the suppression of dissent would not only define his governance but also exacerbate the existing divisions within Byzantine society. This section delves into the steps Constantine took to secure his rule, the institutional and religious reforms he initiated, and the socio-political consequences of his Iconoclastic policies.

Securing the Imperial Authority

The aftermath of the civil war left the Byzantine Empire in a precarious state. While Constantine had emerged victorious, the scars of conflict lingered, and loyalty among the military and civilian populations remained fragile. To solidify his authority, Constantine recognized the importance of projecting strength and stability. He took immediate steps to strengthen the military and ensure that his supporters were well-compensated for their loyalty during the conflict.

One of the first actions Constantine undertook was to reorganize the military hierarchy. He promoted loyal generals and commanders who had supported him during the war, rewarding them with titles and land. This strategy not only reinforced his military leadership but also ensured that those in key positions were personally invested in his rule. By surrounding himself with a loyal cadre of military leaders, Constantine sought to create a buffer against potential dissent and future uprisings.

Moreover, Constantine implemented financial reforms to stabilize the empire's economy, which had been strained by the civil war. He increased taxes on the wealthy and the aristocracy, redirecting funds to bolster the military and support public works projects. This approach, while effective in the short term, alienated some segments of the elite, who resented the increased taxation and the perceived encroachment on their privileges. Nevertheless, Constantine understood that a robust military was essential both for defending the empire and deterring any further challenges to his rule.

Reinforcing Iconoclasm

Central to Constantine's consolidation of power was his unwavering commitment to Iconoclasm. The religious divide that had fuelled the civil war continued to simmer, and Constantine viewed the enforcement of Iconoclastic policies as a means of solidifying his authority and unifying the empire under a single religious doctrine. His father, Leo III, had laid the groundwork for Iconoclasm, and Constantine sought to build upon this foundation with renewed vigour.

In 754, Constantine convened the Council of Hieria, which aimed to formalize the Iconoclastic position within the Byzantine Church. This council marked a significant step in the institutionalization of Iconoclasm, as it rejected the veneration of icons and declared them heretical. The decisions made at Hieria reinforced the imperial stance on Iconoclasm and provided theological justification for the destruction of icons.

Constantine's approach to Iconoclasm was multifaceted. He ordered the removal of icons from churches and public spaces, believing that their presence contributed to superstition and idolatry. Monasteries, which had traditionally been centres of Iconophilia and resistance to Iconoclastic policies, faced intense scrutiny and repression. Many monastic communities were closed, and their leaders were exiled or imprisoned. This harsh treatment was designed to eliminate the sources of opposition and to align the religious landscape with his vision for the empire.

The enforcement of Iconoclasm was not without resistance. Many clergy and laypeople remained steadfast in their adherence to the veneration of icons, viewing the imperial policies as an affront to their faith. As a result, Constantine faced ongoing challenges from both the religious elite and the general populace. The tension reached boiling point as monastic communities became hotbeds of dissent, leading to acts of rebellion against imperial authority.

The Council of Hieria (754 CE): Theological Debates, Political Dynamics, and Long-Term Impact

The Council of Hieria, convened by Emperor Constantine V in 754 CE, stands as one of the most critical councils in Byzantine history, particularly concerning the issue of Iconoclasm – the rejection of religious images. Often labelled the first 'Iconoclast council', it not only reshaped the religious landscape of the Byzantine Empire but also asserted imperial dominance over the Orthodox Church. Although later condemned, the Council of Hieria remains a fascinating case study in the intersection of theology, politics, and imperial ambition.

Historical Background and Prelude to the Council

1. Early Roots of Iconoclasm in Byzantium

Iconoclasm was a relatively new and controversial position in Byzantium by the time of the Council of Hieria. Emperor Leo III, Constantine V's father, began to restrict the use of religious images in the 720s. His policies likely responded to a mix of theological concerns and practical fears, as several external pressures threatened the empire at the time. The Byzantine military had suffered losses to Islamic forces, which Leo III may have viewed as divine punishment for what he saw as idolatry within Christian practices. Iconoclasm thus emerged as both a theological movement and a political reform, aimed at cleansing the empire and seeking divine favour.

Leo III's Iconoclastic policies were controversial and encountered resistance, particularly from monastic communities, which traditionally held strong ties to icon veneration. By the time Constantine V came to power, these policies had fostered significant division within the church and the broader Byzantine society. The stage was set for a definitive ruling on the matter, which Constantine V aimed to establish through the Council of Hieria.

2. Constantine V's Motivations

Constantine V was an ardent Iconoclast who viewed religious images as both a doctrinal error and a political threat. He saw the veneration of icons as a divisive practice that detracted from his vision of a cohesive empire centred on clear religious doctrine and military strength. Additionally, many monastic communities who championed icon veneration held significant influence and resources, which Constantine sought to control or neutralize. By calling the Council of Hieria, Constantine intended to establish an official doctrine that rejected icon veneration and reinforced his authority over both religious and political realms.

Council Proceedings: Theological Debates and Decisions

1. Composition of the Council and Absence of the Patriarch

The Council of Hieria, held at the imperial palace in Hieria near Constantinople, was attended by 338 bishops from across the Byzantine Empire. However, conspicuously absent were the Patriarch of Constantinople and representatives from the other Eastern patriarchates, who either did not support the Iconoclastic stance or were excluded by Constantine. This lack of broader representation meant the council could not be recognized as ecumenical by the church's standards, a point later used by Iconophiles to dispute its legitimacy.

Constantine carefully selected bishops sympathetic to his Iconoclastic policies, ensuring the council would reach a consensus favourable to his goals. His orchestration of the council demonstrated not only his commitment to Iconoclasm but also his willingness to challenge traditional ecclesiastical authority structures by side-lining dissenting voices within the church.

2. Theological Arguments Against Icon Veneration

At the heart of the council's deliberations was a theological rejection of icon veneration, which it branded as heretical. The council argued that icons violated the essential doctrine of Christianity by attempting to depict the divine. According to the council's logic, icons reduced God's transcendence to mere material forms, an act they considered sacrilegious and idolatrous. This was not just a doctrinal argument but a profound statement on the nature of worship and the relationship between the physical and divine realms.

The council's theological stance was partly influenced by early Christian and Judaic traditions that prohibited the use of images in worship. Furthermore, the Iconoclasts argued that icon veneration undermined the Incarnation by presuming that Christ's divine nature could be represented in mere paint and wood. They contended that venerating such images led believers into a form of spiritual blindness, misplacing worship from the Creator to created materials.

3. Iconophile Counterarguments and the Monastic Defence

Although the Iconophile perspective was suppressed at the Council of Hieria, notable theologians such as John of Damascus had previously articulated defences of icon veneration. John argued that icons served as valuable conduits for worship, functioning as visual aids that connected believers to the divine. The Iconophiles also saw icons as a natural extension of the doctrine of the Incarnation, where God had chosen to become visible in human form through Christ. Thus, representing Christ in icons was not idolatry, but rather a reminder of his humanity and his tangible presence in the world.

These defences resonated particularly within monastic communities, which became strongholds of icon veneration. For many monks, icons were indispensable to their spiritual life, symbolizing the visible connection between earth and heaven. Constantine viewed this defence as a challenge to his authority and as a reason to suppress monastic influence through the council's rulings.

4. Declarations and Penalties Imposed by the Council

The Council of Hieria not only condemned the veneration of icons but also prescribed penalties for those who continued to produce or worship religious images. The council's decisions established severe consequences for those who defied the new doctrines, including excommunication, confiscation of property, and, in some cases, imprisonment or exile. This harsh stance reflected Constantine's intent to enforce Iconoclasm not merely as a doctrinal correction but as an essential aspect of his imperial policy. It also marked an escalation in the state's role in policing private belief and religious practices within the empire.

Impact of the Council on Byzantine Society and Culture

1. Religious and Social Turmoil

The council's decrees deepened divisions within Byzantine society, as large segments of the population, particularly the monastic communities and the general populace, held steadfastly to their devotion to icons. These communities resisted the Iconoclastic decrees, with many monks becoming martyrs for the Iconophile cause. This resistance illustrated how deeply ingrained the veneration of icons was in Byzantine spirituality and identity, even as the state sought to eliminate it. The state's persecution of monastic communities fuelled widespread resentment, contributing to the enduring conflict between the imperial court and religious factions.

2. Transformation of Byzantine Art and Architecture

The Iconoclastic policies enforced by the council had a profound impact on Byzantine art and architecture. Churches, monasteries, and even private homes underwent significant alterations as religious images were removed and replaced with symbolic or geometric designs. This led to a unique period in Byzantine art, where cross motifs and other abstract symbols became prominent, reflecting the Iconoclastic aesthetic imposed by Constantine's regime. Artists, who previously specialized in religious imagery, were compelled to adapt to these new restrictions, affecting the evolution of Byzantine art and introducing stylistic changes that distinguished this period from earlier eras.

3. Economic Impact and Confiscation of Monastic Wealth

One of Constantine's aims in enforcing Iconoclasm was to weaken the economic and social power of monastic institutions, which he viewed as centres of resistance to his policies. The Council of Hieria's decrees enabled the state to confiscate monastic properties and redirect funds toward the military and other state functions. Monasteries, which often accumulated wealth through donations from the devout, saw their lands and resources seized, undermining their ability to function as independent centres of religious and economic influence.

This redirection of resources contributed to the strengthening of the Byzantine military, which Constantine viewed as essential to defending the empire. In this way, the council's decrees were not only religious but also a significant element in Constantine's broader fiscal and military strategy.

Legacy and Long-Term Consequences of the Council of Hieria

1. Enduring Controversy and Resurgence of Icon Veneration

Despite Constantine's intentions, the Council of Hieria failed to settle the Iconoclastic controversy permanently. The rejection of icon veneration, although supported by the state, continued to face fierce opposition from many Byzantines. This resistance ultimately led to the Second Council of Nicaea in 787, which overturned the decrees of the Council of Hieria and restored the veneration of icons. However, Iconoclasm would re-emerge in the early ninth century, demonstrating the depth of the controversy and the persistence of Iconoclastic ideas within certain factions of Byzantine society.

The eventual restoration of icon veneration in 843, known as the Triumph of Orthodoxy, symbolized the victory of the Iconophile movement and marked the beginning of a new era in Byzantine religious life. The rejection of the Council of Hieria's rulings highlighted the resilience of Iconophile devotion and underscored the complex relationship between imperial authority and religious practice.

2. Impact of Byzantine Governance and Caesaropapism

The Council of Hieria exemplified the concept of caesaropapism, where the emperor asserted control over church doctrine and religious life. Constantine V's dominance over the council's proceedings established a precedent for imperial involvement in theological matters, a model that would influence Byzantine governance in subsequent centuries. Although later emperors would adopt different stances on religious issues, the Council of Hieria demonstrated how the Byzantine emperor could exercise near-total authority over religious policy, effectively merging political and spiritual leadership within a single office.

3. Shaping of Byzantine Religious Identity

The Council of Hieria, although later discredited by Orthodox tradition, played a critical role in shaping Byzantine religious identity. The controversy over icons forced Byzantines to grapple with questions about the nature of divine representation, the role of images in worship, and the limits of imperial power over religious life. This prolonged debate fostered a more explicit articulation of Orthodox theology, with the Iconophile victory ultimately reinforcing the significance of visual representations as part of Byzantine spirituality.

4. Influence on Later Iconoclastic Movements

The Council of Hieria and the Iconoclastic policies of Constantine V foreshadowed similar debates in later Christian contexts, such as the Protestant Reformation in Western Europe. The theological arguments surrounding Iconoclasm influenced certain reformers who argued against the use of religious images, drawing parallels with the Byzantine Iconoclasts. Although separated by centuries, the debates surrounding the Council of Hieria highlighted issues of idolatry, iconography, and the role of religious imagery – questions that would continue to resonate in later periods of Christian history.

The Role of Monasticism and Dissent

The suppression of monastic communities was one of the most contentious aspects of Constantine's rule. Monks had historically played a significant role in Byzantine society, not only as spiritual leaders but also as educators and custodians of cultural heritage. Their commitment to the veneration of icons made them natural opponents of Constantine's policies.

In response to the increasing tensions, the emperor ordered raids on monasteries suspected of harbouring Iconophiles. These raids often resulted in the destruction of icons and relics, further inflaming the anger of those who supported the veneration of images. The monks, driven by their beliefs and sense of injustice, began to organize resistance against the imperial authority. Skirmishes broke out between imperial forces and monastic militias, resulting in bloodshed and further polarizing society along religious lines.

Despite the challenges posed by dissenting factions, Constantine remained resolute in his pursuit of a unified Iconoclastic church. He sought to marginalize those who opposed him and create a new ecclesiastical order that aligned with his vision. The destruction of icons was framed not only as a religious necessity but also as a patriotic duty – an effort to protect the empire from external and internal threats that were believed to arise from idolatrous practices.

The Impact on Byzantine Society

The Iconoclastic policies implemented by Constantine had profound implications for Byzantine society. While he sought to create a cohesive religious identity, the reality was far more complicated. The enforcement of Iconoclasm deepened existing divisions and alienated significant segments of the population. As the policies unfolded, a culture of resistance emerged among the Iconophile factions, leading to underground networks that sought to preserve the veneration of icons despite the oppressive environment.

In cities like Constantinople, the atmosphere became increasingly charged as conflicts erupted between Iconoclasts and Iconophiles. Public displays of veneration for icons were met with violent reprisals from the imperial authorities, while underground gatherings of supporters of icon veneration sought to protect their beliefs from persecution. This polarization created a rift in Byzantine society that would last well beyond Constantine's reign, setting the stage for future conflicts and debates over the role of icons in the Christian faith.

The religious strife also had socio-political consequences. Constantine's actions against the monastic communities and clergy led to a loss of trust in the imperial authority among large segments of the population. While many supported the Iconoclastic movement, others began to view the emperor as a tyrant who imposed his will on matters of faith. This perception of Constantine would contribute to his legacy as a polarizing figure in Byzantine history, shaping the narratives of both Iconoclasts and Iconophiles for generations.

Efforts to Rebuild the Empire

Recognizing the challenges posed by dissent, Constantine sought to reinforce the administrative structure of the empire to stabilize the situation. He implemented reforms aimed at improving the efficiency of governance and ensuring loyalty among provincial leaders. The reorganization of the themes, the military districts of the empire, played a crucial role in his strategy. By appointing loyal generals as *strategoi* (military governors) and incentivizing them to enforce imperial policies, Constantine aimed to create a network of loyal supporters throughout the empire.

Constantine also focused on diplomatic efforts to secure peace with neighbouring powers, particularly the Arabs to the east and the Bulgars to the north. His military campaigns against these external threats demonstrated his commitment to protecting the empire's borders and restoring stability. By showcasing his military successes, Constantine sought to rally public support and divert attention from the internal strife caused by his Iconoclastic policies.

Moreover, Constantine recognized the importance of propaganda in shaping public perception of his rule. He commissioned works that celebrated his victories and promoted the virtues of Iconoclasm. The creation of new liturgical texts and theological treatises supported the imperial narrative and framed Iconoclasm as a legitimate and necessary defence of the faith. Through these cultural initiatives, Constantine aimed to reinforce his authority and unify the empire under his vision.

Legacy and Long-Term Consequences

While Constantine V's reign was marked by a series of military successes and administrative reforms, the long-term consequences of his policies would be felt long after his death. The schism between Iconoclasts and Iconophiles deepened during his rule, laying the groundwork for future conflicts. The Iconoclastic controversy would continue to reverberate throughout Byzantine history, influencing theological debates and contributing to the eventual downfall of the Isaurian Dynasty.

The harsh measures taken against dissenters and the brutal suppression of monastic communities created a legacy of bitterness and resentment that would not easily fade. As the empire transitioned into the latter half of the eighth century, the unresolved tensions surrounding Iconoclasm would contribute to further instability and internal conflict.

In the broader context of Byzantine history, Constantine's reign represented a critical turning point. His policies and actions illustrated the complexities of governance in a diverse and often fractious empire. The interplay between religion, politics, and military power during his rule highlighted the challenges faced by subsequent emperors, who would grapple with the consequences of his Iconoclastic policies.

Conclusion

The consolidation of power following the civil war of 742–743 marked a defining phase in Constantine V's reign. His commitment to Iconoclasm and the suppression of dissent established a contentious religious landscape that would shape Byzantine society for years to come. Despite his efforts to stabilize the empire through military and administrative reforms, the divisions created by his policies would persist, leading to ongoing conflicts and debates over the nature of faith and authority in the Byzantine world.

As Constantine navigated the complexities of leadership, he faced the challenge of reconciling his vision for the empire with the diverse beliefs and loyalties of his subjects. The struggles of his reign serve as a poignant reminder of the delicate balance between power and faith, authority and dissent, that would define the Byzantine Empire in the centuries to follow.

Section 3: Military Campaigns and Defence of the Empire

Constantine V's reign was characterized by a series of military campaigns that not only defended the Byzantine Empire against external threats but also sought to consolidate his power following the civil war. The military became a vital tool for Constantine, allowing him to project strength, secure borders, and reinforce his authority as emperor. This section examines the various military endeavours undertaken by Constantine, focusing on his strategies, key battles, and the broader implications of his campaigns for the stability and longevity of the Byzantine Empire.

The Military Context of Constantine's Reign

When Constantine ascended to the throne, the Byzantine Empire was embroiled in conflicts on multiple fronts. The rise of Islamic power in the east posed a significant challenge, with the Umayyad Caliphate expanding aggressively into Byzantine territories. The Byzantine Empire had suffered defeats in previous encounters, and the need for a robust military response was critical. Additionally, the north posed its own threats, particularly from the Bulgars, who were increasingly aggressive in their incursions into Byzantine territory.

The challenges were immense, and the resources of the empire were stretched thin, partly due to the civil war that had recently ravaged the land. Constantine recognized that military strength was essential not only for defending the empire but also for legitimizing his rule. He understood that successful campaigns would bolster his standing among his subjects and reaffirm the authority of the Isaurian Dynasty.

Reorganizing the Military Structure

In order to respond effectively to the external threats, Constantine embarked on a military reorganization. He understood that the Byzantine military had to be agile, well-trained, and capable of rapid mobilization in the face of emerging threats. The reforms he implemented aimed to improve the effectiveness of the themes, the military districts that formed the backbone of the Byzantine military system.

One of his key reforms was the enhancement of the role of the *strategoi*, the military governors of the themes. Constantine appointed loyal and capable leaders to these positions, ensuring that they would remain committed to the imperial cause. These *strategoi* were responsible for raising troops, maintaining order, and conducting military campaigns in their respective regions. By empowering the themes, Constantine created a decentralized yet effective military structure that could respond to threats across the empire.

In addition to reorganizing the themes, Constantine invested in the training and equipping of troops. He implemented new training regimens that emphasized mobility, tactics, and the effective use of cavalry, which was a hallmark of Byzantine military success. The emphasis on cavalry would play a crucial role in his campaigns, allowing his forces to execute swift and decisive manoeuvres against enemies.

Campaigns Against the Arabs

One of the most pressing threats to the Byzantine Empire during Constantine's reign came from the Umayyad Caliphate. The Arab armies had made significant inroads into Byzantine territory, and by the 740s, they posed a serious danger to the eastern provinces. Constantine recognized that a robust military response was necessary to reclaim lost territories and prevent further incursions.

In 740, Constantine launched a counter-offensive against the Arabs in the region of Anatolia. His campaign aimed to reclaim lost territory and assert Byzantine dominance in the region. He led a series of coordinated strikes against Arab forces, utilizing the reorganized themes to create a well-structured military campaign. The strategy included engaging in both defensive and offensive manoeuvres, allowing his forces to capitalize on weaknesses in Arab positions.

One notable engagement occurred at the Battle of Acroinon in 740, where Constantine's forces confronted an Arab army attempting to penetrate deep into Byzantine territory. The battle was intense, with both sides suffering significant casualties. However, Constantine's innovative tactics and the mobility of his cavalry proved decisive. By executing flanking manoeuvres and employing surprise attacks, his forces were able to encircle the Arab troops, forcing them into retreat. The victory at Acroinon was a pivotal moment in halting the Arab advance into Anatolia, showcasing the effectiveness of Constantine's military reforms.

Following this success, Constantine continued to campaign against the Arabs, launching a series of raids into enemy territory. His military efforts not only aimed to reclaim lost lands but also sought to disrupt the supply lines and morale of the Arab forces. These campaigns proved to be effective in containing the Arab threat and securing the eastern provinces.

The Defence of Constantinople

While Constantine actively engaged in campaigns in the east, the defence of Constantinople remained a top priority. The city was a symbol of Byzantine power and authority, and its security was essential for the stability of the empire. The memories of the sieges of previous decades loomed large, and Constantine understood that the threat of another siege was ever-present.

To bolster the city's defences, Constantine initiated a series of fortification projects, enhancing the walls and implementing new defensive technologies. The famous Theodosian Walls, already a formidable barrier, were further reinforced under his reign. Constantine also organized a network of lookouts and scouts to provide early warnings of approaching enemies, allowing for better preparedness in the event of a siege.

Constantine's military reforms included the establishment of a standing navy, recognizing the importance of maritime power in protecting the empire's interests. The naval fleet was tasked with securing the Bosporus Strait and patrolling the Aegean Sea, preventing pirate activity and ensuring safe passage for trade routes. The establishment of a strong naval presence not only fortified Constantinople but also projected power across the Mediterranean.

In 746, Constantine faced a significant threat from the Arab forces once again. A large Arab army, aiming to capture Constantinople, laid siege to the city. The defence of Constantinople became a test of resolve for both the emperor and the citizens. Utilizing the fortified walls and the strategic advantages of the city, Constantine organized a robust defence. The Byzantines employed a combination of military tactics, including the use of Greek fire, a secret weapon that devastated enemy ships.

The siege lasted for several months, and the resilience of the Byzantine forces was tested. Despite facing starvation and dwindling supplies, the defenders held firm under Constantine's leadership. The resolve of the people, coupled with the ingenuity of Byzantine military tactics, ultimately led to a successful defence. The Arab forces, unable to breach the walls, eventually withdrew, marking a significant victory for Constantine and the empire.

Campaigns Against the Bulgars

In addition to the Arab threat, the northern borders of the empire faced incursions from the Bulgars. The rise of the Bulgarian state posed a significant challenge to Byzantine authority in the Balkans. Constantine recognized the need for a comprehensive military strategy to deal with this growing power.

The first major conflict with the Bulgars occurred in 759 when they crossed into Byzantine territory, threatening the themes of Thrace and Macedonia. Constantine mobilized a large army, reinforcing the themes in the region and preparing for a decisive confrontation. The Byzantine military had been bolstered by the success of previous campaigns, and the soldiers were motivated by their recent victories.

At the Battle of Pliska in 759, Constantine faced the Bulgarian forces head-on. The battle was fierce, characterized by heavy fighting and significant casualties on both sides. Constantine's forces employed the tactics honed during previous campaigns, utilizing cavalry charges and well-coordinated infantry manoeuvres. The Bulgars, despite their initial successes, were unable to withstand the onslaught of the Byzantine military.

The Battle of Pliska (759 CE): A Byzantine Victory Amidst Protracted Conflict

The Battle of Pliska in 759 CE was one of several significant clashes between the Byzantine Empire and the Bulgarian Khanate in the ongoing struggle for dominance in the Balkan region. This battle, while less well-documented than the more famous encounter in 811 CE, showcases the persistent conflict between the Byzantines and Bulgarians, as well as Emperor Constantine V's determination to secure Byzantine influence in the Balkans. Constantine's victory in this engagement temporarily bolstered Byzantine morale and demonstrated his tactical acumen. However, the win did little to resolve the long-standing tension between the two powers.

Background to the Battle: Byzantine-Bulgarian Rivalry

The Byzantine Empire and the Bulgarian Khanate had been in conflict over the control of territories in the Balkans since the establishment of the First Bulgarian Empire in 681 CE. Both empires aimed to dominate the strategically-important region, which served as a gateway between Eastern Europe and the Byzantine heartland. The Bulgarians had gained substantial power and territory under previous leaders, creating a formidable buffer against Byzantine expansion.

Emperor Constantine V, one of the more militarily aggressive Byzantine emperors of the eighth century, pursued numerous campaigns to curb Bulgarian influence and reclaim disputed lands. This focus on military endeavours led to a series of engagements between the two empires over several decades, including the Battle of Anchialus in 763 and other skirmishes near Thrace and Moesia.

In 759 CE, Khan Vinekh of Bulgaria led his forces into the region, threatening Byzantine defences near Pliska, the capital of the Bulgarian Empire. This movement presented an opportunity for Constantine V to counter the Bulgarian advance and reinforce Byzantine control over critical border territories.

Military Preparations and Strategic Objectives

Byzantine Forces and Strategy

Constantine V mobilized a substantial Byzantine army, likely composed of experienced tagmata troops from Constantinople, as well as provincial soldiers from the themes of Thrace and Macedonia. Known for his attention to detail and strategic planning, Constantine prepared his forces carefully, aiming to meet the Bulgarians on favourable terrain and to leverage the disciplined nature of his troops.

The Byzantine strategy was relatively straightforward: Constantine intended to lure the Bulgarian forces into a pitched battle where the Byzantines' superior organization and equipment could give them an advantage. Byzantine infantry were well-equipped with spears, swords, and the distinctive round shields often used by Byzantine foot soldiers. Archers and cavalry also played a central role in Constantine's battle plans, allowing him to exploit the open battlefield with ranged attacks and rapid manoeuvres.

Bulgarian Forces and Tactics

Khan Vinekh's Bulgarian army was comprised mainly of mounted troops, reflecting the Bulgarian emphasis on cavalry in warfare. Bulgarian horsemen were known for their speed and agility, which made them formidable in both skirmishes and full-scale battles. Vinekh aimed to exploit the mobility of his forces by drawing the Byzantines into vulnerable positions, from where Bulgarian riders could use hit-and-run tactics to weaken and demoralize them.

Unlike the later battle in 811, which occurred within a well-planned ambush site, the Battle of Pliska in 759 unfolded in a more open setting. Both forces were able to manoeuvre freely, and the Bulgarians hoped to use the surrounding terrain to their advantage. However, Vinekh's approach would be tested by Constantine's disciplined command over the Byzantine forces.

The Battle Unfolds

The battle began with a series of skirmishes, as Bulgarian horsemen attempted to harass the Byzantine lines and provoke a disorderly advance. Constantine V, however, kept his forces in formation, directing his cavalry and archers to respond with coordinated counterattacks. The Byzantines' discipline held, and the Bulgarian tactics failed to break their lines.

After several hours of manoeuvring, Constantine ordered a full-scale assault. Byzantine cavalry, supported by archers, charged into the Bulgarian formations, breaking through their defences and disrupting their cohesion. The well-armoured Byzantine cataphracts proved particularly effective against the lighter-armed Bulgarian horsemen, who struggled to withstand the onslaught.

Constantine's use of combined arms – the coordination of infantry, cavalry, and archers – overwhelmed the Bulgarian forces. The Bulgarian army, unable to regroup effectively, began to suffer heavy casualties. Khan Vinekh realized that his forces were outmatched and ordered a retreat, but by then the Byzantines had gained the upper hand.

Outcome and Aftermath

The Byzantine victory at Pliska was decisive, with Bulgarian forces suffering significant losses. Constantine V's triumph reinforced Byzantine dominance in the region, albeit temporarily, as the Byzantine army was unable to capitalize fully on the win to secure a lasting peace. Despite the setback, the Bulgarians maintained their independence and continued to challenge Byzantine authority in subsequent years.

Constantine's victory bolstered his reputation as a capable military leader, one determined to maintain Byzantine control over contested borderlands. This victory at Pliska, like the later one at Anchialus, underscored Constantine's commitment to an aggressive foreign policy aimed at curbing the influence of neighbouring powers.

Short-Term Impact on Byzantine-Bulgarian Relations

In the immediate aftermath, the Battle of Pliska forced Khan Vinekh into a defensive posture. The loss weakened his position among the Bulgarian nobility, who began to question his leadership. In response, Vinekh sought peace with the Byzantines, but this move was unpopular among the Bulgarian elite, who viewed Constantine's campaigns as an existential threat to Bulgarian sovereignty. Consequently, Vinekh was eventually overthrown, and subsequent Bulgarian rulers continued to resist Byzantine incursions.

Long-Term Influence on Byzantine Military Strategy

The victory at Pliska also had long-term implications for Byzantine military thinking. Constantine V's success in this battle and others during his reign reinforced the value of a disciplined, well-equipped army capable of responding flexibly to the fast-moving cavalry tactics commonly used by the Bulgarians and other steppe-based powers. Future Byzantine emperors would take note of these strategies, and the Byzantine military continued to adapt its tactics to counter the cavalry-based armies of the region.

However, Constantine's campaigns, though successful, did not result in a lasting peace. The aggressive stance taken by the Byzantines only fuelled further animosity between the two empires, setting the stage for decades of intermittent warfare that would ultimately culminate in future battles, including the catastrophic defeat of the Byzantine army at Pliska in 811 under Emperor Nikephoros I.

Legacy of the Battle of Pliska (759 CE)

The Battle of Pliska in 759 CE marked an important, if temporary, assertion of Byzantine power in the Balkans. Constantine V's success underscored his reputation as a warrior-emperor who prioritized the security of the empire's borders and aimed to assert dominance over neighbouring states. His victory at Pliska was emblematic of his broader policy of containment and confrontation with the Bulgarian Khanate.

While the battle did not bring lasting peace, it demonstrated the tactical flexibility and strength of the Byzantine military under Constantine's leadership. His campaigns against Bulgaria helped to develop Byzantine tactics, especially in combined-arms warfare and the coordination of cavalry, infantry, and archers. In this regard, the battle contributed to the evolving Byzantine military tradition that would continue to develop over subsequent centuries.

Ultimately, the battle and Constantine's broader Bulgarian campaigns solidified his legacy as an emperor determined to protect Byzantine interests in the Balkans. However, the underlying tensions between the Byzantine and Bulgarian states remained unresolved, as the Bulgarians continued to grow in power and influence in the region. The intermittent peace that followed proved fragile, with both sides bracing for future conflicts that would continue to shape the balance of power in south-eastern Europe.

The victory at Pliska established Byzantine dominance in the region and forced the Bulgars to retreat. Constantine capitalized on this victory by negotiating a peace treaty that secured the borders and established tributary relations with the Bulgarian state. This approach not only prevented further conflict but also allowed for the stabilization of the empire's northern frontiers.

The Broader Implications of Constantine's Military Campaigns

Constantine V's military campaigns had profound implications for the Byzantine Empire. His successes against both the Arabs and the Bulgars reinforced Byzantine authority and showcased the effectiveness of his military reforms. The victories helped restore confidence in the empire's military capabilities and strengthened the resolve of the citizens.

Moreover, the successful defence of Constantinople against the Arab siege solidified Constantine's status as a formidable leader. His ability to unite the military and civilian populations in defence of the city fostered a sense of communal identity and pride. The resilience displayed during the siege became a source of inspiration for future generations, reinforcing the idea that the Byzantine Empire could withstand external threats.

However, while the military successes bolstered Constantine's reputation, they also contributed to the complexities of governance. The emphasis on military campaigns and the allocation of resources to defence often came at the expense of social and economic stability. The strains of ongoing warfare placed significant burdens on the populace, leading to increased taxation and military conscription. This imbalance contributed to underlying tensions that would resurface in the years to come.

Additionally, the focus on military endeavours reinforced the imperial ideology that equated military success with divine favour. Constantine positioned himself as a defender of the faith, framing his campaigns against the Arabs and Bulgars as holy wars. This rhetoric not only served to legitimize his rule but also heightened the religious fervour surrounding military endeavours, complicating the already intricate relationship between faith and politics within the empire.

Conclusion

The military campaigns of Constantine V were pivotal in shaping the course of Byzantine history during the eighth century. His strategic leadership, coupled with reforms to the military structure, allowed him to confront external threats effectively and defend the integrity of the empire. The victories over the Arabs and Bulgars bolstered his authority and reaffirmed the strength of the Byzantine military.

However, these successes were not without their costs. The ongoing military efforts strained resources and contributed to societal tensions that would continue to influence the empire long after Constantine's reign. As he navigated the complexities of governance, Constantine V left a lasting legacy defined by both military prowess and the enduring challenges of leadership in a diverse and often fractious empire.

Chapter 3

The Religious and Cultural Landscape of Constantine V

Section 1: Iconoclasm and Its Impact on Byzantine Society

The reign of Constantine V marked a pivotal moment in the Byzantine Empire, characterized by significant religious upheaval and cultural transformation. At the heart of this transformation was the Iconoclastic movement, which sought to eliminate the veneration of icons within the Christian faith. This section explores the roots of Iconoclasm, the motivations behind Constantine V's policies, and the profound effects these measures had on Byzantine society, including the response from various social groups, the cultural ramifications, and the long-term implications for the Church and the state.

The Roots of Iconoclasm

The roots of the Iconoclastic movement can be traced back to theological debates about the nature of God and the appropriate expressions of faith. By the time of Constantine V, the Christian Church had been grappling with the question of idolatry for centuries. The Second Commandment, which prohibits the making of graven images, was a significant point of contention for those who believed that the veneration of icons was tantamount to idolatry.

Iconoclasm gained momentum under Constantine's father, Leo III, who issued an edict in 726 that forbade the veneration of icons. Leo's motivations were both theological and political; he sought to unify the empire under a singular religious doctrine and believed that the veneration of icons divided Christians. The Iconoclasts argued that the use of images was not only unnecessary but also detrimental to true worship.

This theological debate was compounded by the socio-political landscape of the empire. The rise of Islamic power in the east and the experiences of military defeat led some Byzantine leaders to view the veneration of icons as a source of divine displeasure. They believed that by rejecting icons, they could restore God's favour and strengthen the empire against external threats. This perspective gained traction during Constantine V's reign, setting the stage for a more aggressive enforcement of Iconoclasm.

Constantine V's Iconoclastic Policies

Upon ascending to the throne, Constantine V inherited his father's Iconoclastic agenda and embraced it with fervour. He viewed the promotion of Iconoclasm as a means of consolidating power and unifying the empire. To this end, he enacted a series of policies that aimed to eliminate the veneration of icons, framing these measures as essential to the defence of the faith and the stability of the empire.

One of the first actions Constantine took was to convene the Council of Hieria in 754. This council represented a significant turning point in the Iconoclastic movement, as it formally rejected the veneration of icons and declared it heretical. The decisions made at Hieria not only solidified the Iconoclastic stance within the Church but also provided theological justification for the destruction of images.

The council's rulings were accompanied by a series of edicts that mandated the removal of icons from churches and public spaces. Churches that displayed images were often raided, and their icons were destroyed. Constantine's approach was not merely punitive; he actively sought to re-educate the clergy and laity about the supposed dangers of icon veneration, portraying it as a misguided practice that led to idolatry and divine wrath.

In addition to the destruction of icons, Constantine instituted a crackdown on monasteries, which were often centres of Iconophile sentiment. Many monasteries faced closure, and their leaders were exiled or imprisoned. The monastic communities, dedicated to the veneration of icons, resisted these measures, resulting in violent confrontations with imperial forces. The suppression of monasticism became a hallmark of Constantine's Iconoclastic policies, and the consequences of this repression would reverberate throughout Byzantine society.

Responses from the Clergy and the Laity

The response to Constantine V's Iconoclastic policies varied widely across Byzantine society. While some segments of the clergy and laity supported the Iconoclastic movement, many others staunchly opposed it. The religious landscape became increasingly polarized, with fervent Iconophiles viewing the destruction of icons as an attack on their faith.

Prominent bishops and theologians emerged as vocal opponents of Iconoclasm. Figures such as Saint John of Damascus and Theodore the Studite defended the veneration of icons, arguing that images served as important tools for teaching and devotion. They maintained that icons were not objects of worship but rather windows to the divine, helping the faithful to connect with the spiritual realm. These arguments were rooted in a deep understanding of Christian theology and the historical role of icons in the Church.

The opposition from the clergy was met with severe repression. Many bishops who refused to adhere to Constantine's policies were deposed, exiled, or imprisoned. The Iconophiles became targets of state persecution, creating a culture of fear and division within the Church. The tension between Iconoclasts and Iconophiles escalated, leading to conflicts in churches, public spaces, and even within families.

The laity, too, was deeply divided. While some embraced the Iconoclastic movement as a means of restoring the empire's fortunes, many ordinary Christians were unwilling to part with their icons. For them, the images represented a tangible connection to their faith, their community, and their personal spirituality. The destruction of these icons was perceived as an affront to their religious identity and cultural heritage.

The struggle between Iconoclasts and Iconophiles extended beyond theological disputes; it became a cultural battleground. Churches that had been decorated with icons for centuries were stripped of their visual history, and the loss of these images was felt acutely by communities that had relied on them for spiritual inspiration and guidance. The pain of this loss created a rift that would persist for generations.

Cultural Ramifications of Iconoclasm

The impact of Constantine V's Iconoclastic policies extended into the cultural fabric of Byzantine society. The removal of icons from churches and public life led to a significant shift in the artistic expression of faith. Iconoclasm forced artists and craftsmen to re-evaluate their roles and the purpose of their work. Many artists who had dedicated their lives to creating religious imagery were left without a means of expression, leading to a decline in artistic production.

With the decline of iconography came a shift toward other forms of religious expression. Mosaics, frescoes, and decorative patterns became more prevalent as artists sought to find ways to express spirituality without violating the edicts against icons. This transition reflected an adaptation to the changing religious landscape, but it also signalled a loss of the rich visual culture that had characterized Byzantine Christianity.

In the broader context of Byzantine culture, the emphasis on Iconoclasm contributed to a climate of suspicion and division. The questioning of established religious practices led to broader societal implications, as individuals began to scrutinize not only the role of icons but also the authority of the Church and the emperor. The conflicts surrounding Iconoclasm fostered a culture of dissent that would eventually contribute to a more profound questioning of imperial authority and the relationship between Church and state.

Political Implications of Iconoclastic Policies

The religious and cultural upheaval brought about by Constantine V's Iconoclastic policies had significant political implications. The struggle between Iconoclasts and Iconophiles became entwined with issues of loyalty and governance. The emperor's aggressive stance on Iconoclasm was perceived by some as an extension of his political power, raising concerns about the relationship between secular authority and religious belief.

Many in the empire began to view the Iconoclastic policies as a means for Constantine to consolidate power rather than as a genuine religious reform. The perception that the emperor was prioritizing his political agenda over the spiritual needs of the populace fuelled resentment among segments of the population. As the opposition grew, the opposition to the emperor's authority became increasingly vocal, leading to protests, riots, and acts of defiance against imperial edicts.

This dissent was particularly pronounced among the monastic communities, which had historically served as centres of spiritual and intellectual life within the empire. The repression of monasticism not only alienated the clergy but also led to a broader backlash against the emperor's policies. Monks and their supporters became symbols of resistance, rallying the faithful around the preservation of icons and traditional practices.

The political ramifications of Iconoclasm extended beyond the immediate conflict between factions. The divisions created by the Iconoclastic controversy would shape the future of the Byzantine Empire, contributing to ongoing instability and challenges to imperial authority. The failure to reconcile the religious divide between Iconoclasts and Iconophiles laid the groundwork for future conflicts and power struggles that would define Byzantine politics for centuries to come.

The Legacy of Constantine V's Iconoclasm

The legacy of Constantine V's Iconoclastic policies is complex and multifaceted. While his actions were intended to unify the empire under a singular religious doctrine, they ultimately deepened divisions within Byzantine society. The Iconoclastic movement became a defining issue of the eighth and ninth centuries, influencing theological debates, artistic expression, and political dynamics.

The repercussions of Iconoclasm extended well beyond Constantine's reign. Subsequent emperors faced the challenge of reconciling the conflicting factions within Church and society. The oscillation between Iconoclasm and Iconophilia became a recurring theme in Byzantine history, resulting in cycles of repression and resistance that would shape the empire's religious identity.

Moreover, the cultural loss associated with the destruction of icons had lasting effects on Byzantine art and spirituality. The decline of iconography and the shift towards alternative forms of religious expression altered the artistic landscape, marking a significant departure from the rich tradition that had characterized Byzantine Christianity. This transformation would influence subsequent generations of artists and theologians as they grappled with the implications of Iconoclastic ideology.

Conclusion

Constantine V's Iconoclastic policies marked a turning point in the religious and cultural landscape of the Byzantine Empire. His aggressive stance against the veneration of icons reflected a complex interplay of theological, political, and social motivations. The impact of these policies was profound, leading to deep divisions within society, a decline in artistic expression, and challenges to imperial authority.

As the empire grappled with the consequences of Iconoclasm, the struggle for religious identity and cultural continuity became a defining feature of Byzantine life. The legacy of this period would echo through the centuries, shaping the trajectory of the empire and its relationship with faith, art, and authority. The enduring questions raised during Constantine V's reign about the nature of worship, the role of images, and the power of the state would continue to resonate in the Byzantine world and beyond.

Section 2: Cultural Developments and Intellectual Life

The reign of Constantine V was not only marked by military conflicts and religious upheaval but also by significant cultural developments that shaped the Byzantine Empire's identity. During this period, the cultural landscape underwent transformations in art, literature, education, and philosophy, influenced by the broader social and political changes brought about by Constantine's policies, particularly his Iconoclastic stance. This section explores the cultural developments of the time, the role of education and intellectual life, and the interplay between culture and politics within Byzantine society.

The Artistic Landscape in the Context of Iconoclasm

The Iconoclastic movement, with its emphasis on the destruction of religious images, had a profound impact on the artistic landscape of the Byzantine Empire. The cultural expression that flourished in the centuries prior to Constantine V's reign faced significant challenges due to the policies aimed at eliminating the veneration of icons. Artists and craftsmen, whose work was intimately connected to religious expression, found themselves at a crossroads.

Despite the restrictions, the period was not devoid of artistic innovation. Artists adapted to the changing religious climate by exploring new forms of artistic expression. Mosaics and frescoes began to dominate, as these art forms could convey religious themes without directly violating the Iconoclastic decrees. The use of abstract patterns, intricate designs, and symbolic representations became more pronounced in ecclesiastical architecture and decorative arts, allowing artists to maintain a connection to spiritual themes while adhering to the demands of Iconoclasm.

In churches that had previously been adorned with icons, mosaics depicting biblical scenes, saints, and allegorical figures began to take their place. The use of colour, light, and perspective in these mosaics aimed to create an ethereal quality, emphasizing the divine presence rather than the physical form of Christ or the saints. While this shift represented a significant departure from traditional iconography, it also opened new avenues for artistic expression and allowed for the continuation of religious art within the constraints of Iconoclasm.

Additionally, the emergence of non-religious themes in art became more pronounced during this time. As the rigid restrictions of Iconoclasm took hold, artists began to explore secular subjects, drawing on themes from mythology, history, and daily life. This diversification reflected broader cultural trends and the influence of classical antiquity, which continued to resonate in Byzantine society. The blending of religious and secular themes in art would set the stage for future artistic developments in the Byzantine Empire, culminating in the eventual restoration of icon veneration in later centuries.

Education and Intellectual Life

Education and intellectual life during Constantine V's reign played a crucial role in shaping the cultural identity of the Byzantine Empire. The education system, rooted in the classical traditions of antiquity, emphasized the study of literature, philosophy, rhetoric, and the sciences. However, the turbulent political and religious landscape during this period also influenced educational practices and intellectual discourse.

The rise of monasticism had a profound impact on education in Byzantine society. Monasteries served as centres of learning, preserving classical texts and religious manuscripts while also providing instruction in theology and philosophy. Monastic schools became important venues for the dissemination of knowledge, producing scholars and theologians who would contribute to the intellectual life of the empire.

Prominent figures emerged during this period, contributing to theological debates and philosophical discourse. Scholars such as John of Damascus, an influential theologian and philosopher, defended the veneration of icons in his writings and became a prominent voice against the Iconoclastic policies of Constantine V. His works, including '*The Fount of Wisdom*', offered a synthesis of Christian theology and Greek philosophy, emphasizing the compatibility of faith and reason. John's arguments against Iconoclasm were rooted in a deep understanding of both scripture and the traditions of the Church, and his writings had a lasting impact on Byzantine theology.

The educational landscape also underwent changes as a result of Constantine V's Iconoclastic policies. The closure of many monasteries led to a decline in traditional modes of education. However, this vacuum prompted a re-examination of educational practices, with some secular institutions emerging to fill the gap. These institutions began to adopt a more comprehensive approach to education, incorporating not only religious studies but also subjects such as rhetoric, grammar, and history.

The revival of interest in classical literature and philosophy was another significant development during this time. As Byzantine scholars sought to reconcile their Christian faith with the legacy of antiquity, they engaged with the works of ancient Greek and Roman thinkers. This intellectual engagement laid the groundwork for the eventual revival of classical learning in the later Byzantine period, particularly during the Renaissance.

The Interplay of Culture and Politics

The relationship between culture and politics in the Byzantine Empire during Constantine V's reign was complex and dynamic. The emperor recognized the power of culture as a tool for governance and control. By promoting certain cultural developments and suppressing others, he sought to reinforce his authority and unify the empire under a shared identity.

Constantine's policies regarding education, art, and religion were intimately tied to his political agenda. The emphasis on Iconoclasm not only sought to establish religious orthodoxy but also served to consolidate the emperor's political power. By positioning himself as a defender of true faith, Constantine aimed to rally support among the populace and secure loyalty from the military and the clergy.

However, the repercussions of these policies were not entirely predictable. The suppression of Iconophiles and the monastic communities led to significant social tensions. As the emperor faced resistance from those who viewed his policies as oppressive, the interplay between culture and politics became increasingly fraught. The cultural divide between Iconoclasts and Iconophiles mirrored broader societal divisions, challenging the notion of a unified Byzantine identity.

The political landscape of the time also influenced cultural expression. The ongoing military conflicts and external threats shaped the narratives within literature and art. Works produced during this period often reflected themes of struggle, resilience, and divine intervention, resonating with a populace grappling with the realities of war and uncertainty. The need for unity in the face of external challenges became a recurring theme, and cultural expressions began to serve as vehicles for reinforcing loyalty to the emperor and the state.

Literary Developments and Cultural Production

The literary landscape of the Byzantine Empire during Constantine V's reign was marked by significant developments in both religious and secular literature. The tensions surrounding Iconoclasm spurred a rich body of writings that addressed the controversies of the time, reflecting the complex interplay between faith, culture, and politics.

In addition to the theological works of figures like John of Damascus, various other genres of literature flourished during this period. Poetry, historical writings, and hagiography (the biographies of saints) became popular forms of expression. These literary forms served not only to entertain but also to educate and inspire the faithful.

Historical writings from this period often sought to contextualize the current events within the broader narrative of Byzantine history. Historians aimed to provide moral lessons and reflections on the consequences of political and religious decisions. The works of historians such as Theophanes the Confessor offer valuable insights into the political and religious dynamics of the era, chronicling events and providing commentary on the implications of Constantine's policies.

Moreover, hagiographies became a significant literary form, particularly as the cult of saints continued to play a vital role in Byzantine spirituality. The lives of saints were celebrated not only for their piety and virtues but also for their resilience in the face of persecution. Hagiographies often reflected the struggles of the faithful against the backdrop of Iconoclasm, serving to inspire devotion and bolster the spirits of communities facing religious repression.

The period also witnessed a growing interest in secular literature, with themes drawn from classical antiquity gaining prominence. Works that explored philosophical concepts, moral dilemmas, and human experiences began to emerge alongside religious texts. The blending of secular and religious themes in literature reflected the complexities of Byzantine identity and the ongoing dialogue between faith and reason.

The Role of Women in Cultural Life

The cultural developments during Constantine V's reign also encompassed the roles and contributions of women in Byzantine society. While the patriarchal structure of society often limited women's formal participation in public life, they played significant roles in the preservation and transmission of culture within the domestic sphere.

Women were instrumental in the production of religious artefacts, including textiles, manuscripts, and other decorative arts. Many women participated in monastic communities, contributing to the preservation of religious texts and engaging in artistic production. Monastic life provided women with opportunities for education and spiritual fulfilment, allowing them to engage with theological debates and express their faith through art and writing.

Prominent women such as empresses and noblewomen also wielded influence during this period. The empresses served as patrons of the arts and played a vital role in the promotion of religious practices. Their involvement in the cultural life of the empire helped to shape public perceptions of the imperial family and its connection to the Church.

Women's contributions to literature and religious life often went unrecognized in the historical record, yet their roles were crucial in maintaining the cultural continuity of Byzantine society. The legacy of women in this era can be seen in the enduring traditions of Byzantine art, literature, and spirituality that would influence future generations.

The Role of Women in the Cultural Sphere during Constantine V's Reign

The Byzantine Empire was rich in artistic, literary, and religious traditions, and women played a critical role in sustaining and enriching these aspects of cultural life. Despite societal limitations on their public roles, Byzantine women engaged deeply in the cultural sphere through contributions in art, literature, music, and the preservation of spiritual traditions. In particular, noblewomen, empresses, and monastic women became central to the preservation of Byzantine cultural identity, even amidst Constantine V's Iconoclastic policies.

Women as Patrons and Custodians of Byzantine Art

During the eighth century, women of the Byzantine aristocracy were often patrons of the arts, commissioning works that adorned churches, convents, and even private homes. These commissions included mosaics, frescoes, illuminated manuscripts, and religious artefacts that symbolized their devotion. Despite Constantine V's Iconoclastic stance, many noblewomen continued to support artists and artisans who created works aligned with traditional Orthodox imagery, although in more discreet settings. In these spaces, they fostered the continuity of visual culture that emphasized religious themes, often adapting the content to reflect their own spiritual convictions.

Artisans working under the patronage of these women were sometimes asked to create subtle religious symbols that could pass as secular designs or nature motifs, allowing icons to exist in a concealed form. Women's involvement in commissioning art reflected both their spiritual resilience and their determination to preserve Byzantine artistic heritage, even under restrictions. For example, personal devotional objects like *enkolpia* (pendants bearing religious images) and *crosses* served as concealed tokens of faith. These items not only reinforced personal piety but also symbolized a quiet defiance of imperial policy.

Literary Contributions and the Education of Women

Education, although generally limited for women in Byzantine society, was more accessible for women of noble or imperial background. Empresses and high-ranking noblewomen often received instruction in literature, theology, and history, allowing them to participate in the intellectual life of the court and to influence cultural conversations. Their education often extended to the reading and preservation of sacred texts, classical literature, and chronicles, which were crucial to the empire's intellectual continuity.

Women in religious communities, particularly nuns, played a central role in copying manuscripts and preserving theological writings. Despite Constantine's Iconoclastic policies, convents served as vital centres for the transcription of religious texts, including those that promoted Iconophile doctrines. The labour of female scribes in these convents helped to ensure that Orthodox teachings survived the Iconoclastic controversies, enabling future generations to access a rich repository of Byzantine theological and cultural knowledge.

Women also contributed original works, including hymns, poems, and theological reflections. These works sometimes reflected their personal experiences of faith, devotion, and the challenges of living in an era of religious conflict. The writings of Byzantine women were often preserved within religious communities and offered a unique perspective on the spiritual life of the empire, highlighting the intellectual and emotional resilience of women during times of upheaval.

Women's Influence on Byzantine Music and Hymnography

Music and hymnography held a special place in Byzantine worship, and women were deeply involved in this cultural and spiritual practice. Byzantine hymns, sung during liturgical services, played an essential role in reinforcing religious beliefs, particularly in an era when literacy was limited and oral tradition remained strong. Noblewomen and empresses, who often had the resources to support choirs and musicians, were patrons of Byzantine liturgical music.

In convents, nuns were known to compose and perform hymns that celebrated the Orthodox faith, using music as a form of worship and, subtly, as resistance to Iconoclasm. Hymns written by female monastics occasionally included references to saints and martyrs who were venerated by Iconophiles, subtly asserting their beliefs without directly opposing imperial edicts. The preservation and creation of these hymns not only reinforced the spiritual life of monastic communities but also contributed to the broader Byzantine musical tradition, with melodies and lyrical themes that would endure through subsequent generations.

The Role of Women in the Preservation of Oral and Folk Traditions

In Byzantine society, women were often the primary custodians of oral and folk traditions, including legends, tales, and spiritual stories passed down through generations. Within their families and communities, women shared stories that conveyed moral lessons, historical knowledge, and cultural values. This form of cultural preservation was particularly important during Constantine V's reign, as the Iconoclastic policies threatened traditional modes of religious expression.

Oral traditions often celebrated the lives of saints and martyrs who had defended the veneration of icons, effectively preserving Iconophile sentiments within Byzantine culture. By sharing these stories, women reinforced a sense of spiritual continuity that persisted despite official prohibitions on icons. These traditions became part of a quiet resistance, ensuring that younger generations retained a connection to Orthodox beliefs even as the empire's official stance shifted. Through these shared stories, Byzantine women helped preserve cultural memory, creating a legacy that would eventually support the restoration of icons in later periods.

The Cultural Influence of Women in Religious Communities

Religious communities, especially convents, offered Byzantine women an opportunity to engage in cultural and intellectual pursuits that were otherwise limited in secular society. Convents often functioned as centres of education, art, and literature, allowing women to explore theological, literary, and artistic disciplines that might be inaccessible in other social contexts. Nuns in these communities often became skilled in iconography, manuscript illumination, and the creation of religious textiles, each of which reflected the Byzantine artistic tradition.

Some convents were known to produce embroidered textiles used in church services, which included elaborate designs that conveyed religious themes, albeit with less emphasis on icons. These textiles, including altar cloths, vestments, and ceremonial banners, became an alternative means of expressing devotion and preserving religious artistry. Such works underscored the adaptability of Byzantine women in maintaining cultural traditions, even within the limitations imposed by Iconoclasm.

Moreover, religious communities provided an environment where women could exchange ideas and preserve Iconophile beliefs, fostering a subculture that retained traditional Orthodox practices. This environment not only supported the spiritual life of the women involved but also allowed them to contribute to the broader Byzantine cultural legacy. By preserving artistic skills and theological texts, women in convents ensured that Byzantine religious culture remained vibrant, even under the pressures of imperial Iconoclasm.

Empresses as Cultural Mediators

As empresses, Constantine's wives, especially Tzitzak (Irene of Khazaria), served as mediators between different cultures. Tzitzak's background introduced Khazar cultural elements into the Byzantine court, influencing court dress and customs. Her presence bridged Byzantine and Khazar traditions, symbolizing a cultural synthesis that extended beyond political alliances. This blending of customs had a lasting impact on the Byzantine elite, who began to incorporate aspects of Khazar dress and ceremonial practices into their own.

Additionally, the empress's ability to sponsor or influence cultural events allowed her to play a subtle but powerful role in shaping the tastes and values of the court. While Constantine V's reign was marked by strict control over religious imagery, empresses could promote cultural works that maintained Byzantine identity through less contentious means. Whether through literature, music, or ceremonial practices, these cultural contributions helped to sustain a sense of Byzantine tradition that remained resilient despite official Iconoclastic policies.

Conclusion: Women as Cultural Custodians of Byzantine Legacy

Women's roles in the cultural sphere during Constantine V's reign reveal their resilience and adaptability in preserving Byzantine traditions. From commissioning art to sustaining oral traditions, from creating hymns to preserving sacred texts, women played an indispensable role in nurturing the cultural and spiritual fabric of Byzantine society. Empresses and noblewomen, though constrained in public life, found ways to support the arts and foster diplomacy. Monastic women, meanwhile, preserved Orthodox culture within convents, reinforcing traditions that sustained the empire's spiritual foundation.

Through their contributions, Byzantine women ensured that the empire's cultural identity remained intact, even amidst intense religious reforms. Their legacy, often recorded indirectly through art, literature, and preserved texts, contributed to the Byzantine Empire's lasting influence on Eastern Christianity and medieval culture. By acting as custodians of faith and culture, these women reinforced the spiritual and artistic resilience of Byzantium, leaving an enduring legacy that would inspire future generations long after the Iconoclastic era had ended.

Cultural Exchanges and Influences

The cultural landscape of the Byzantine Empire was not isolated; it was shaped by interactions with neighbouring cultures and civilizations. Trade routes, diplomatic relations, and military encounters facilitated exchanges of ideas, artistic styles, and technological innovations.

The contact with the Islamic world, particularly during the expansion of the Umayyad Caliphate, had a profound impact on Byzantine culture. Despite the tensions arising from military conflicts, the interaction with Islamic scholars, artists, and traders led to the exchange of knowledge and ideas. The transmission of scientific and philosophical works from the Islamic world influenced Byzantine intellectual life, contributing to a richer understanding of various disciplines.

Artistic influences also flowed across cultural boundaries. The incorporation of certain Islamic motifs and styles into Byzantine art reflects the complexity of these interactions. While the Iconoclastic movement sought to establish a distinct Byzantine identity, the fluidity of cultural exchange challenged rigid notions of artistic tradition.

Cultural Exchanges between the Byzantine Empire and the Umayyad Caliphate during Constantine V's Reign

Despite their political and military rivalries, the Byzantine Empire and the Umayyad Caliphate engaged in vibrant intellectual, artistic, and scientific exchanges during the eighth century. Although Constantine V's reign was marked by internal upheavals, particularly the Iconoclast controversy, there were significant ongoing interactions between the two empires, shaped both by the proximity of their borders and the rich cultural legacies of the civilizations that had coexisted for centuries.

Intellectual and Philosophical Exchanges

One of the most notable, though often underappreciated, aspects of Byzantine-Umayyad interactions during Constantine V's reign was the transfer of intellectual traditions between the two empires. Both the Byzantine and Umayyad Caliphates were heirs to the ancient intellectual traditions of Greece, Rome, and Persia. However, despite significant political tension, especially in the aftermath of the

Islamic conquest of Byzantine territories in the early eighth century, there was a slow but steady exchange of philosophical and scientific ideas across borders.

Transmission of Greek Philosophy to the Islamic World

The Byzantine Empire, with its continuing attachment to Greco-Roman intellectual traditions, was a crucial conduit for the transmission of classical knowledge. In the post-Classical era, Byzantine scholars, particularly in Constantinople and Antioch, were the primary preservers of Greek philosophical texts. During Constantine V's reign, the Byzantine state maintained institutions of learning, such as the Academy of Constantinople, which played a significant role in preserving the works of ancient philosophers, particularly Aristotle, Plato, and Galen. However, it is important to note that the political and religious climate in the Byzantine Empire under Constantine V, especially due to the Iconoclast controversy, made intellectual engagement with certain kinds of ancient Greek texts less central to state policy. As a result, many classical texts were translated and transmitted across borders, where they found fertile ground in the Umayyad Caliphate.

In the Umayyad Empire, which ruled vast territories stretching from Spain to Central Asia, Greek philosophy – particularly works on logic, metaphysics, and ethics – began to be translated into Arabic. While much of this was initiated by Christian Syriac-speaking scholars working within the caliphate, it had a significant influence on the intellectual development of the Muslim world. The translation movement of the eighth century was particularly active in centres like Baghdad and Damascus, the capitals of the Umayyads, and later the Abbasids. These translations were often carried out by Christian scholars or bureaucrats who had been trained in Greek philosophical traditions and had access to Byzantine manuscripts. This is especially significant because many of these early translations were drawn from texts that had been preserved and studied in Byzantine institutions, making the Byzantine Empire an intellectual bridge between the ancient Greek world and the burgeoning Islamic intellectual world.

The interpretation and adaptation of Greek thought within the Islamic world laid the groundwork for the rise of Islamic philosophy in the subsequent centuries. Figures like Al-Kindi and Al-Farabi, who were influenced by the neoplatonic and Aristotelian traditions preserved by the Byzantines, would build upon these ideas in the Islamic Golden Age, ultimately influencing the intellectual revival of medieval Europe during the Renaissance. Thus, while Constantine V was engaged in a theological and political struggle within his own empire, the very intellectual divide created by his Iconoclastic policies contributed indirectly to a dynamic intellectual exchange between East and West, Christian and Muslim worlds.

Byzantine Influence on Islamic Theology and Logic

Although Constantine V's reign was characterized by a theological focus on the Iconoclastic controversy, which rejected religious images, it was also an era of consolidation for Christian theological orthodoxy. Interestingly, some of the theological debates of the time found parallel developments in the Islamic world, particularly as the Umayyad Caliphate began to formalize its own theological understanding. During Constantine's reign, Byzantine scholars wrestled with debates concerning the nature of Christ, the role of images, and the nature of salvation – issues that were also highly debated in early Islamic theology. While the theological questions of Byzantine Christians and Muslims did not always align, the intellectual dialogues between Christian and Muslim scholars, particularly through Christian merchants and diplomats, helped bridge the religious divide.

In addition, the Byzantine traditions of dialectical reasoning and philosophical logic influenced early Muslim thinkers. As the Umayyads became more involved in the political and intellectual life of the empire, they began to utilize logic and philosophical reasoning as tools of political legitimacy. Greek logic – in the form of syllogisms and deductive reasoning – became a cornerstone of Islamic scholasticism, especially in religious and legal contexts. The Byzantine legacy of translating and preserving texts like Aristotle's *Organon*, a work of logic, and various treatises on ethics and metaphysics, would reverberate across the intellectual landscape of the Islamic world, especially as it intersected with later theological development.

Artistic and Architectural Influences

Although Constantine V's Iconoclasm led to a reduction in the production of religious icons in the Byzantine Empire, the Iconoclast period was not a time of total artistic stagnation. While religious images were banned, the artistic tradition of Byzantium remained highly vibrant in other domains such as secular art, architecture, and mosaics. At the same time, the Umayyads, having conquered large portions of Byzantine territories, began to incorporate Byzantine aesthetic and architectural traditions into their own art.

Iconoclast Art and Its Influence on Islamic Art

One of the key cultural exchanges during this period was the mutual influence between Byzantine and Umayyad art, particularly in the context of non-figural art. In the wake of Constantine V's Iconoclastic policies, Byzantine art began to emphasize abstract and geometric designs, reducing the representation of human or divine figures in religious settings. This shift had a profound effect on the visual culture of the Byzantine Empire, resulting in the development of intricate mosaics, frescoes, and decorative patterns that focused on symbolic motifs, such as crosses, floral arrangements, and stylized patterns.

This type of art found fertile ground in the Umayyad Empire, where the prohibition of images (especially figural representations) was already central to Islamic theology. The Umayyads, while influenced by Byzantine architectural forms such as domes, arches, and mosaics, employed these elements in ways that reflected their religious beliefs. The Great Mosque of Damascus (705 CE), one of the most significant architectural works of the Umayyad period, is a prime example of the cultural fusion between the Byzantine and Islamic traditions. The Byzantine-style mosaics in the mosque, which avoid depicting human figures but instead feature lush landscape scenes, exemplify how the Umayyads took inspiration from Byzantine non-figural art.

In addition to architecture, the luxurious metalwork and textile industries of the Umayyads were influenced by Byzantine techniques. The Byzantine use of enamel work, goldsmithing, and the fine production of silk fabrics found their counterparts in Umayyad workshops, particularly those in cities like Damascus and Baghdad. These fine arts continued to flourish in both empires and reflected the intermingling of Byzantine craftsmanship with Islamic decorative traditions.

Mosaics, Calligraphy, and Decorative Arts

The decorative arts saw the most significant cross-cultural exchange during this period. While the Byzantines focused on mosaics, painted iconography, and luxury goods, the Umayyads began to develop their own Islamic calligraphy and decorative patterns, influenced in part by Byzantine geometric precision. The intricate calligraphic patterns that would later dominate Islamic art in the Abbasid period were already beginning to take form during the Umayyad period. The careful placement of inscriptions and verses from the Quran, combined with geometric ornamentation, reflected a growing artistic sophistication in the Muslim world that was inspired by Byzantine designs.

Scientific and Medical Knowledge Transfer

The Byzantine Empire and the Umayyad Caliphate shared an intellectual commitment to preserving and expanding upon ancient scientific knowledge. During Constantine V's reign, Byzantine scholars – especially those working in medicine, astronomy, and geometry – continued to influence the development of scientific knowledge in the Islamic world. While Constantine V himself was more focused on religious and military matters, his empire continued to produce texts and discoveries that would later influence Islamic scholars.

The Transmission of Medical Knowledge

One of the most significant areas of exchange was in medicine. Byzantium, inheriting much of its medical knowledge from the Greeks, particularly from Hippocrates and Galen, was a major centre for the study and practice of medicine. Byzantine physicians were highly skilled in surgical techniques, anatomy, and the use of herbal medicines. Many of these practices and texts were transmitted to the Umayyad Caliphate, where they were studied, preserved, and expanded upon. One notable example was the transmission of Galen's medical writings, which were translated into Arabic by Christian scholars working in the Umayyad court.

The hospital system in the Umayyad Caliphate also drew upon Byzantine precedents, as the Byzantine Empire had a long-standing tradition of institutional medicine. The Bimaristan (the Islamic hospital), which emerged in the Umayyad and later Abbasid periods, was influenced by Byzantine models, and became a centre for both the treatment of patients and the study of medicine.

Astronomy and Mathematics

Similarly, Byzantine contributions to astronomy and mathematics provided foundational knowledge for Umayyad scholars. While Constantine V did not directly promote the study of these sciences, his empire's scientific infrastructure laid the groundwork for later developments. Byzantine astronomical texts and mathematical theories – particularly in geometry and astrology – were passed on through intermediary Christian scholars and traders, and adapted by Muslim scholars, who refined these practices into more sophisticated astronomical models. These scientific exchanges, in turn, influenced later Islamic astronomy, particularly in regions like Al-Andalus and Persia, and later played a pivotal role in the European Renaissance.

Conclusion: The Lasting Legacy of Byzantine-Umayyad Cultural Exchanges

Despite the tension and religious division that characterized the political landscape of the eighth century, the cultural exchanges between the Byzantine Empire and the Umayyad Caliphate were significant and far-reaching. Through these exchanges, the Byzantine Empire's intellectual, artistic, and scientific legacies were transmitted to the Umayyad world, where they were absorbed and further developed. The result was a fusion of cultural traditions that enriched both civilizations and laid the foundations for future developments in the Islamic world.

In philosophy, art, and science, the Byzantine-Umayyad interactions contributed to the growth of an intellectual environment that not only enriched the Islamic Golden Age but also had a lasting impact on medieval Europe. As Byzantine scholars and Muslim intellectuals shared and adapted each other's works, the cultural boundaries between the two empires blurred, fostering an exchange of knowledge and creativity that transcended religious and political divides. These exchanges would ultimately shape the course of history in the medieval Mediterranean and beyond, laying the groundwork for the intellectual revival of the Renaissance in Europe.

The Byzantine Empire's role as a conduit of knowledge during the reign of Constantine V, despite the Iconoclastic policies that sought to erase religious images, underscores the complex legacy of the empire as both a preserver of ancient knowledge and a catalyst for the transmission of ideas to the broader world. The result was an enduring cultural legacy that continues to resonate in both Western and Islamic intellectual traditions today.

Overall Conclusion

The cultural developments during the reign of Constantine V were characterized by a complex interplay of artistic innovation, intellectual engagement, and societal transformation. The Iconoclastic movement, while restrictive, prompted new forms of artistic expression and philosophical discourse, allowing Byzantine culture to adapt to the changing religious landscape.

Education and intellectual life flourished, driven by the tensions surrounding Iconoclasm and the enduring legacy of classical antiquity. Literature, art, and education became intertwined with the political and religious struggles of the time, reflecting the resilience of Byzantine society in the face of challenges.

As the Byzantine Empire navigated the turbulent waters of religious conflict and cultural change, it laid the groundwork for future developments that would shape its identity. The legacy of this period is evident in the rich tapestry of Byzantine culture, which continued to evolve in response to internal and external influences, ultimately contributing to the enduring legacy of the empire in the annals of history.

Section 3: Political Implications of Iconoclasm

The reign of Constantine V was characterized by a turbulent and contentious relationship between politics and religion, particularly due to his fervent Iconoclastic policies. His aggressive stance against the veneration of icons not only had profound theological and cultural ramifications but also sparked political unrest and social divisions within the Byzantine Empire. This section delves into the political implications of Constantine V's Iconoclasm, examining the responses from various social groups, the challenges to imperial authority, and the long-lasting legacy of his reign.

The Iconoclast Policies and Their Justifications

Constantine V ascended to the throne in 741 amidst a backdrop of social unrest and military threats. He inherited a politically fragmented empire, plagued by internal divisions and external pressures. In this context, he adopted an Iconoclastic policy, believing that the veneration of icons was detrimental to the true practice of Christianity and posed a threat to the unity of the empire. His views were rooted in the belief that the use of icons could lead to idolatry, a position that resonated with certain theological traditions but alienated significant segments of Byzantine society.

To justify his policies, Constantine employed a combination of theological arguments and political rhetoric. He claimed that the veneration of icons undermined the authority of the Church and the state, positioning himself as the defender of the true Christian faith against what he deemed superstitious practices. In his view, Iconoclasm was not merely a religious reform but a necessary political manoeuvre to consolidate his power and unify the empire under a singular vision of orthodoxy.

The Iconoclast movement was not merely a theological debate but a broader ideological struggle that reflected the tensions between different factions within Byzantine society. Constantine's Iconoclasm appealed to segments of the military, urban elites, and certain clerical groups who believed that a return to a more austere form of Christianity would strengthen the empire against external threats, particularly from the expanding Islamic Caliphate.

Responses from the Church and Monastic Communities

One of the most significant challenges to Constantine V's Iconoclastic policies came from the Church and monastic communities, which were pivotal in the preservation of Byzantine religious traditions and the veneration of icons. The monastic movement, which had flourished in the Byzantine Empire, was deeply rooted in the veneration of holy images. Monasteries served as centres of spiritual life and artistic production, producing some of the most revered icons of the time.

The reaction from monastic communities was swift and vehement. Monks, many of whom were staunch defenders of icon veneration, viewed Constantine's policies as an attack on their spiritual practices and the very essence of their faith. They argued that icons served as vital conduits for divine grace and expressed the mysteries of Christianity in a way that words alone could not. As a result, many monastic leaders actively opposed Constantine's edicts, leading to a period of intense conflict between the emperor and monastic communities.

Prominent figures, such as the monk and theologian John of Damascus, emerged as vocal opponents of Iconoclasm. John articulated a compelling defence of icons in his writings, arguing that the veneration of images was a legitimate expression of Christian faith, grounded in the Incarnation of Christ. He contended that since Christ took on human form, it was permissible to depict him in art. John's treatises not only countered the theological justifications for Iconoclasm but also galvanized support for the Iconophile cause among the clergy and laypeople alike.

The resistance from monastic communities and Iconophiles led to significant social tensions. Monks were often targeted by the imperial authorities, facing persecution, imprisonment, and exile. The conflicts between Iconoclasts and Iconophiles became emblematic of broader societal divisions, leading to violent confrontations and a growing atmosphere of distrust and resentment within Byzantine society.

Military and Political Consequences

Constantine V's Iconoclastic policies had far-reaching military and political consequences for the Byzantine Empire. As the tensions between Iconoclasts and Iconophiles escalated, the social fabric of the empire began to fray. This unrest manifested in several ways, including revolts, civil strife, and challenges to the imperial authority.

The military, which had initially supported Constantine's policies, began to fracture as divisions emerged between Iconoclast and Iconophile factions within its ranks. Some military leaders, particularly those with close ties to monastic communities, expressed their opposition to the emperor's stance, leading to a crisis of loyalty among the troops. This internal discord undermined the effectiveness of the Byzantine military, particularly during a time when the empire faced external threats from Arab invasions and other adversaries.

The rise of provincial leaders and local aristocrats also posed challenges to Constantine's authority. In regions where Iconophiles held significant influence, resistance to the emperor's policies manifested in open rebellion. Figures like the Byzantine general Artabasdos, who was an Iconophile, capitalized on discontent with Constantine's Iconoclastic measures, leading a rebellion against the emperor in 742. This revolt highlighted the growing divide within the empire and the potential for civil conflict driven by religious and ideological differences.

Constantine's attempts to suppress dissent only intensified the backlash. His measures included the exile of prominent Iconophile leaders, the closure of monasteries, and the imposition of harsh penalties for those who continued to venerate icons. These actions, while intended to reinforce his authority, ultimately alienated key segments of the population and exacerbated the divisions within Byzantine society.

The Role of Empresses and the Imperial Family

The political implications of Iconoclasm were further complicated by the roles played by empresses and the imperial family. Women in the Byzantine imperial family often wielded significant influence over religious and political matters, and their positions could either support or challenge the emperor's policies.

Empresses such as Eudokia, who expressed their support for the veneration of icons contributed to the tension between the imperial authority and the Iconophile movement. The imperial family's alignment with either the Iconoclast or Iconophile factions could sway public opinion and mobilize supporters or opponents of the emperor. In cases where empresses actively defended the veneration of icons, they became targets of Constantine's policies, further complicating the political landscape.

The impact of Iconoclasm on the imperial family was evident in the later reign of Constantine V's son, Leo IV, who took a more moderate approach to the issue of Iconoclasm. The legacy of Constantine's strict policies influenced Leo's decisions, leading to a complex interplay of religious and political considerations that would shape the future of the empire. The tension between the Iconoclast and Iconophile factions continued to resonate within the imperial court, reflecting the broader societal struggles over faith and identity.

The Aftermath of Iconoclasm and the Enduring Legacy of Constantine V

The political ramifications of Constantine V's Iconoclastic policies extended well beyond his reign. The divisions that emerged during this period set the stage for the later Iconoclastic controversies that would define Byzantine history for centuries to come. The tensions between Iconoclasts and Iconophiles continued to shape political alliances, religious practices, and cultural expression long after Constantine's death in 775.

The eventual restoration of icons in the early ninth century, spearheaded by the Empress Theodora, represented a significant turning point in Byzantine religious life. This restoration was not merely a theological victory for Iconophiles; it was also a political act that sought to heal the divisions within the empire. The legacy of Constantine V's reign, characterized by conflict and strife, served as a cautionary tale for future emperors navigating the delicate balance between religious authority and imperial power.

The theological debates surrounding Iconoclasm continued to influence the development of Byzantine thought and spirituality. The questions raised during this period regarding the nature of worship, the role of images in religious practice, and the relationship between faith and politics remained relevant throughout Byzantine history. The Iconoclastic controversies served as a backdrop for later theological developments and debates, shaping the trajectory of the Eastern Orthodox Church and its identity.

Furthermore, the Iconoclast policies of Constantine V contributed to the broader historical narrative of the Byzantine Empire as it navigated the complexities of religious identity, political authority, and cultural expression. The legacy of this period is evident in the enduring traditions of Byzantine art, theology, and literature, which would continue to evolve in response to the challenges posed by both internal divisions and external threats.

Conclusion

The political implications of Constantine V's Iconoclastic policies were profound and far-reaching. The tensions and conflicts that arose during his reign reflected deeper societal divisions within Byzantine culture, challenging the notions of unity and authority within the empire. The responses from various social groups, including the Church, monastic communities, the military, and the imperial family, shaped the political landscape and contributed to a legacy of conflict and resilience.

As the Byzantine Empire grappled with the consequences of Iconoclasm, it laid the groundwork for future developments in religious, cultural, and political life. The struggles of this era would echo through the centuries, influencing the trajectory of the empire and shaping its identity in the face of ongoing challenges. The legacy of Constantine V serves as a reminder of the complexities inherent in the interplay between faith, culture, and politics, a theme that remains relevant in the study of history and the understanding of human experience.

Section 4: Economic Implications of Iconoclasm

The reign of Constantine V (741–775) was marked not only by religious and cultural upheaval but also by significant economic ramifications stemming from his Iconoclastic policies. As the Byzantine Empire grappled with the tensions between Iconoclasts and Iconophiles, its economic landscape was inevitably influenced by the political and social turmoil of the time. This section explores the economic implications of Constantine V's policies, examining their effects on trade, agriculture, taxation, and the overall economic stability of the empire.

Trade Dynamics in the Iconoclastic Era

Trade played a crucial role in the economic vitality of the Byzantine Empire, serving as a conduit for the exchange of goods, ideas, and cultural influences. However, the period of Constantine V's reign saw disruptions in trade routes and practices due to the prevailing political and religious conflicts. The Iconoclastic policies, which led to internal divisions and civil strife, had a direct impact on trade dynamics.

The Byzantine Empire was strategically located at the crossroads of Europe and Asia, making it a pivotal centre for commerce. Major trade routes connected the empire to the Silk Road and facilitated trade with regions such as the Middle East, North Africa, and Western Europe. The wealth generated from trade contributed to the empire's economic stability and supported the imperial treasury.

However, the Iconoclastic controversy created an environment of uncertainty and instability. The tensions between Iconoclasts and Iconophiles often spilled over into social unrest, impacting commercial activities. Merchants, fearful of political repercussions or disruptions caused by civil strife, became wary of engaging in trade. This caution led to a decline in the volume of trade, particularly in regions where Iconophile sentiments were strong.

Moreover, the empire faced external threats from Arab incursions during this period, which further complicated trade dynamics. The Muslim conquests had already altered trade routes, and the Byzantine Empire found itself in direct competition with the expanding Islamic Caliphate. The military conflicts and territorial losses not only disrupted traditional trade networks but also diverted resources and attention away from economic development.

Despite these challenges, certain regions of the empire experienced a degree of economic resilience. The coastal cities, such as Constantinople, continued to thrive as major trade hubs, benefiting from their strategic locations. The bustling markets of Constantinople remained a focal point for merchants from diverse backgrounds, fostering cultural exchanges and economic activities. Nonetheless, the overall trade environment was characterized by a heightened sense of caution and instability, influenced by the political climate.

Agricultural Production and Taxation Policies

Agriculture was the backbone of the Byzantine economy, providing sustenance for the population and generating revenue for the state. During Constantine V's reign, agricultural production faced various challenges, influenced by both natural factors and the socio-political landscape shaped by Iconoclasm.

The empire relied heavily on peasant farmers who cultivated the land, and agricultural output was crucial for feeding the population and supporting the military. However, the tensions arising from the Iconoclastic policies created an atmosphere of uncertainty for rural communities. The imposition of harsh penalties on Iconophiles, particularly within monastic communities, disrupted agricultural practices and the management of agricultural estates.

Monastic landholdings, which played a vital role in agricultural production, faced direct challenges due to the suppression of monastic communities. The confiscation of monastic properties under Constantine V's regime significantly impacted agricultural output. Monasteries were often centres of agricultural innovation, and their closure resulted in a decline in productivity in regions reliant on their stewardship.

The taxation policies implemented by Constantine V further complicated the agricultural landscape. To fund military campaigns and maintain the imperial treasury, the emperor imposed increased taxes on landowners and peasants alike. The burden of taxation fell heavily on rural communities, exacerbating social tensions and resentment towards the imperial authority.

Peasants, who already faced the challenges of natural disasters and poor harvests, found it increasingly difficult to meet tax obligations. The combination of rising taxes and declining agricultural productivity contributed to widespread economic hardship. This discontent among the rural population fuelled resistance against the imperial authority, particularly in regions where Iconophile sentiments were strong.

Despite these challenges, certain agricultural regions continued to thrive due to favourable conditions and effective land management. Areas such as Anatolia, with its fertile plains and favourable climate, remained productive, contributing to the overall economic resilience of the empire. However, the disparities in agricultural output and the unequal burden of taxation highlighted the economic challenges faced by different regions within the empire.

The Impact of Iconoclasm on the Urban Economy

The economic implications of Iconoclasm extended to urban centres, where trade, craftsmanship, and artisan production flourished. Cities like Constantinople served as vibrant economic hubs, but the political and social unrest stemming from the Iconoclastic controversy had tangible effects on urban economies.

As tensions escalated between Iconoclasts and Iconophiles, urban centres became focal points for conflict. Demonstrations and protests against the emperor's policies often erupted in cities, disrupting daily life and economic activities. The atmosphere of fear and uncertainty deterred investment and commerce, affecting the livelihoods of merchants and artisans.

Craftsmanship, which thrived in Byzantine cities, faced challenges during this period. Skilled artisans who produced religious artefacts, including icons, found themselves at odds with imperial policies. Many artisans were forced to abandon their traditional practices, leading to a decline in the production of religious art and crafts. The economic repercussions of this decline extended beyond individual artisans; entire workshops and guilds faced uncertainty and financial strain.

However, despite the challenges, urban economies displayed resilience in the face of adversity. The demand for non-religious goods and services increased as citizens sought to adapt to the changing cultural landscape. The production of textiles, pottery, and other crafts continued, reflecting the adaptability of urban economies to the shifting demands of society.

The relationship between urban economies and imperial authority was complex. The emperor relied on the loyalty of urban elites and merchants to support his policies and maintain stability. However, the discontent among urban populations, exacerbated by the repercussions of Iconoclasm, posed a threat to the emperor's authority. As social tensions rose, urban elites began to navigate the precarious balance between supporting imperial authority and addressing the grievances of their constituents.

Taxation and Economic Policy

Constantine V's economic policies, particularly regarding taxation, had a significant impact on the overall economic stability of the Byzantine Empire. The emperor's need for revenue to fund military campaigns and maintain imperial authority led to the imposition of increased taxes on various segments of society. These policies, while aimed at strengthening the state, ultimately exacerbated social tensions and economic hardship.

The taxation system in the Byzantine Empire was already complex, relying on various forms of taxation, including land taxes, poll taxes, and customs duties. Under Constantine V, the pressures of ongoing military conflicts necessitated a re-evaluation of taxation policies. The emperor sought to expand the tax base by increasing rates and introducing new forms of taxation, which disproportionately affected the rural and urban poor.

The increased burden of taxation on peasants led to widespread discontent. Many rural communities faced the dual challenges of rising taxes and declining agricultural productivity, resulting in economic strain. Peasant revolts and protests against tax policies became more frequent as communities pushed back against the imperial authority. This unrest highlighted the vulnerabilities of the Byzantine economy and the potential for civil strife driven by economic grievances.

Moreover, the reliance on taxation to fund military campaigns placed additional strain on the economy. As the empire faced external threats, military expenditures surged, diverting resources from other areas of economic development. The focus on military funding often overshadowed the need for infrastructure improvements and support for trade, contributing to a cycle of economic instability.

The imperial treasury's reliance on taxation also shaped the relationship between the emperor and various social groups. Urban elites, who played a crucial role in the economy, sought to maintain their influence and protect their interests. The tension between the emperor's need for revenue and the demands of urban elites created a complex political landscape, where alliances and rivalries influenced economic policies and practices.

Long-Term Economic Consequences

The economic implications of Constantine V's Iconoclastic policies had lasting effects on the Byzantine Empire, shaping its trajectory long after his reign. The tensions and conflicts arising from Iconoclasm contributed to social divisions, undermining the unity that Constantine sought to achieve.

In the years following Constantine V's reign, the empire continued to grapple with the economic repercussions of his policies. The divisions between Iconoclasts and Iconophiles persisted, influencing political alliances and shaping economic practices. The struggles of rural communities against oppressive taxation and economic hardship laid the groundwork for future revolts and challenges to imperial authority.

Moreover, the legacy of Constantine V's Iconoclastic policies can be seen in the broader narrative of Byzantine history. The theological debates and cultural tensions surrounding Iconoclasm would reverberate throughout subsequent centuries, impacting the development of the Eastern Orthodox Church and the socio-political landscape of the empire.

The economic challenges faced during this period also set the stage for future reforms. As the empire sought to address the grievances of its citizens, leaders would eventually implement changes to taxation, land management, and agricultural practices. These reforms aimed to restore stability and foster economic resilience in the face of ongoing challenges.

Conclusion

The economic implications of Constantine V's Iconoclastic policies were profound and far-reaching. The interplay between trade, agriculture, taxation, and social unrest shaped the economic landscape of the Byzantine Empire during his reign. While the emperor sought to consolidate power and unify the empire through his policies, the repercussions were often counterproductive, leading to social divisions and economic instability.

The economic challenges of this period underscore the complexities of governance in the Byzantine Empire, where religious, political, and economic factors intertwined to shape the lived experiences of its citizens. The legacy of Constantine V's reign serves as a reminder of the intricate relationship between faith, culture, and economics in the Byzantine world, with lasting implications for the empire's future trajectory.

Chapter 4

Military Reforms and Campaigns of Constantine V

Section 1: Military Reforms and Strategies

The Byzantine Empire, particularly during the reign of Constantine V (741–775), faced significant military challenges that necessitated substantial reforms and strategic innovations. Constantine's ascension to the throne came at a time when the empire was grappling with external threats from the expanding Islamic Caliphate and internal divisions exacerbated by his controversial policies. This section examines the military reforms and strategies implemented by Constantine V, detailing the transformations in the Byzantine military structure, the significance of these reforms, and the outcomes of his military campaigns.

Context of Military Challenges

Upon Constantine V's accession to the throne in 741, the Byzantine Empire was in a precarious position. The loss of territories in the eastern provinces to Arab forces had weakened the empire's borders, and ongoing military threats from various fronts posed significant challenges to the stability of the state. The Islamic Caliphate, having expanded rapidly since the early seventh century, threatened to overrun Byzantine territories and undermine the empire's authority in the region.

In addition to external threats, internal conflicts further complicated the military landscape. The Iconoclastic policies pursued by Constantine V had created divisions within society, resulting in discontent among certain military factions, particularly those sympathetic to Iconophile sentiments. The emperor recognized that a cohesive and effective military force was essential for both defending the empire and consolidating his power amid social unrest.

Reorganization of the Military Structure

To address the military challenges he faced, Constantine V initiated a series of reforms aimed at reorganizing and strengthening the Byzantine army. Central to these reforms was the restructuring of the military hierarchy and the establishment of new command structures to enhance operational efficiency.

One of the key reforms was the emphasis on the theme system, which involved the reorganization of the military into regional units known as themes. Each theme was responsible for the defence of a specific territory and was comprised of local troops, often composed of free peasants who were granted land in exchange for military service. This system allowed for a more rapid mobilization of forces and enabled the empire to tap into local resources and manpower.

The establishment of themes also fostered a sense of local loyalty and commitment to the empire. By integrating military service with land ownership, Constantine sought to create a dedicated class of soldiers who were invested in the defence of their regions. This not only bolstered the military ranks but also provided stability to rural economies, as soldiers were often drawn from the agricultural populace.

Moreover, Constantine V recognized the importance of professionalizing the military. He sought to enhance the training and discipline of troops, implementing new standards for recruitment and military education. The emperor emphasized the need for experienced and well-trained soldiers, which was crucial for maintaining effectiveness in the face of external threats.

Strategic Innovations and Tactical Developments

In addition to structural reforms, Constantine V introduced various strategic innovations and tactical developments that significantly impacted Byzantine military operations. His approach to warfare was characterized by a combination of traditional Byzantine strategies and new tactics that reflected the evolving nature of conflict in the eighth century.

One of the most notable innovations was the emphasis on mobile warfare. Recognizing the need for flexibility in the face of a dynamic battlefield, Constantine encouraged the development of lighter cavalry units and skirmishers who could manoeuvre quickly and strike decisively. This shift away from reliance on heavy infantry allowed Byzantine forces to adapt to different combat situations and exploit vulnerabilities in enemy formations.

The emperor also implemented improvements in siege warfare. The Byzantine army was known for its sophisticated siege techniques, and under Constantine's leadership these methods were refined further. The use of specialized siege equipment, such as battering rams and catapults, became more prevalent, enhancing the effectiveness of Byzantine forces in besieging enemy fortifications.

Constantine V's military reforms extended to naval forces as well. The Byzantine navy played a crucial role in protecting trade routes and coastal cities from maritime threats. The emperor recognized the significance of naval power in defending the empire's interests and sought to bolster the fleet through increased funding and the construction of new ships. This emphasis on naval strength was particularly relevant given the ongoing Arab naval expansion in the Mediterranean.

The Role of the Military Elite

The success of Constantine V's military campaigns was heavily reliant on the support of the military elite, including generals and local commanders who played crucial roles in executing the emperor's strategies. Constantine recognized the importance of cultivating strong relationships with these leaders, many of whom were vital in rallying troops and maintaining loyalty to the imperial authority.

The Byzantine military aristocracy, known as the *stratiotes*, became instrumental in supporting the emperor's military initiatives. These landholding soldiers, who were often also local leaders, provided the manpower and resources necessary for sustaining military campaigns. Constantine's reforms, which emphasized the integration of military service with land ownership, further solidified the loyalty of the *stratiotes* to the emperor.

Moreover, the military elite were often tasked with overseeing the training and organization of troops within their respective themes. By empowering local commanders and granting them authority over military affairs, Constantine ensured that his reforms were effectively implemented at the regional level.

Challenges and Limitations

Despite the successes achieved through Constantine V's military reforms and campaigns, challenges remained. The ongoing conflict with the Arabs necessitated constant vigilance, and the empire faced difficulties in sustaining prolonged military engagements. The economic strain resulting from military expenditures, coupled with the need for effective resource management, presented ongoing obstacles to the Byzantine military efforts.

Additionally, the internal divisions within Byzantine society, stemming from the Iconoclastic controversy, created an environment of instability that could undermine military effectiveness. The tensions between Iconoclasts and Iconophiles manifested in various forms, including dissent within the military ranks. Some soldiers and commanders were sympathetic to the Iconophile cause, leading to potential challenges to imperial authority and cohesion within the armed forces.

The emperor also faced external challenges from emerging powers, such as the Bulgarian Khanate to the north. As the Byzantine Empire sought to consolidate its power in the east, it was also compelled to address threats from the Bulgarian tribes, which necessitated a multifaceted military strategy.

Legacy of Military Reforms

The military reforms and campaigns of Constantine V left a lasting impact on the Byzantine Empire. The restructuring of the military through the theme system became a defining feature of Byzantine military organization in subsequent centuries. The emphasis on local loyalty and rapid mobilization proved effective in defending the empire against external threats and maintaining stability within its borders.

Moreover, the innovations in military tactics and strategies laid the groundwork for future military successes. The emphasis on mobility, combined with advanced siege techniques, would continue to shape Byzantine military doctrine. These reforms ensured that the Byzantine army remained a formidable force capable of adapting to changing circumstances on the battlefield.

The legacy of Constantine V's military policies extended beyond his reign. His efforts to fortify the eastern frontier and reclaim lost territories contributed to the empire's resilience in the face of external threats. The victories achieved during his campaigns not only boosted Byzantine morale but also instilled a sense of renewed confidence in the imperial authority.

Conclusion

Constantine V's military reforms and strategies were critical to the Byzantine Empire's efforts to navigate the challenges of the eighth century. The restructuring of the military, emphasis on local loyalty, and innovations in tactics laid the groundwork for a more cohesive and effective fighting force. While external threats and internal divisions posed significant challenges, the legacy of Constantine's military initiatives would endure, shaping the trajectory of the Byzantine military in the years to come.

As the empire continued to grapple with the complexities of warfare and governance, the achievements of Constantine V in the realm of military reform would serve as a testament to the resilience of the Byzantine state in the face of adversity.

Section 2: Military Campaigns and Battles

Constantine V's reign was marked by a series of military campaigns that were pivotal in defending the Byzantine Empire against formidable external threats, particularly from the Arab forces. These campaigns not only showcased his military reforms and strategic innovations but also reflected the broader geopolitical struggles of the era. This section explores the key military campaigns and battles of Constantine V, examining their contexts, strategies, outcomes, and lasting implications for the Byzantine Empire.

The Landscape of Conflict

By the time Constantine V ascended to the throne in 741, the Byzantine Empire was embroiled in a protracted struggle against the Islamic Caliphate. The rapid expansion of Arab forces throughout the early eighth century had resulted in significant territorial losses for the empire, particularly in the eastern provinces. The emergence of the Umayyad Caliphate as a dominant power in the region posed a direct threat to Byzantine stability and security.

The military landscape was further complicated by internal divisions fuelled by the ongoing Iconoclastic controversy. The tensions between Iconoclasts and Iconophiles created factions within the military, leading to challenges in maintaining a unified front against external adversaries. Recognizing the need for cohesive military action, Constantine sought to assert his authority and solidify his power through a series of military campaigns.

The Campaign Against the Umayyads

One of the most significant challenges facing Constantine V was the ongoing conflict with the Umayyad Caliphate. The Arab forces, having secured victories in previous engagements, posed a persistent threat to Byzantine territory. Constantine V aimed to reclaim lost lands and restore Byzantine authority in the east through strategic military action.

In 743, Constantine V launched a campaign to reclaim territories in Asia Minor that had fallen under Arab control. This campaign marked the beginning of a series of military actions aimed at pushing back the Umayyad forces and reasserting Byzantine dominance in the region. The campaign involved a combination of direct military engagement and diplomatic efforts to rally support from local populations discontented with Arab rule.

The Byzantine army, bolstered by the theme system, was able to mobilize local forces rapidly. Constantine V's strategy relied on the element of surprise, utilizing the mobility of his cavalry and infantry to strike swiftly against Arab garrisons. His forces engaged in several key battles, showcasing the effectiveness of the reforms he had implemented.

The Battle of the Upper Cilicia (744)

One of the most notable engagements during this campaign was the Battle of Upper Cilicia in 744. The Byzantines sought to intercept an Arab force that was advancing into Byzantine territory, aiming to secure the strategic region of Cilicia, known for its fertile lands and crucial trade routes. Constantine V led his troops into battle, demonstrating his commitment to overseeing military operations personally.

The battle was characterized by a series of tactical manoeuvres that exemplified the reforms Constantine had implemented. Utilizing a combination of cavalry charges and infantry formations, the Byzantine forces engaged the Arab army in a series of skirmishes before launching a decisive assault. The element of surprise and the effectiveness of Constantine's mobile forces contributed to a significant Byzantine victory at Upper Cilicia.

The success at Upper Cilicia had far-reaching implications. It not only bolstered Byzantine morale but also demonstrated the effectiveness of Constantine's military reforms in the face of external threats. Following this victory, the emperor was able to consolidate Byzantine control over parts of Cilicia, enhancing the empire's strategic position in the region.

The Siege of Amoria (746)

Following the successful campaign in Cilicia, Constantine V turned his attention to Amoria, a city that had become a stronghold for Arab forces. The siege of Amoria in 746 represented a critical phase in the ongoing conflict with the Umayyad Caliphate. This campaign highlighted the emperor's determination to reclaim lost territories and reassert Byzantine authority in the face of external adversaries.

Constantine's approach to the siege involved a combination of military might and strategic planning. The emperor recognized the importance of securing the city to disrupt Arab supply lines and reinforce Byzantine control over the surrounding regions. The siege was meticulously planned, with the Byzantine forces encircling the city to cut off reinforcements and supplies.

Throughout the siege, Constantine V demonstrated his commitment to utilizing advanced siege technologies, employing battering rams and other equipment to breach the city's fortifications. The Byzantine forces maintained a steady pressure on the city, executing a series of coordinated assaults to weaken the defences.

Despite facing fierce resistance from the Arab garrison, the determination of the Byzantine forces ultimately prevailed. The city of Amoria fell to Constantine's troops after several weeks of siege, resulting in a significant victory for the Byzantine Empire. The capture of Amoria not only enhanced Byzantine territorial control but also dealt a psychological blow to Arab forces, signalling the resurgence of Byzantine military power in the region.

Campaigns Against the Bulgarians

In addition to the threat posed by the Umayyads, Constantine V faced challenges from the Bulgarian tribes to the north. The Bulgarians had emerged as a formidable power in the Balkans, and their incursions into Byzantine territory posed significant challenges to the empire's stability. Recognizing the need to address this northern threat, Constantine launched military campaigns aimed at securing the empire's borders.

In 754, Constantine V led a campaign against the Bulgarians, seeking to re-establish Byzantine authority in the region. The campaign was marked by a series of confrontations with Bulgarian forces, culminating in the Battle of the River Iskar. This battle exemplified Constantine's strategic acumen, as he utilized the terrain to his advantage and executed a coordinated assault against the Bulgarian forces.

The Byzantine army, equipped with improved tactics and organization, managed to achieve a decisive victory over the Bulgarians at Iskar. The successful outcome of this battle allowed Constantine to solidify Byzantine control over the Balkan territories and deter future incursions from the north.

In the aftermath of the campaign, Constantine V sought to establish a more permanent presence in the region. He fortified key fortifications and strengthened defensive structures along the northern frontier, ensuring that the empire was better equipped to respond to future threats from the Bulgarian tribes.

The Defence of Constantinople

Constantine V's military efforts extended beyond regional campaigns; he also recognized the strategic importance of Constantinople as the empire's capital. Throughout his reign, the emperor focused on fortifying the city against potential sieges and assaults, particularly from the Arab forces.

The city of Constantinople, renowned for its formidable walls and defences, faced repeated threats from the Umayyad Caliphate. In 746, the Umayyad forces launched a massive naval campaign aimed at besieging the city. Constantine V, fully aware of the stakes, mobilized his resources to defend the capital.

The defence of Constantinople was characterized by a combination of military preparedness and diplomatic manoeuvring. Constantine strengthened the city's defences by reinforcing the walls and bolstering the garrison. The Byzantine navy played a crucial role in repelling the Arab fleet, utilizing effective naval tactics to disrupt their supply lines and prevent their forces from establishing a foothold.

The successful defence of Constantinople against the Arab siege was a defining moment for Constantine V's reign. The ability of the Byzantine forces to withstand the siege demonstrated the resilience of the empire and solidified Constantine's reputation as a capable military leader. The victory not only ensured the survival of the capital but also marked a turning point in the broader conflict with the Umayyad Caliphate.

The Campaign Against the Saracens

The culmination of Constantine V's military efforts came in 760 with a series of campaigns against the Saracens, a term often used to refer to the various Muslim forces opposing the Byzantine Empire. The Byzantine army, bolstered by the reforms implemented by Constantine, embarked on a series of coordinated strikes against Arab positions in Asia Minor.

The campaigns were marked by a focus on reclaiming territories that had been lost to the Saracens. Constantine's strategy involved a combination of direct military engagement and guerrilla tactics, utilizing the element of surprise to harass and disrupt enemy forces.

In the spring of 760, the Byzantine forces launched a coordinated attack on the Arab garrison at Kinnasrin, a strategic city that served as a hub for Arab military operations in the region. The attack was meticulously planned, with Constantine personally overseeing the military preparations.

The Byzantine forces, employing improved siege technologies and strategies, laid siege to Kinnasrin, cutting off reinforcements and supplies. After weeks of intense fighting, the city fell to the Byzantine army, resulting in a significant victory that bolstered Byzantine control over the region.

Following the success at Kinnasrin, Constantine V continued his campaigns against Arab forces, securing victories at key locations throughout Asia Minor. These military successes helped to re-establish Byzantine authority and deter further incursions from Arab forces.

The Legacy of Military Campaigns

The military campaigns of Constantine V had lasting implications for the Byzantine Empire. Through a combination of effective military reforms, strategic planning, and decisive engagements, the emperor was able to reclaim lost territories, bolster Byzantine authority, and deter external threats.

The victories achieved during Constantine's campaigns instilled a sense of renewed confidence in the Byzantine military. The reforms he implemented not only enhanced the army's effectiveness but also laid the groundwork for future military successes. The theme system, which emphasized local loyalty and rapid mobilization, became a defining feature of Byzantine military organization in the years to come.

Moreover, the successful defence of Constantinople against external threats solidified the city's reputation as a bastion of resilience and military might. The ability to withstand sieges and repel invaders served as a testament to the strength of Byzantine defences and the strategic acumen of its leaders.

However, the military successes of Constantine V also highlighted the ongoing challenges faced by the Byzantine Empire. The internal divisions stemming from the Iconoclastic controversy continued to pose obstacles to imperial authority. The complexities of managing a diverse empire, coupled with the persistent threats from various fronts, underscored the need for sustained military vigilance.

Conclusion

The military campaigns of Constantine V represented a critical period in the history of the Byzantine Empire. Through a combination of reforms, strategic innovations, and decisive engagements, the emperor successfully defended the empire against formidable adversaries, reclaiming lost territories and solidifying Byzantine authority. The legacy of these military efforts would endure, shaping the future trajectory of the Byzantine military and influencing the empire's interactions with external powers.

As the empire navigated the complexities of warfare and governance in the eighth century, the achievements of Constantine V in military affairs would serve as a foundation for future leaders, ensuring that the Byzantine Empire remained a formidable force in the face of adversity.

Section 3: Naval Strategies and Maritime Campaigns

The Byzantine Empire, renowned for its military prowess, faced significant challenges not only on land but also at sea. The Mediterranean Sea served as a crucial arena for conflict during the eighth century, where naval power became essential for defending trade routes, protecting coastal cities, and asserting dominance over rival powers. Under the leadership of Constantine V, the Byzantine navy underwent significant reforms and engaged in a series of maritime campaigns that showcased the strategic importance of naval forces in the broader context of Byzantine military operations. This section explores the naval strategies and maritime campaigns of Constantine V, examining their implications for the empire's security and its interactions with external adversaries.

The Importance of Naval Power

By the time Constantine V ascended to the throne in 741, the Mediterranean had become a theatre of conflict as various powers sought to expand their influence. The Arab forces, having established the Umayyad Caliphate, posed a significant threat to Byzantine control over key maritime routes and coastal territories. The Arab navy had demonstrated its capabilities in previous engagements, leading to a precarious situation for the Byzantine Empire.

Recognizing the critical role of naval power, Constantine V sought to revitalize the Byzantine navy, which had suffered from neglect in the years prior to his reign. A strong navy was essential for several reasons:

- **Defence of Trade Routes:** The Mediterranean was a vital conduit for trade and commerce. Protecting maritime trade routes from piracy and enemy naval forces was essential for the economic stability of the empire.
- **Protection of Coastal Cities:** Many Byzantine cities were situated along the coast and were vulnerable to naval assaults. A robust naval presence was crucial for defending these urban centres from enemy invasions.
- **Projection of Power:** A formidable navy allowed the Byzantine Empire to project its power beyond its borders, engaging in offensive operations against adversaries and asserting dominance over key maritime territories.
- **Support for Land Campaigns:** Naval forces could provide critical support for land operations by transporting troops, supplies, and equipment, enabling coordinated military actions.

Reforms and Strengthening the Navy

To bolster the effectiveness of the Byzantine navy, Constantine V implemented a series of reforms aimed at enhancing its capabilities. These reforms included the following:

- **Increased Funding and Resources:** Understanding the financial demands of a strong navy, Constantine allocated resources to rebuild and maintain the fleet. This included investment in shipbuilding and the maintenance of existing vessels.
- **Naval Infrastructure:** The emperor recognized the importance of having well-equipped naval bases and ports. He focused on improving existing facilities and establishing new ones to ensure that the navy could operate efficiently.
- **Training and Recruitment:** Constantine emphasized the need for well-trained sailors and naval officers. He established training programmes to improve the skills of the crew, ensuring that they could effectively operate ships and engage in naval warfare.
- **Innovation in Ship Design:** The Byzantine navy began to experiment with new ship designs and technologies. The development of larger and more manoeuvrable vessels enhanced the navy's combat capabilities and allowed for more effective engagement with enemy forces.
- **Coordination with Land Forces:** Recognizing the interdependence of naval and land operations, Constantine emphasized the importance of coordination between the navy and the army. Joint training exercises and strategic planning helped to ensure that both branches could work effectively together in military campaigns.

The Defence of Constantinople

One of the primary responsibilities of the Byzantine navy during Constantine V's reign was the defence of Constantinople, the empire's capital and a vital centre of trade and culture. The city's strategic location made it a target for various adversaries, particularly the Arab forces, which sought to establish dominance in the region.

In 746, the Umayyad Caliphate launched a significant naval campaign aimed at besieging Constantinople. This assault was part of a broader strategy to weaken Byzantine control in the eastern Mediterranean. Constantine recognized the imminent threat posed by the Arab fleet and mobilized his naval forces to defend the city.

The defence of Constantinople involved a combination of tactics, including the deployment of fire ships – vessels equipped with incendiary materials designed to set enemy ships ablaze. The use of Greek fire, a powerful incendiary weapon, became a hallmark of Byzantine naval warfare. Its introduction marked a turning point in naval engagements, allowing Byzantine forces to counter larger enemy fleets effectively.

During the siege, the Byzantine navy engaged in several skirmishes with the Arab fleet, utilizing their superior manoeuvrability and knowledge of the local waters. The combination of naval tactics and the effective use of Greek fire contributed to the eventual repulsion of the Arab forces. The successful defence of Constantinople not only safeguarded the city but also solidified the reputation of the Byzantine navy as a formidable force in maritime warfare.

Naval Engagements in the Aegean Sea

In addition to defending Constantinople, Constantine V sought to project Byzantine strength into the Aegean Sea, where rival powers posed threats to trade and security. The Aegean was a critical area for Byzantine commerce, and control over its waters was essential for maintaining economic stability.

Throughout his reign, Constantine ordered several naval expeditions aimed at engaging with Arab and pirate forces operating in the Aegean Sea. One notable engagement was the Battle of Samos in 760, where Byzantine naval forces confronted an Arab fleet that had been raiding coastal settlements.

The battle exemplified the effectiveness of the reforms implemented by Constantine V. The Byzantine navy, equipped with well-trained sailors and advanced ships, was able to engage the enemy effectively. Utilizing tactics that emphasized mobility and coordination, the Byzantine forces achieved a decisive victory, disrupting Arab naval operations in the region.

Following the success at Samos, Constantine V ordered further naval campaigns to secure Byzantine interests in the Aegean. These expeditions targeted pirate strongholds and Arab raiding parties, contributing to the reestablishment of maritime security in the region.

The Battle of Syllaeum (762)

Another significant naval engagement during Constantine V's reign was the Battle of Syllaeum in 762. This confrontation occurred as Byzantine naval forces sought to reassert control over maritime routes threatened by a coalition of Arab fleets. The battle marked a turning point in the naval conflict between the Byzantine Empire and the Umayyad Caliphate.

The Byzantine navy, led by skilled commanders, engaged the Arab fleets in a series of skirmishes before the decisive confrontation at Syllaeum. Constantine V's emphasis on coordination between naval and land forces played a crucial role in the planning of this battle. The Byzantine fleet, supported by land-based artillery, was able to capitalize on the element of surprise and effectively outmanoeuvre the enemy.

The victory at Syllaeum not only solidified Byzantine naval supremacy in the Aegean Sea but also sent a powerful message to rival powers regarding the resilience of the Byzantine navy. The battle demonstrated the effectiveness of Constantine's naval reforms and the impact of advanced tactics on naval engagements.

Challenges and Limitations

Despite the successes achieved by the Byzantine navy, challenges persisted throughout Constantine V's reign. The financial demands of maintaining a strong naval presence often strained imperial resources. The need for continuous investment in shipbuilding, training, and naval infrastructure placed significant pressure on the imperial treasury.

Additionally, the complexities of naval warfare required constant innovation and adaptation. As enemy forces developed new tactics and technologies, the Byzantine navy needed to remain vigilant and responsive to evolving threats. The introduction of new ships and weapons systems among rival powers posed challenges that required ongoing strategic planning.

Moreover, the ongoing internal divisions stemming from the Iconoclastic controversy created an environment of instability that could undermine military effectiveness. The tensions between factions within society had the potential to impact recruitment and the overall cohesion of naval forces.

Legacy of Naval Strategies

The naval strategies and maritime campaigns of Constantine V left a lasting impact on the Byzantine Empire. The reforms he implemented transformed the Byzantine navy into a formidable force capable of defending the empire's maritime interests and projecting power beyond its borders.

The emphasis on naval power became a defining characteristic of Byzantine military policy in subsequent centuries. The successes achieved during Constantine's reign laid the groundwork for future naval engagements and shaped the empire's approach to maritime warfare.

Moreover, the successful defence of Constantinople and victories in the Aegean established the Byzantine navy as a critical component of the empire's military apparatus. The ability to engage effectively in naval warfare not only safeguarded trade routes but also contributed to the overall stability of the Byzantine Empire.

Conclusion

Constantine V's naval strategies and maritime campaigns played a crucial role in shaping the course of Byzantine military history. Through a combination of reforms, strategic planning, and decisive engagements, the emperor revitalized the Byzantine navy and ensured its effectiveness in defending the empire's interests. The victories achieved at sea bolstered Byzantine power and solidified the navy's reputation as a formidable force in the Mediterranean.

As the Byzantine Empire continued to navigate the complexities of warfare and governance in the eighth century, the legacy of Constantine V's naval initiatives would endure, influencing future generations of Byzantine leaders and shaping the empire's interactions with rival powers.

Section 4: Political and Administrative Reforms

The reign of Constantine V was not only defined by military campaigns and naval strategies but also by significant political and administrative reforms that reshaped the Byzantine Empire. Recognizing the need for a strong, centralized authority to respond effectively to both internal challenges and external threats, Constantine implemented a series of reforms aimed at enhancing the governance of the empire. This section explores the political landscape of the Byzantine Empire during his reign, examining the key reforms that Constantine V enacted and their lasting implications for the structure and function of imperial administration.

The Political Context

When Constantine V ascended to the throne in 741, the Byzantine Empire faced a multitude of challenges. The ongoing Iconoclastic controversy, which divided the empire along theological lines, created internal strife and weakened imperial authority. Additionally, the external threat from the Arab forces and other neighbouring powers loomed large, necessitating a cohesive and effective government capable of responding to military and political exigencies.

Constantine recognized that to stabilize the empire and restore imperial authority, he needed to address both the political fragmentation caused by the Iconoclastic controversy and the administrative inefficiencies that had developed over time. His reign marked a turning point in Byzantine governance, characterized by a commitment to centralization, reform, and efficiency.

Centralization of Power

One of the key features of Constantine V's political reforms was the centralization of imperial authority. Recognizing the dangers of localism and factionalism, he sought to strengthen the power of the emperor and diminish the influence of regional elites. This process involved several measures aimed at consolidating control over the administration and military:

- **Reorganization of the Themes:** Constantine restructured the theme system, which was a key feature of Byzantine governance. The themes were military districts that combined civil and military authority, allowing for efficient local governance and rapid mobilization of forces. By reorganizing these districts and appointing loyal commanders, Constantine ensured that the military was directly under imperial control, reducing the potential for regional revolts.
- **Appointment of Loyal Officials:** To reinforce central authority, Constantine V appointed officials who were loyal to the emperor rather than local aristocrats. This practice not only curtailed the power of regional elites but also facilitated the implementation of imperial policies throughout the empire. The use of a meritocratic system for appointments helped to ensure that capable administrators filled key positions.
- **Reduction of Aristocratic Influence:** Constantine actively worked to diminish the power of the aristocracy, whose influence had historically undermined imperial authority. By restricting their access to key administrative positions and concentrating power in the hands of loyal officials, Constantine aimed to create a more cohesive and centralized government. This shift was crucial for maintaining stability and unity within the empire.

Administrative Reforms

In addition to centralizing political power, Constantine V implemented significant administrative reforms that enhanced the efficiency of governance. These reforms addressed issues of bureaucracy, taxation, and local administration:

- **Streamlining Bureaucracy:** Recognizing the complexities of Byzantine bureaucracy, Constantine sought to streamline administrative processes. He reduced the number of unnecessary bureaucratic layers, allowing for quicker decision-making and more effective governance. This reorganization facilitated better communication between the central government and local authorities.
- **Taxation Reforms:** The fiscal stability of the empire was critical for sustaining military campaigns and administrative functions. Constantine implemented reforms aimed at improving tax collection and ensuring equitable taxation. By creating a more efficient tax system, he sought to alleviate the burdens on the peasantry while increasing revenue for the state.
- **Land and Property Administration:** Constantine V recognized the importance of land management in sustaining the empire's agricultural economy. He implemented policies to regulate land ownership and ensure that land was used productively. This included measures to prevent the consolidation of land in the hands of a few powerful families, which could destabilize the agrarian economy.
- **Judicial Reforms:** To improve the administration of justice, Constantine reformed the legal system. He sought to ensure that legal processes were more accessible to ordinary citizens and that justice was administered fairly. By establishing clear legal codes and reducing corruption within the judiciary, Constantine aimed to enhance public trust in the legal system.

Religious Policy and Iconoclasm

The Iconoclastic controversy was a defining issue of Constantine V's reign, significantly impacting the political and religious landscape of the Byzantine Empire. Constantine, a staunch Iconoclast, sought to enforce his policies against the veneration of icons, which he believed were contrary to true Christian worship.

- **Iconoclastic Measures:** Constantine V implemented policies aimed at suppressing the Iconophile movement, which had gained significant support among the populace and clergy. He convened synods to condemn the veneration of icons and promoted the destruction of icons in churches. This approach created tensions between the imperial authority and religious factions, leading to protests and resistance from Iconophiles.

- **Centralization of Religious Authority:** Constantine sought to centralize religious authority in the hands of the emperor. By asserting control over ecclesiastical appointments and decisions, he aimed to ensure that the church remained aligned with imperial policies. This strategy was aimed at minimizing dissent and reinforcing the emperor's authority as both a political and religious leader.
- **Impact on Society:** The religious policies of Constantine V had far-reaching consequences for Byzantine society. The suppression of Iconophiles led to social unrest and division within communities. While his reforms strengthened the imperial authority in the short term, they also generated long-lasting animosities that would continue to influence Byzantine politics.

Military Integration with Governance

One of the hallmarks of Constantine V's reign was the integration of military and administrative functions. This approach was particularly important given the ongoing threats facing the empire:

- **Military Command Structure:** Constantine centralized military command under the emperor, ensuring that the military was responsive to imperial authority. He appointed *strategoi* (military commanders) who were loyal to him and tasked with maintaining order in their respective themes. This structure facilitated rapid mobilization of forces in response to external threats.
- **Militarization of Local Administration:** In the themes, local administrators were often required to maintain a military presence, blurring the lines between civil and military authority. This militarization ensured that local leaders were equipped to respond to threats and maintain order within their districts.
- **Training and Preparation:** Constantine emphasized the importance of military training for both soldiers and local leaders. Regular drills and preparations for potential invasions became integral to governance, ensuring that the empire was always ready to respond to external challenges.

Challenges to Reforms

Despite the ambitious reforms implemented by Constantine V, his reign was not without challenges. The political landscape remained volatile, and various factors threatened the stability of his reforms:

- **Opposition from Iconophiles:** The Iconoclastic policies faced significant opposition from factions within the church and society. Iconophiles, who advocated for the veneration of icons, often resisted imperial authority. This internal dissent created social tensions that could undermine the stability of the empire.
- **Regional Resistance:** The centralization of power and reduction of local aristocratic influence often led to resentment among regional elites. Some areas resisted the emperor's reforms, leading to localized revolts and challenges to imperial authority. The balance between centralization and local governance remained delicate.
- **Economic Strain:** The ambitious administrative and military reforms required significant financial resources. Economic strain, particularly in times of military conflict, posed challenges to maintaining the necessary funding for these initiatives. Taxation reforms, while aimed at improving revenue, were often met with resistance from the populace.

Legacy of Political and Administrative Reforms

The political and administrative reforms of Constantine V left a lasting legacy on the Byzantine Empire. His efforts to centralize authority, streamline bureaucracy, and integrate military and governance structures shaped the future trajectory of Byzantine administration:

- **Strengthened Central Authority:** The reforms implemented during Constantine's reign laid the groundwork for a stronger imperial authority. Subsequent emperors would build upon these changes, enhancing the centralization of power and establishing a more cohesive governance structure.
- **Militarization of Governance:** The integration of military and administrative functions became a defining characteristic of Byzantine governance. The theme system, with its emphasis on local military command, continued to play a critical role in responding to external threats and maintaining internal stability.
- **Enduring Social Divisions:** While the reforms strengthened imperial authority, they also left enduring divisions within Byzantine society. The tensions between Iconoclasts and Iconophiles persisted, influencing political dynamics for generations. The religious controversies initiated during Constantine's reign would continue to shape Byzantine history.
- **Model for Future Reforms:** The administrative reforms of Constantine V served as a model for future Byzantine emperors facing similar challenges.

The emphasis on centralization, efficiency, and military readiness remained central to the governance of the empire in subsequent centuries.

Conclusion

Constantine V's political and administrative reforms were instrumental in shaping the Byzantine Empire during a tumultuous period. His efforts to centralize power, streamline governance, and integrate military and administrative functions addressed the pressing challenges of the era. While his reforms faced opposition and were not without challenges, their legacy endured, influencing the structure and function of Byzantine administration for generations.

As the empire navigated the complexities of governance and warfare in the eighth century, the reforms of Constantine V laid the foundation for a more cohesive and resilient Byzantine state, ensuring its survival and adaptability in the face of adversity.

Section 5: Legacy and Long-Term Impact

The reign of Constantine V marked a transformative period in the Byzantine Empire's history. Known for his sweeping reforms across military, political, and religious domains, Constantine V left an indelible legacy that continued to influence the empire long after his death in 775. While he was a divisive figure – revered by some and reviled by others – his impact on Byzantine governance, military structure, and religious policy reshaped the empire's institutions and society in fundamental ways. This section examines Constantine V's enduring legacy, analyzing the long-term effects of his policies and assessing their contributions to the empire's resilience and development.

Strengthening the Military: A Legacy of Preparedness

One of Constantine V's most enduring legacies was the strengthening of the Byzantine military. His reforms laid the groundwork for a more resilient and disciplined army, ensuring that the empire could effectively defend its borders and respond to external threats.

- **Professionalization of the Army:** Constantine's efforts to improve the quality of military recruitment, training, and equipment brought a level of professionalism to the Byzantine armed forces that had not been seen before. By establishing training programs for soldiers and encouraging meritocratic promotions, Constantine ensured that the army was not only loyal to the emperor but also highly skilled. This professionalism contributed to the army's effectiveness in defending the empire from

Arab invasions and Slavic incursions, both during his reign and in subsequent generations.

- **Theme System as a Model for Military Organization:** The reorganization of the themes (military districts) became a model of military and administrative efficiency, influencing Byzantine military structure for centuries. By integrating local soldiers into these regions and aligning military duties with administrative roles, Constantine created a self-sustaining system that reduced the need for mercenaries and ensured a steady supply of trained soldiers. This system provided the Byzantine Empire with a level of stability that was especially valuable during times of crisis.
- **Long-Term Stability in Border Defence:** The emphasis on disciplined military units stationed within the themes allowed the Byzantine Empire to maintain its borders more effectively. The defensive infrastructure and well-prepared soldiers stationed across the empire's territories created a formidable barrier against invasions. For centuries, the theme system remained the backbone of Byzantine defence, demonstrating the lasting success of Constantine's military reforms.

Political Centralization and Administrative Efficiency

Constantine V's efforts to centralize imperial authority and streamline the administration had far-reaching consequences for Byzantine governance. His policies fostered a culture of bureaucratic efficiency and reinforced the authority of the emperor, helping to consolidate imperial power.

- **Strengthened Central Authority:** Constantine's insistence on centralization, especially in the appointment of officials loyal to the emperor, reinforced the central authority of the Byzantine state. By reducing the influence of regional elites and bringing the themes under imperial control, Constantine curtailed the power of potentially rebellious local aristocrats and ensured that the empire's administration was aligned with the emperor's vision. This legacy of centralized control proved invaluable in maintaining cohesion and stability in the Byzantine Empire, especially during times of external threats.
- **Administrative Efficiency:** Constantine's streamlining of the Byzantine bureaucracy led to a more efficient and responsive government. By reducing redundant positions, consolidating administrative processes, and prioritizing merit-based appointments, he fostered an environment in which government officials could carry out their duties effectively. This administrative culture of efficiency contributed to the resilience of

the Byzantine state, helping it to withstand periods of crisis and recover more quickly from setbacks.

- **Enhanced Tax Collection and Fiscal Stability:** Constantine's reforms to the taxation system and land administration addressed the economic pressures facing the empire. By improving tax collection mechanisms and implementing policies to prevent the concentration of land in the hands of powerful elites, Constantine increased the state's revenue and promoted a more equitable distribution of land. This fiscal stability not only strengthened the empire's economy but also provided the necessary resources to fund military campaigns and public projects, supporting Byzantine resilience in the long term.

Religious Policy and the Enduring Impact of Iconoclasm

The religious policies of Constantine V, particularly his support for Iconoclasm, had profound implications for Byzantine society and religious life. His stance on the veneration of icons divided Byzantine society, leaving an ideological legacy that persisted for generations.

- **Institutionalizing Iconoclasm:** Constantine's enforcement of Iconoclastic policies institutionalized the movement and brought it to the forefront of Byzantine religious life. He convened church councils, passed laws against the veneration of icons, and promoted Iconoclast clergy. While this policy aimed to unify the church under the emperor's authority, it also alienated a large portion of the population, especially monks and the Iconophile faithful. The schism created by Iconoclasm contributed to social unrest and polarized communities, with lasting consequences for the Byzantine Empire.
- **Legacy of Religious Division:** The Iconoclastic policies of Constantine V intensified the theological divide within Byzantine society. The persecution of Iconophiles, destruction of religious art, and suppression of monasteries led to a lingering resentment among those who opposed Iconoclasm. This legacy of division resurfaced repeatedly in Byzantine politics and hindered efforts at religious reconciliation for decades. Even after the eventual restoration of icons under Empress Irene and later emperors, the scars left by Constantine's Iconoclastic policies remained a source of tension in Byzantine society.
- **Reinforcement of Imperial Authority Over the Church:** Constantine's assertion of authority over religious matters reinforced the notion that the emperor held supremacy in both secular and religious affairs. This precedent of imperial control over the church continued to shape

Byzantine religious policy, as future emperors sought to exercise authority over ecclesiastical decisions. Constantine's legacy in this regard influenced the Byzantine concept of '*symphonia*', where the emperor and church operated in a close relationship, though with the emperor typically in a dominant position.

Cultural and Artistic Legacy: The Loss and Transformation of Byzantine Art

Constantine V's Iconoclastic policies also had a significant impact on Byzantine art and culture. The prohibition of religious images led to the destruction of countless works of art, altering the course of Byzantine artistic expression.

- **Destruction of Religious Art:** Under Constantine's orders, icons and religious artwork were systematically destroyed. This loss was profound, as many irreplaceable works of religious art, including frescoes, mosaics, and icons, were removed or defaced. The Iconoclastic movement thus created a cultural vacuum, depriving future generations of access to some of the empire's greatest artistic achievements.
- **Shift Toward Secular Art and Symbolism:** In response to the prohibition of religious icons, Byzantine artists turned their attention to secular themes and abstract designs. This shift led to a new style of Byzantine art that focused on geometric patterns, floral motifs, and symbolic representations. Although this period is often seen as a loss in terms of religious art, it also marked a transformation in Byzantine artistic traditions, showcasing the adaptability of Byzantine culture.
- **Enduring Debate over Iconography:** Constantine's legacy sparked an ongoing debate within Byzantine society regarding the role of images in religious worship. Even after Iconoclasm was formally repudiated, the discussion surrounding the proper use of religious images persisted. This debate influenced Byzantine art for centuries, shaping the empire's approach to religious representation and contributing to the unique stylistic qualities of Byzantine iconography that emerged after the restoration of icons.

Economic Impacts and Land Reforms

The economic policies implemented by Constantine V, particularly his land and taxation reforms, had a lasting impact on the Byzantine economy. His focus on preventing the concentration of land ownership and promoting agricultural productivity contributed to a more stable and sustainable economic base for the empire.

- **Redistribution of Land:** Constantine's policies aimed at redistributing land and preventing large estates from monopolizing resources created a more balanced economic landscape. By ensuring that land was distributed among smallholders and peasant farmers, he strengthened the economic foundations of rural communities, which were essential for the empire's agricultural production.
- **Strengthening the Peasantry:** By supporting small landowners, Constantine bolstered the Byzantine peasantry, who formed the backbone of the empire's economy and military. The land reforms not only enhanced agricultural output but also provided a reliable source of recruits for the theme system, as soldiers were often drawn from rural communities. This connection between landownership and military service created a mutually beneficial relationship that supported both the economy and the empire's defence.
- **Long-Term Fiscal Benefits:** The improvements in tax collection and land management contributed to the financial stability of the empire. By increasing state revenue, Constantine ensured that the empire had the resources necessary to fund public projects, maintain the military, and support administrative functions. This fiscal foundation proved valuable during times of crisis, allowing the Byzantine Empire to endure and recover from setbacks.

Influence on Successor Emperors and Byzantine Governance

The impact of Constantine V's reforms extended beyond his reign, influencing the policies of successor emperors and shaping the principles of Byzantine governance.

- **Blueprint for Future Military and Administrative Reforms:** Constantine's emphasis on military preparedness and administrative efficiency served as a blueprint for future emperors facing similar challenges. His reforms provided a foundation for military and political stability, demonstrating the importance of a centralized, well-organized administration in maintaining the empire's resilience. Many subsequent emperors looked to Constantine's reign as a model for strengthening imperial authority and reinforcing the military.
- **Enduring Model of Centralized Governance:** Constantine's commitment to centralizing power and curbing the influence of the aristocracy became an enduring feature of Byzantine governance. Future emperors continued to implement policies aimed at consolidating authority, ensuring that the emperor held ultimate control over the state. This centralization

contributed to the longevity of the Byzantine Empire, allowing it to maintain internal cohesion despite external pressures.

- **Legacy of Pragmatism and Adaptability:** Constantine's pragmatic approach to governance, which prioritized the needs of the empire over ideological or traditional considerations, became a hallmark of Byzantine leadership. His willingness to adapt and reform based on practical concerns rather than adherence to established custom set a precedent for future emperors, fostering a culture of adaptability that enabled the Byzantine Empire to survive and thrive in a changing world.

Conclusion: A Complex and Enduring Legacy

Constantine V's legacy is a complex one, marked by both significant achievements and deep controversies. His reforms strengthened the Byzantine military, centralized the administration, and enhanced the empire's fiscal stability. These accomplishments contributed to the resilience of the Byzantine state, enabling it to withstand the challenges of the eighth century and beyond. However, his Iconoclastic policies left a legacy of religious division that continued to affect Byzantine society for generations.

Ultimately, Constantine V's reign represents a pivotal period in Byzantine history. His legacy, characterized by both innovation and contention, left a profound impact on the empire's military, political, and cultural institutions. As the Byzantine Empire navigated the challenges of the medieval period, the reforms of Constantine V provided a foundation for stability, adaptability, and strength – qualities that would sustain the empire through both triumphs and trials.

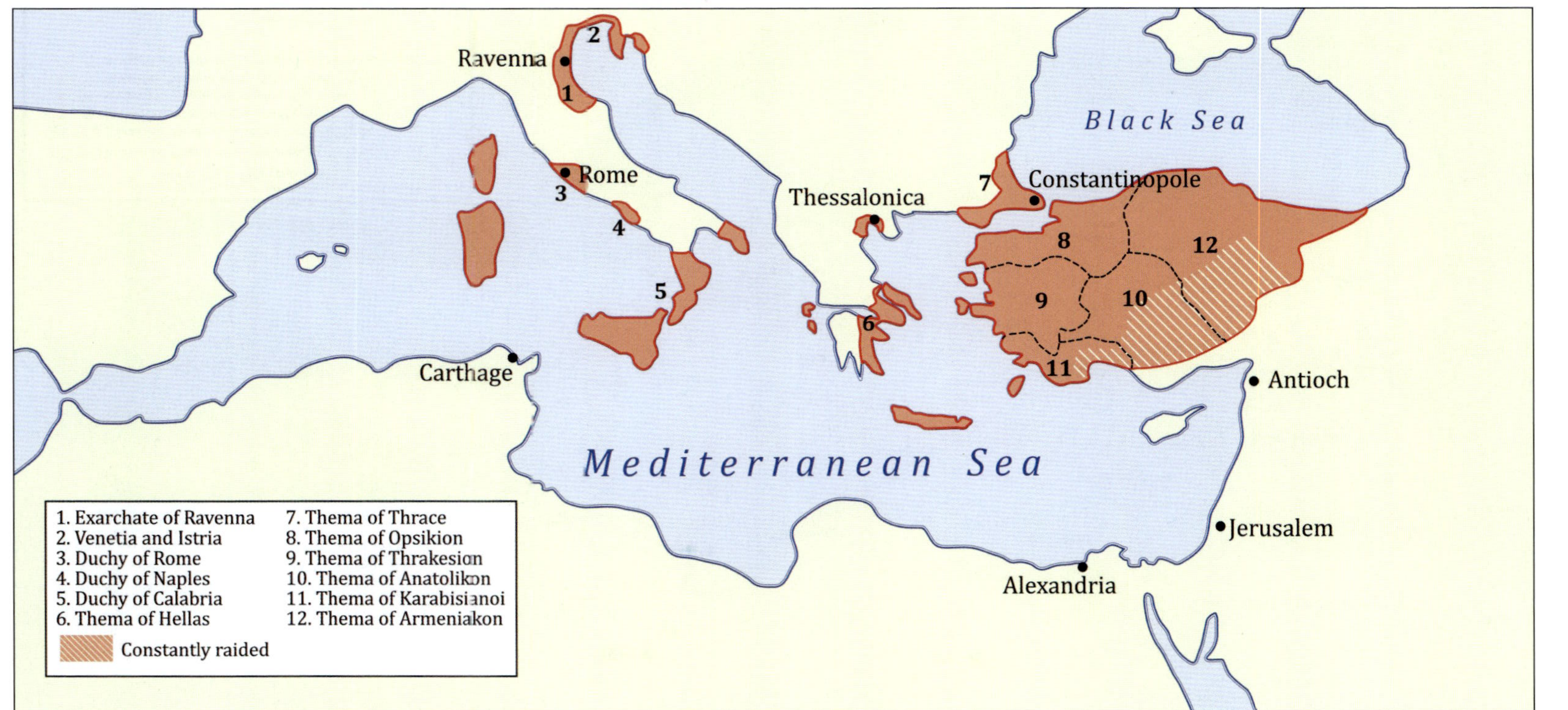

Byzantine Empire in the year 717 CE. (*Amonixinator via Wikimedia Commons, CC BY-SA 3.0*)

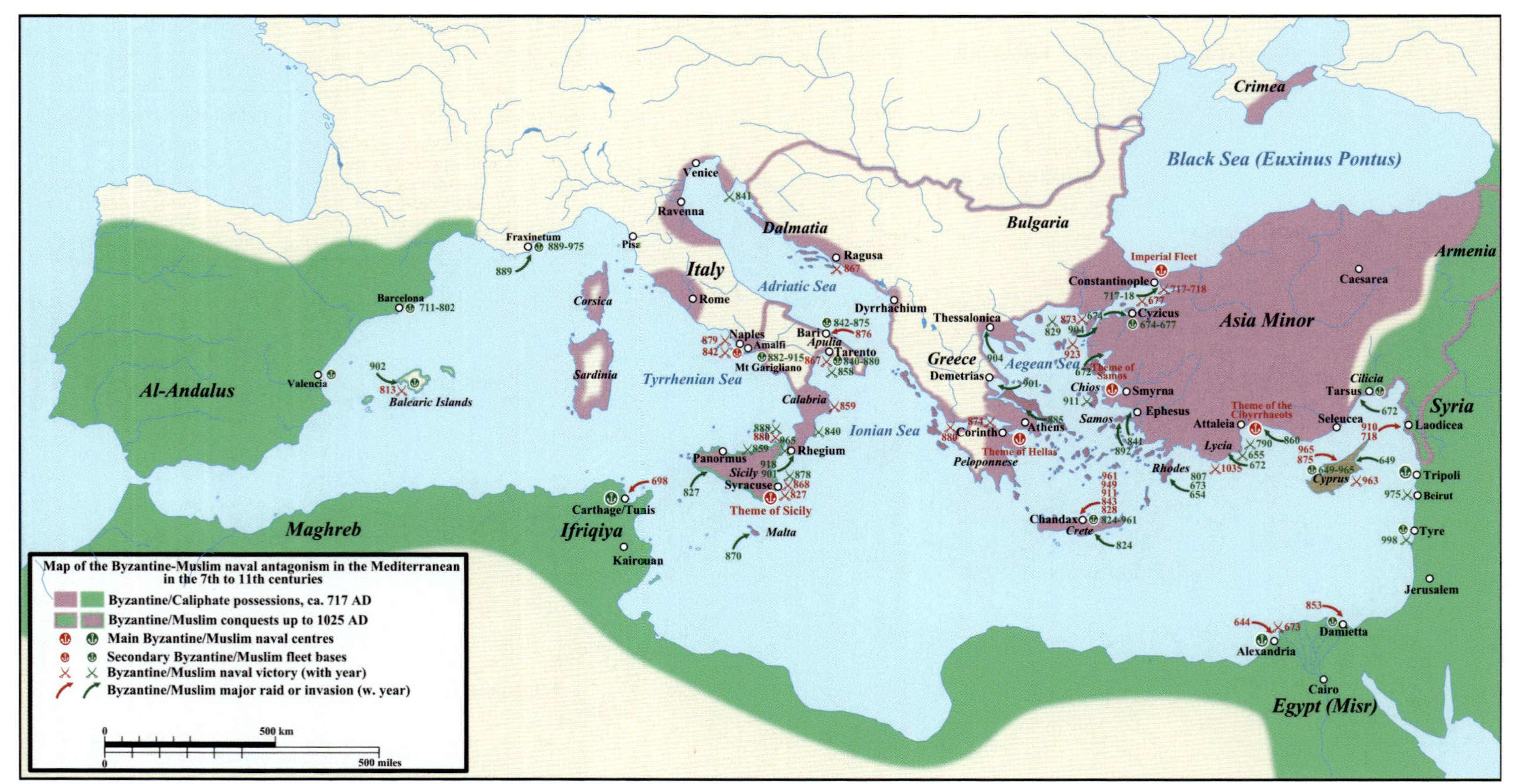

Byzantine and Abbasid naval warfare, eighth century. (*Szajci via Wikimedia Commons, CC BY-SA 4.0*)

Asia Minor in 780 CE. (*Cplakidas via Wikimedia Commons, CC BY-SA 3.0*)

Constantinople in the eighth century. (*Cplakidas via Wikimedia Commons, CC BY-SA 3.0*)

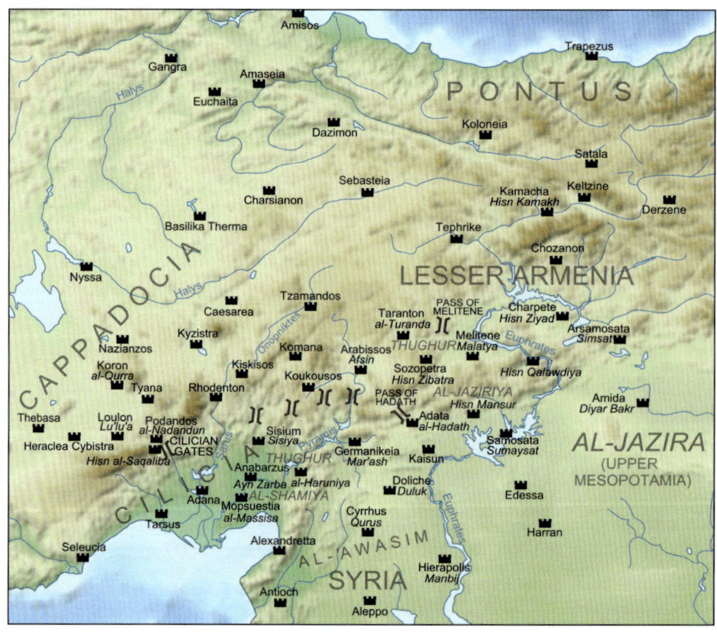

Arab and Byzantine Frontier in the eighth century. (*Cplakidas via Wikimedia Commons, CC BY-SA 3.0*)

yzantine and Bulgarian Wars during the reign of Constantine V. (*Kandi via Wikimedia Commons, C BY-SA 4.0*)

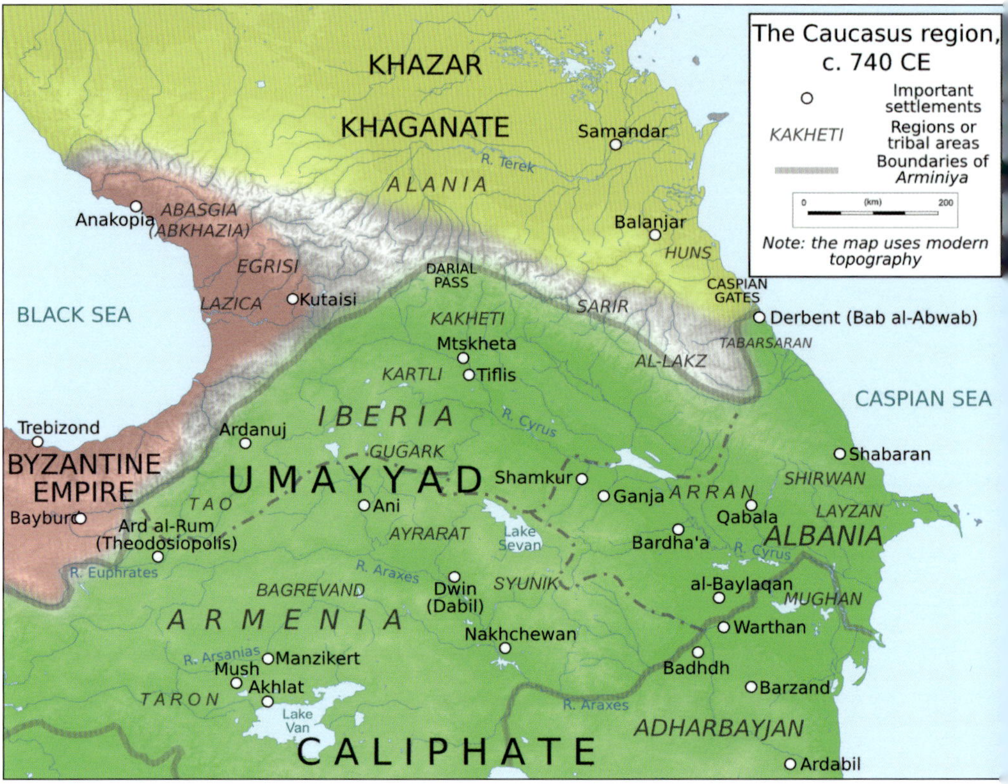

Map of the Caucuses in 740 CE. (*Constantine Plakidas via Wikimedia Commons, CC BY-SA 4.0*)

Reinforced Walls of Constantinople. (*GFDL via Wikimedia Commons, CC BY-SA 3.0*)

Depiction of Constantine V. (*Public domain*)

Solidus of Constantine V. (*Classical Numismatic Group, Inc. http://www.cngcoins.com*)

Solidus of the Usurper Artabasdos. (*Dumbarton Oaks via Wikimedia Commons/public domain*)

Solidus of Leo III and Constantine V (reverse side). (*Classical Numismatic Group, Inc. http://www.cngcoins.com*)

Solidus of Leo III and Constantine V. (*Classical Numismatic Group, Inc. http://www.cngcoins.com*)

Use of Greek fire in battle. (*John Strylitzes depiction/public domain*)

Seventh Ecumenical Council held in 787 CE. (*Public domain*)

Iconoclastic art as a simple cross in the Hagia Irene. (*Carole Raddato via Wikimedia Commons CC BY-SA 2.0*)

Chapter 5

Administrative Overhauls and Centralization

Section 1: The Administrative Reforms of Constantine V

Constantine V's administrative reforms represented a profound shift in the Byzantine government's structure, as he pursued greater centralization and efficiency to consolidate imperial authority. These reforms were instrumental in strengthening the state apparatus, bringing about a leaner, more effective government that could better address the internal and external challenges facing the empire. Constantine's efforts were not without controversy, as they often curtailed the power of regional elites and met resistance from established aristocratic circles. However, his policies laid the groundwork for a more cohesive and stable Byzantine state, providing a model that would influence subsequent emperors.

Centralization of Authority: A Response to Decentralized Power

A critical component of Constantine's reforms was his drive to centralize power, a strategy he deemed essential to maintaining control over a vast and diverse empire. Byzantine territory, stretching across various ethnic, linguistic, and religious groups, was challenging to govern uniformly, and previous administrations had often delegated power to regional aristocrats, military officials, and local governors. This decentralized approach, while sometimes necessary, allowed local leaders to amass significant influence, occasionally leading to internal divisions and even rebellions against the central government.

- **Curtailing Aristocratic Influence:** Constantine viewed the concentration of power among local elites as a threat to imperial stability, particularly as these figures could leverage their authority to challenge or undermine the emperor. To mitigate this, he enacted policies that limited the autonomy of regional governors and curbed the privileges of wealthy landowners. One of his primary tactics involved redistributing administrative positions to loyal, lower-ranking officials who owed their positions to Constantine rather than to noble birth or wealth. By placing his supporters in key administrative roles, Constantine weakened the influence of the traditional aristocracy and reduced the risk of insubordination.

- **Streamlining Governance through the Imperial Court:** Constantine concentrated decision-making within the imperial court, making it the central hub of administration. Unlike previous emperors who had relied on a sprawling bureaucracy with considerable autonomy, Constantine restructured the government to ensure that officials reported directly to the emperor or his close advisers. This move allowed him to maintain oversight of critical decisions and to ensure that imperial directives were followed consistently throughout the empire. Although this approach increased the demands on Constantine's time and attention, it proved effective in asserting the authority of the throne over all levels of administration.
- **Restructuring Provincial Administration:** Under Constantine's reforms, provinces (or *'themes'*) were reorganized to promote loyalty to the central government. Governors were held accountable directly to the emperor, with their powers more tightly regulated to prevent abuses. This reorganization allowed Constantine to establish a more reliable administrative framework, as he appointed officials who shared his vision of a strong, centralized state. While provincial leaders continued to oversee local affairs, Constantine's policies ensured that they remained firmly under imperial control.

Bureaucratic Efficiency and the Role of the Theme System

A hallmark of Constantine's reign was his approach to military and administrative alignment, particularly through the theme system, which he further restructured to streamline governance and ensure a more responsive military force. The theme system had already been introduced by earlier emperors, but Constantine's refinements emphasized efficiency and reinforced its role as a dual administrative and military institution.

- **Strengthening the Theme System:** The themes were originally established as military districts, each managed by a *strategos* (general) who commanded troops and also governed civilian affairs within their jurisdiction. Constantine expanded the role of the '*strategoi*', integrating them more deeply into the administrative framework and holding them accountable to imperial oversight. This helped consolidate both military and administrative control in the hands of officials loyal to the emperor, creating a tightly-knit network that could respond swiftly to both external threats and internal matters.
- **Supporting Soldiers and Local Economy:** Constantine's reforms provided soldiers with land within the themes, encouraging them to settle in their

assigned regions and participate in local agriculture. This arrangement not only incentivized loyalty among soldiers but also bolstered the local economy, as soldiers cultivated land and contributed to regional stability. This model created a symbiotic relationship between the military and the populace, ensuring that soldiers were invested in the well-being of their regions and that local economies had a degree of protection from economic downturns.

- **Administrative Streamlining within the Themes:** Within each theme, Constantine established a simplified hierarchy of officials responsible for specific aspects of governance, including tax collection, law enforcement, and infrastructure maintenance. This organization allowed the themes to operate with greater efficiency, as responsibilities were clearly delineated and overlapping roles reduced. By reducing bureaucratic redundancies, Constantine created a more functional and responsive administrative system that could better serve the needs of both the government and the populace.

Fiscal Reforms and Enhanced Revenue Collection

One of the most impactful aspects of Constantine's administrative reforms was his focus on fiscal policy. Recognizing the importance of a stable revenue stream for maintaining the empire's military and administrative functions, Constantine implemented measures to improve tax collection and reduce financial inefficiencies. His fiscal policies were aimed at creating a more equitable system that could sustain the demands of the empire's expanding infrastructure and military needs.

- **Taxation Reform and Redistribution:** Constantine restructured the taxation system to ensure a fairer distribution of the tax burden across social classes. Wealthy landowners, who had previously enjoyed certain exemptions, were now required to contribute their fair share, while lower-income citizens were afforded greater protections against excessive taxation. This move not only increased revenue but also strengthened the loyalty of the peasantry, who saw Constantine as a ruler willing to hold the elite accountable. By placing limits on tax exemptions, Constantine prevented the wealthiest classes from undermining the financial stability of the state.
- **Revenue Collection Mechanisms:** Constantine introduced new regulations to improve the consistency of revenue collection, with an emphasis on reducing fraud and corruption within the tax system. He appointed trusted officials to oversee taxation, ensuring that funds were

collected in accordance with imperial standards. This increased oversight helped minimize revenue losses and contributed to a more predictable fiscal environment, which allowed him to fund his military campaigns and administrative projects with greater confidence.

- **Investment in Infrastructure and Public Works:** Constantine's fiscal reforms also allowed him to invest in public infrastructure, which he saw as essential to the stability and prosperity of the empire. Roads, fortifications, and aqueducts were constructed or improved under his administration, facilitating trade and communication across the empire. These projects not only enhanced the quality of life for Byzantine citizens but also strengthened Constantine's support base, as the public recognized the tangible benefits of his investments.

Addressing Corruption and Strengthening Accountability

Recognizing that corruption could undermine even the most well-intentioned reforms, Constantine took steps to address dishonesty within the government. He implemented policies aimed at improving transparency and accountability among officials, signalling his commitment to a more ethical administration.

- **Anti-Corruption Measures:** Constantine established a system of checks and balances to monitor officials at various levels of government, creating a network of inspectors tasked with investigating allegations of corruption. These inspectors reported directly to the emperor or his close advisers, allowing Constantine to address issues of mismanagement or abuse of power swiftly. By implementing a zero-tolerance policy toward corruption, Constantine sought to maintain the integrity of his administration and reassure the public of his commitment to just governance.
- **Punitive Actions Against Corruption:** Constantine did not shy away from making examples of corrupt officials, often imposing severe punishments to deter others from engaging in similar activities. Public trials and confiscation of property were common consequences for those found guilty of corruption, reinforcing the message that abuse of power would not be tolerated. This approach helped cultivate a more accountable administration, as officials became more cautious in their actions, knowing that Constantine was vigilant in his oversight.
- **Building a Culture of Loyalty and Merit:** Constantine promoted officials based on merit and loyalty rather than social standing, a departure from the traditional aristocratic system. This policy encouraged talented individuals from lower social classes to pursue careers in the bureaucracy, diversifying the administrative class and infusing it with new perspectives.

By rewarding competence and dedication, Constantine fostered a culture within the government that valued service to the empire above personal ambition.

Impact on Byzantine Society and Long-Term Consequences

Constantine's administrative overhauls had far-reaching effects on Byzantine society, creating a more centralized and responsive government that could better serve the needs of the state. His reforms altered the balance of power within Byzantine society, empowering the central government at the expense of regional elites and reinforcing the emperor's role as the ultimate authority.

- **Shifts in Social Dynamics:** By curtailing the influence of the aristocracy and promoting officials based on merit, Constantine created a more inclusive government that reflected the diversity of Byzantine society. This shift allowed individuals from a wider range of backgrounds to participate in the administration, breaking down some of the traditional barriers that had favoured the elite. Over time, this contributed to a more dynamic and flexible government, capable of adapting to changing circumstances and challenges.
- **Strengthening the Emperor's Authority:** Constantine's reforms reinforced the idea of the emperor as the supreme authority within the Byzantine state, a legacy that would shape Byzantine governance for centuries. By centralizing power and reducing the autonomy of regional officials, Constantine ensured that future emperors would inherit a more stable and controllable administration. This centralization provided a foundation for stability, enabling the Byzantine Empire to withstand external threats and internal discord with greater resilience.
- **Legacy of Efficiency and Reform:** Constantine's administrative overhauls set a precedent for subsequent rulers, who would continue to refine and expand upon his policies. His emphasis on efficiency, accountability, and centralization became defining features of the Byzantine government, influencing the way future emperors approached governance. Constantine's legacy as a reformer persisted long after his death, shaping the Byzantine administrative framework and ensuring that his vision of a strong, unified state remained a central tenet of imperial policy.

These administrative overhauls illustrate Constantine V's vision of a centralized, efficient, and loyal state apparatus. His reforms not only strengthened the Byzantine government but also redefined the relationship between the emperor, his officials, and the subjects they governed, creating a legacy of stability and resilience that would endure through successive generations.

Section 2: Economic Policies for Stability and Growth

Constantine V's reign is often remembered for his military achievements and religious reforms, but his economic policies also played a crucial role in solidifying Byzantine stability. Recognizing the importance of a strong economy in supporting both defence and governance, Constantine implemented several financial and economic reforms aimed at creating a sustainable and equitable system. These reforms were instrumental in consolidating imperial control, stabilizing the empire's finances, and preparing it for future challenges. This section explores the multifaceted approach Constantine V took in managing the Byzantine economy, focusing on taxation, land redistribution, currency stability, and infrastructure development.

Tax Reforms and Fiscal Policies

A cornerstone of Constantine V's economic strategy was his overhaul of the Byzantine tax system. Previous emperors had grappled with inefficiencies and inequalities within the tax structure, which often placed a disproportionate burden on the lower classes while allowing wealthy landowners to escape full taxation. Constantine sought to create a more balanced and efficient system, both to increase revenue and to reduce social unrest.

- **Equitable Tax Distribution:** One of Constantine's primary aims was to ensure a fairer distribution of tax burdens across different social classes. To achieve this, he introduced measures that targeted wealthier segments of society, particularly landowning aristocrats and large estate holders, who had historically enjoyed significant tax privileges. By enforcing stricter tax collection and reducing exemptions, Constantine increased state revenue while addressing inequalities that had long favoured the elite. This policy shift was popular among the peasantry and urban middle classes, who saw the emperor's tax reforms as a means of reducing the exploitative practices of wealthy landlords.
- **Enhanced Tax Collection Efficiency:** Constantine introduced new regulations to streamline tax collection, which involved training officials specifically for the task and setting up a hierarchical reporting structure. By appointing loyal administrators with clear accountability to the imperial court, Constantine minimized the risk of fraud and corruption. This oversight helped ensure that collected taxes actually reached the

state treasury, reducing the revenue losses that had previously hampered imperial finances. Additionally, he restructured the bureaucracy to eliminate redundant positions, resulting in a more efficient and cost-effective tax administration.

- **Peasant Protections Against Over-Taxation:** To maintain social stability, Constantine was careful to protect the peasantry from excessive taxation. His reforms imposed limits on the taxes that local landlords could levy, shielding peasants from exploitative practices. This not only improved the lives of the rural populace but also ensured a steady source of agricultural productivity, as peasants were less likely to abandon their lands under Constantine's protections. By securing the loyalty of the rural population, Constantine strengthened the economic backbone of the empire, providing a reliable base of agricultural and tax revenue to support his other initiatives.

Land Redistribution and Agrarian Policy

Constantine's economic reforms also extended to land distribution, a critical issue in a predominantly agrarian society. Land ownership was closely tied to wealth and power, with large estates held by the aristocracy creating disparities in wealth distribution and occasionally fuelling regional rebellions. By implementing land reforms, Constantine sought to strengthen the empire's economic stability and increase agricultural productivity.

- **Redistribution to Loyal Soldiers and Smallholders:** One of Constantine's most impactful policies was the redistribution of land to loyal soldiers and smallholders. By granting soldiers land within the themes (military districts), Constantine not only rewarded them for their service but also incentivized them to stay within their regions, cultivating the land and contributing to local stability. This policy transformed soldiers into landed peasants, binding them to their regions and reducing the likelihood of desertion or rebellion. For smallholders, access to land provided a measure of security and independence, fostering loyalty to the emperor among the rural populace.
- **Breaking Up Large Estates:** Constantine's land policies were also designed to reduce the concentration of wealth and power held by aristocratic landowners. By breaking up large estates and redistributing land to small farmers, he weakened the economic dominance of the aristocracy and curbed their influence in provincial matters. This move was not without controversy, as it angered some members of the elite, but it succeeded in creating a more equitable economic landscape that

supported the empire's long-term stability. Smallholders became more self-sufficient, which in turn supported local economies and provided a stable tax base.

- **Promotion of Agricultural Productivity:** Constantine encouraged agricultural productivity by investing in infrastructure that supported farming. Irrigation projects, improved storage facilities, and the construction of new roads enabled farmers to transport goods to markets more easily, boosting local economies. Constantine's administration also provided farmers with resources such as seed stock and basic tools, reducing barriers to entry for smallholders. This emphasis on agricultural development enhanced food security within the empire, mitigating the risks of famine and creating a surplus that could be stored or traded.

Currency Reforms and Stabilization

Constantine V recognized that a stable currency was essential for economic growth and the smooth functioning of trade, both domestically and internationally. During his reign, he implemented measures to ensure currency stability and prevent inflation, which had posed challenges to previous emperors.

- **Minting Policies and Standardization:** Constantine standardized the production and purity of Byzantine coins, particularly the gold *solidus*, which was the empire's primary currency. By regulating the purity and weight of coins, Constantine ensured that Byzantine currency remained stable and reliable, a significant factor in maintaining economic stability. This standardization boosted both domestic and international confidence in Byzantine currency, facilitating trade across borders. Byzantine coins, renowned for their reliability, became widely accepted in trade networks from the Mediterranean to the Middle East, further enhancing the empire's economic reach.
- **Combating Inflation:** To prevent inflation, Constantine implemented policies that limited excessive minting of coins. By carefully controlling the money supply, he preserved the value of Byzantine currency, protecting the empire's purchasing power and preventing the destabilization that often accompanied inflation. This control over the money supply also safeguarded the savings of citizens, encouraging them to participate in the economy without fear of devaluation. Constantine's currency reforms helped stabilize prices, fostering a predictable economic environment that benefited both merchants and consumers.
- **Fostering Trade Relations:** Constantine's currency reforms also made Byzantine currency a valuable asset in international trade. Merchants

from neighbouring empires and trading partners preferred the Byzantine *solidus* due to its consistent purity, which allowed the empire to act as a central hub in Mediterranean trade. Constantine encouraged this position by promoting policies that facilitated trade with foreign merchants, who relied on Byzantine coins as a stable means of exchange. This influx of foreign currency and goods further boosted the economy, enriching Byzantine cities and increasing the availability of goods within the empire.

Infrastructure Development and Public Works

Constantine understood that a robust infrastructure was essential for economic growth, especially in a sprawling empire like Byzantium. His investments in public works not only supported economic activity but also reinforced the connectivity and unity of the empire.

- **Roads and Transportation Networks:** Constantine prioritized the construction and maintenance of roads, particularly those connecting strategic military and economic centres. These roads facilitated the movement of troops, supplies, and goods, which was essential for both defence and trade. Improved transportation networks reduced travel times and costs, enabling merchants to transport goods more efficiently. The increased ease of movement contributed to the economic vitality of urban and rural areas alike, as merchants could reach a broader range of markets and consumers had access to a wider variety of products.
- **Fortifications and Security Infrastructure:** Constantine invested in fortifications, particularly along vulnerable borders and key trade routes. These fortifications served a dual purpose, protecting the empire from invasions while also safeguarding trade routes from banditry. By enhancing security, Constantine created a more stable environment for commerce, as merchants could conduct their business with greater confidence. The increase in trade volume generated revenue for the state through customs duties and taxes, contributing to the empire's economic prosperity.
- **Urban Development and Public Amenities:** Constantine also invested in the development of urban centres, which served as hubs of trade, governance, and culture. By funding public amenities such as marketplaces, public baths, and aqueducts, Constantine improved the quality of life in Byzantine cities, attracting both merchants and skilled artisans. The expansion of marketplaces, in particular, fostered economic growth by providing spaces for commercial exchange. These improvements not only enhanced urban life but also reinforced the emperor's image as

a benefactor and protector of the public good, further solidifying his support base.

Impact on Different Social Classes

Constantine's economic policies had a significant impact on the social structure of Byzantine society, affecting different classes in various ways. By redistributing wealth and fostering economic stability, Constantine aimed to create a more equitable society, though his policies were met with both support and resistance.

- **The Peasantry and Smallholders:** For the peasantry and smallholders, Constantine's policies brought about improvements in land ownership, tax protections, and agricultural support. Access to land allowed peasants to achieve a level of economic independence, and the protections against excessive taxation provided them with greater security. As a result, the peasantry became more loyal to Constantine, viewing him as a ruler who looked out for their interests. This strengthened the bond between the emperor and the rural population, providing a stable base for both economic productivity and military recruitment.
- **The Aristocracy and Landed Elites:** Constantine's reforms were less favourable to the aristocracy, particularly wealthy landowners who had previously enjoyed significant privileges. By imposing stricter taxation and redistributing land to soldiers and smallholders, Constantine reduced the economic and political influence of the elite. While this generated resentment among some aristocrats, it also prevented them from amassing enough power to challenge the emperor, reducing the likelihood of regional rebellions and internal strife.
- **Urban Merchants and Artisans:** Constantine's economic policies benefited urban merchants and artisans, as increased trade and improved infrastructure created new opportunities for commerce. Byzantine cities flourished under Constantine's rule, with expanded marketplaces and stable currency providing a conducive environment for economic growth. For artisans, the emperor's investment in public works and urban development created a steady demand for skilled labour, contributing to a vibrant urban economy.

Long-Term Effects and Legacy

Constantine V's economic policies had long-lasting effects on the Byzantine Empire, shaping its economic structure for generations. By implementing fairer taxation, fostering agricultural productivity, stabilizing currency, and enhancing infrastructure, Constantine laid the groundwork for a more resilient economy.

- **Sustainable Revenue for Future Administrations:** Constantine's reforms created a stable and sustainable revenue stream, providing future emperors with the financial resources needed to address new challenges. By creating a more equitable tax system and protecting the economic interests of the peasantry, Constantine established a foundation of fiscal stability that would support the empire's continued prosperity.
- **Strengthening the Byzantine Economy's Resilience:** Constantine's focus on agricultural productivity, infrastructure, and currency stability ensured that the Byzantine economy could withstand external shocks, such as invasions or natural disasters. His policies created a self-sufficient and resilient economic base, one capable of sustaining the empire through periods of turmoil.
- **A Model for Future Reforms:** Constantine's economic strategies served as a model for subsequent emperors, who would build upon his reforms to further strengthen the Byzantine economy. His emphasis on fairness, stability, and infrastructure investment influenced Byzantine economic policy for centuries, leaving a lasting legacy of prosperity and resilience.

Constantine V's economic policies were essential to the stability and growth of the Byzantine Empire. Through targeted tax reforms, land redistribution, currency stabilization, and infrastructure development, Constantine transformed the Byzantine economy into a more equitable and sustainable system. His policies not only strengthened the empire's financial foundation but also reshaped the social fabric, creating a more unified and resilient state.

Section 3: Effects on the Peasantry and Nobility

Constantine V's reign was marked by sweeping reforms that reshaped the Byzantine Empire's social and economic structures. His policies aimed at centralizing power and creating a more efficient state significantly impacted the lives of both peasants and the nobility. By redistributing land, altering tax policies, and increasing government control over local governance, Constantine attempted to reduce the social stratification that had allowed the nobility to grow disproportionately powerful. While these reforms strengthened the emperor's control, they also sparked tensions and changed the balance of power within Byzantine society. This section will delve into the effects of Constantine V's policies on the peasantry and the nobility, highlighting both the challenges and the benefits experienced by these groups.

Constantine's Vision for Social Balance and Unity

Constantine V's approach to governance was driven by a vision of a strong, centralized state where the emperor held supreme authority. Recognizing the historical challenges posed by powerful noble families and their expansive estates, Constantine aimed to curb the influence of the aristocracy and bolster the stability of the empire by empowering the peasantry. This vision was revolutionary for a Byzantine emperor, as it sought to reduce the entrenched privileges of the nobility while increasing the autonomy and stability of the rural population. By shifting resources and privileges toward the peasantry and away from the aristocracy, Constantine hoped to create a more balanced social structure, where wealth and power were not concentrated in the hands of a few.

- **Reducing Noble Influence:** Constantine sought to reduce the influence of the nobility on local governance by implementing reforms that limited their control over lands and people. His vision was to establish a direct relationship between the emperor and the peasantry, thereby bypassing the traditional role of noble intermediaries. This move aligned with Constantine's broader strategy of centralization, where loyalty to the emperor superseded all other allegiances.
- **Empowering the Peasantry:** Constantine understood that a stable and loyal peasantry was crucial to the empire's economic productivity and military strength. By redistributing land and ensuring fairer taxation, he aimed to protect peasants from exploitation by noble landlords. This policy not only increased peasant loyalty to the emperor but also contributed to the empire's stability by creating a larger class of smallholders who were financially independent and less likely to rebel against the state.

The Peasantry: Gains and Challenges Under Constantine V

The impact of Constantine V's reforms on the peasantry was profound, with both positive and challenging aspects. While his policies provided peasants with more land, protections against exploitation, and reduced tax burdens, they also placed new demands on them. These changes fundamentally altered the lives of Byzantine peasants, giving them more economic opportunities and autonomy, but also greater responsibility to the state.

- **Increased Access to Land:** Constantine's policies granted more peasants access to land, particularly in regions where land had previously been concentrated in the hands of noble families. By redistributing confiscated or reclaimed lands to soldiers and small farmers, Constantine increased the number of smallholders across the empire. This shift not only improved the livelihoods of peasant families but also reduced their dependence on noble landlords. With their own land, peasants had a vested interest in maintaining stability within the empire, as they now had tangible assets to protect.

- **Protections from Noble Exploitation:** One of Constantine's key reforms was to limit the ability of nobles to extract excessive rents and taxes from peasants. Prior to his reign, noble landlords often imposed heavy burdens on peasants, leading to widespread discontent and, in some cases, open rebellion. Constantine enacted legal protections that restricted the rents landlords could charge and imposed penalties on nobles who overtaxed their tenants. This policy was popular among the peasantry, who viewed Constantine as a ruler who was willing to protect them from abuse.
- **Economic Security and Social Mobility:** Constantine's land policies and tax protections gave peasants greater economic security and, in some cases, the opportunity for social mobility. Smallholders who managed their land effectively could achieve a degree of wealth and status that had previously been out of reach for most rural families. This improvement in economic standing fostered loyalty to the emperor, as peasants recognized that their newfound stability was the result of Constantine's reforms.
- **New Responsibilities and Military Obligations:** While Constantine's policies offered benefits, they also came with new responsibilities. Many peasant smallholders were required to serve in the military as part of their land grants. This military obligation was a double-edged sword, as it provided peasants with a sense of duty and an opportunity to serve the empire but also imposed a significant burden on families, particularly during times of war. Despite the challenges, most peasants viewed this responsibility as an honourable duty, which strengthened their loyalty to the state.

The Nobility: Resistance, Adaptation, and Loss of Influence

Constantine's reforms placed considerable pressure on the Byzantine nobility, whose traditional privileges and power were significantly curtailed. While some nobles resisted these changes, others adapted by finding new ways to maintain their influence within Constantine's centralized system. The impact of Constantine's policies on the nobility was complex, leading to both loss of autonomy and forced adaptation to the new political landscape.

- **Reduction of Land and Wealth:** The redistribution of land was one of the most contentious aspects of Constantine's reforms. By breaking up large estates and redistributing land to smallholders and soldiers, Constantine directly challenged the economic power of the aristocracy. This reduction in landholdings limited the ability of nobles to accumulate wealth and reduced their capacity to exercise control over local populations. Many aristocrats viewed these changes as an attack on their traditional privileges and status, fuelling resentment toward the emperor.

- **Diminished Political Influence:** Constantine's centralization efforts weakened the nobility's role in local governance. By appointing loyal officials directly answerable to the imperial court, Constantine bypassed the traditional networks of noble influence. This move was particularly evident in military districts (themes), where the appointment of military governors (*strategoi*) limited the political autonomy of local aristocrats. Constantine's reliance on a merit-based system of administration, rather than aristocratic patronage, further diminished the power of noble families, making it difficult for them to challenge imperial authority.
- **Adaptation through Military and Bureaucratic Roles:** Despite these setbacks, some members of the nobility found ways to adapt to Constantine's system. By serving in the military or taking on administrative roles within the centralized bureaucracy, these nobles maintained a degree of influence within the empire. Constantine's merit-based promotions allowed some aristocrats to rise through the ranks, provided they demonstrated loyalty and competence. This adaptation reflected the nobility's resilience and their ability to adjust to the changing political landscape, even as their traditional privileges were curtailed.
- **Cultural and Social Adjustments:** The diminishing influence of the aristocracy also led to shifts in Byzantine culture. The once-dominant culture of aristocratic patronage and luxury gave way to a more meritocratic ethos, where loyalty and service to the emperor were prioritized over noble lineage. This shift was evident in the increased emphasis on martial virtues, as Constantine's military-focused policies elevated the status of soldiers and military officers within Byzantine society. Some aristocrats embraced these changes, adopting a more austere lifestyle and participating in the emperor's campaigns, while others struggled to reconcile the loss of their traditional privileges with Constantine's new order.

Social Tensions and Conflicts

The redistribution of power and wealth under Constantine V inevitably generated social tensions, as the competing interests of peasants and nobles created friction. While the peasantry generally supported Constantine's reforms, the nobility often resisted them, leading to a complex social dynamic marked by both cooperation and conflict.

- **Resistance Among the Nobility:** Resistance to Constantine's policies was not uncommon among the nobility, particularly in regions where powerful families had deep-rooted influence. Some aristocrats openly defied the emperor's orders, refusing to relinquish lands or pay taxes. In extreme cases, noble opposition led to localized rebellions, as disgruntled aristocrats sought to challenge imperial authority. Constantine responded to these uprisings with swift repression, using his military power to quell resistance and reassert control.
- **Peasant Loyalty and Support:** In contrast to the nobility, the peasantry generally supported Constantine's reforms, viewing the emperor as a protector of their interests. This loyalty was particularly strong in rural areas where peasants had experienced significant improvements in their economic standing and protection from exploitation. The peasantry's support played a critical role in enabling Constantine to implement his policies, as their backing provided him with a stable base of support that counterbalanced noble opposition.
- **Impact on Social Cohesion:** While Constantine's policies were largely successful in reducing the power of the nobility and empowering the peasantry, they also created social divisions that lingered beyond his reign. The tensions between peasants and nobles, as well as between loyalist and dissident aristocrats, reflected deeper conflicts over the direction of Byzantine society. Constantine's efforts to centralize power and create a more equitable system often pitted different social groups against one another, leading to a complex social fabric marked by both unity and division.

Long-Term Effects and Legacy

The social changes brought about by Constantine V's policies had a lasting impact on Byzantine society, shaping the relationships between the peasantry, the nobility, and the imperial state for generations to come.

- **A More Equitable Society:** By redistributing wealth and limiting the power of the nobility, Constantine V contributed to the development of a more equitable society, where social mobility was possible for those willing to serve the empire. His policies laid the foundation for a more balanced distribution of power, reducing the dominance of the aristocracy and strengthening the empire's stability.

- **Loyalty to the Imperial State:** Constantine's reforms fostered a sense of loyalty to the imperial state among the peasantry, who recognized that their improved economic conditions were the result of the emperor's policies. This loyalty provided the Byzantine Empire with a stable and committed base of support, which would prove essential in maintaining social cohesion during times of crisis.
- **Enduring Tensions with the Nobility:** Despite his success in curbing noble power, Constantine's policies also left a legacy of tension between the nobility and the imperial state. Future emperors would continue to face challenges from aristocratic families who sought to reclaim their lost privileges and influence. This ongoing struggle between the nobility and the emperor remained a defining feature of Byzantine politics, shaping the empire's social dynamics for centuries.

Constantine V's reign represented a transformative period in Byzantine history, as his policies reshaped the social and economic structures of the empire. By empowering the peasantry and curbing the influence of the nobility, Constantine created a more centralized and equitable system that strengthened the empire's stability and resilience. His reforms, while controversial, left a lasting legacy that continued to influence Byzantine society for generations.

Section 4: Innovations and Long-Term Effects of Constantine V's Policies on Governance and the Economy

Constantine V's reign was characterized by significant reforms that reshaped the Byzantine Empire's political and economic landscape. These changes had lasting consequences that reverberated throughout the centuries, shaping the governance structures and economic foundations of the empire long after his death. This section will examine the innovations introduced by Constantine V, focusing on the lasting effects of his policies on governance, administration, and the economy. It will also explore how his reforms influenced later emperors and the empire's ability to adapt to external challenges in the centuries that followed.

Administrative Reforms and Centralization

One of the defining features of Constantine V's reign was his emphasis on centralizing power and reducing the influence of the aristocracy and regional elites. This shift in governance was one of his most enduring innovations and laid the groundwork for the future development of the Byzantine Empire's political structure.

- **Reduction of Aristocratic Power:** Constantine V's reforms diminished the political and military power of the aristocracy, shifting authority directly into the hands of imperial officials. He reduced the nobility's ability to influence local governance and military leadership, replacing many aristocratic figures with loyal bureaucrats and military officers. This created a more centralized administration that was less susceptible to the influence of powerful families.
- **Influence on Later Governance:** In the centuries following Constantine V's reign, his centralization policies were expanded upon by subsequent emperors. The Byzantine Empire saw a continued trend toward a more bureaucratic government, where imperial power was consolidated through the creation of a more structured and hierarchical administration. This development allowed the emperor to exert greater control over the empire, preventing any single family or faction from gaining too much power and challenging imperial authority.
- **Military and Administrative Integration:** Constantine's introduction of the theme system (the division of the empire into military districts or 'themes') had lasting effects on the governance of the Byzantine Empire. This system allowed for greater integration between military and civilian administration, ensuring that military leaders (*strategoi*) were also responsible for local governance. This dual role helped maintain stability and allowed the empire to mobilize its military forces more efficiently in times of crisis.
- **Professional Bureaucracy and Fiscal Management:** Constantine's reforms also established the foundations of a more professional bureaucracy. He invested in the development of administrative structures that were focused on efficient tax collection and financial management. This fiscal discipline ensured that the empire could maintain its administrative functions and military capabilities, even in times of war or economic distress.
- **Legacy in Bureaucratic Innovation:** Over the centuries, the Byzantine bureaucracy grew increasingly complex, with the creation of various offices and positions designed to oversee the empire's finances, military, and legal matters. Constantine's emphasis on efficient administration helped to create a system that was both adaptable and resilient, ensuring that the empire could manage its resources effectively.

Economic Reforms: Long-Term Impact on Agricultural and Military Economies

Constantine V's economic reforms were a major innovation in the way the Byzantine state interacted with its subjects. By redistributing land to smallholders, improving tax collection methods, and encouraging agricultural productivity, Constantine helped to stabilize the Byzantine economy, a feat that would have far-reaching effects on the empire's future.

- **Redistribution of Land and Agricultural Reform:** Constantine's land redistribution policies ensured that smallholders received land directly from the state. This shifted land from the hands of the powerful aristocracy to those who were more dependent on the emperor and the state. As a result, the Byzantine economy became more reliant on small, independent farmers, who were often required to serve in the military in exchange for land.
- **Impact on Agricultural Stability:** This policy contributed to greater agricultural productivity, as smallholders were more motivated to work their land, knowing they would directly benefit from its yield. By stabilizing the agricultural economy, Constantine created a solid economic base that would sustain the empire for years. The policy also mitigated the risks associated with noble-led agricultural estates, which were often vulnerable to mismanagement or exploitation.
- **Long-Term Effects on Military Economy:** The redistribution of land also had significant consequences for the Byzantine military. The land grants given to soldiers were a key part of the army's recruitment strategy, as soldiers were often provided with land in exchange for their service. This system, known as the *pronoia*, created a class of landholding soldiers who were financially invested in the success of the empire. This arrangement proved to be effective for several centuries, as the army had a steady supply of trained soldiers who had a personal stake in the defence of the empire.
- **Taxation and Financial Stability:** Constantine's taxation reforms aimed to make the Byzantine tax system more efficient and equitable. He simplified the process and restructured the tax burden, which helped prevent tax evasion and corruption. These reforms allowed the state to generate a steady stream of revenue, which could then be used for military campaigns, public works, and imperial administration.
- **Sustaining the Imperial System:** Constantine's reforms set the stage for a system of taxation that would support the empire's military and administrative needs for centuries. The efficiency of the Byzantine tax system became one of the empire's key strengths, allowing it to fund military campaigns and maintain public infrastructure even in difficult

times. This financial stability was crucial for the empire's survival, particularly during the crises of the seventh and eighth centuries.

- **Encouraging Trade and Urban Development:** Constantine's economic policies also encouraged trade and urban growth. By stabilizing the economy and providing incentives for infrastructure development, Constantine helped to promote urbanization and the growth of Byzantine cities. This, in turn, led to greater commercial activity and wealth generation, contributing to the empire's economic resilience in the long term.

The Long-Term Effects of Constantine's Religious Policies

Constantine V's religious policies, particularly his Iconoclastic stance, had a profound effect on the cultural and religious landscape of the Byzantine Empire. While his Iconoclasm was controversial during his reign, it set the stage for a broader shift in the empire's religious policies that had long-term effects on both the Byzantine Church and the political structures of the empire.

- **Iconoclasm and Its Impact on Religious Authority:** Constantine V's vigorous pursuit of Iconoclasm – his opposition to the veneration of religious icons – challenged the power of the Orthodox Church and reshaped the relationship between church and state. By removing icons from churches and forbidding their use, Constantine aimed to establish greater imperial control over religious affairs. This policy had significant long-term consequences for the church's role in Byzantine society.
- **Legacy of Religious Control:** In the years following Constantine's reign, his Iconoclastic policies continued to influence the relationship between the emperor and the church. The emperor's authority over religious matters became more firmly entrenched, and the church was forced to adapt to the emperor's demands. This shift in power dynamics contributed to the Byzantine state's increasing control over religious affairs, which would remain a key feature of Byzantine governance for centuries.
- **Social and Cultural Effects:** The Iconoclastic controversy also had a lasting cultural impact, particularly in terms of art and religious practice. While the rejection of icons was eventually reversed by later emperors, the debates surrounding Iconoclasm led to a more philosophical and theological approach to religious practice. This intellectual engagement with religious matters became a hallmark of Byzantine culture in the centuries that followed.

- **Religious Polarization and Political Control:** The Iconoclastic policies also had a polarizing effect on Byzantine society. While some segments of the population supported Constantine's efforts to rid the church of what he considered to be idolatrous practices, others vehemently opposed these reforms. This division created lasting tensions between the emperor and various religious factions, which would influence the political landscape of the empire for years to come.

Impact on the Successive Generations

Constantine V's policies left a profound legacy on the Byzantine Empire's governance, economy, and religious practices. While not all of his reforms endured unchanged, the fundamental principles of centralization, military integration, and economic stability continued to influence subsequent generations of Byzantine rulers.

- **The Centralization of Power:** The emphasis on imperial control and the reduction of aristocratic power remained a key feature of Byzantine governance in the centuries after Constantine V. Successive emperors, particularly in the ninth and tenth centuries, continued to centralize political authority and expand the role of the emperor in both secular and religious matters. This trend towards a strong, centralized government helped the Byzantine Empire withstand external pressures, such as invasions and economic challenges.
- **Military and Economic Resilience:** Constantine's reforms in military organization and land distribution provided a foundation for a more resilient empire. The continued use of the *pronoia* system, where land was granted in exchange for military service, ensured that the Byzantine military remained a powerful and well-trained force. At the same time, the economic stability created by Constantine's tax and land policies provided the resources necessary to sustain this military power.
- **Religious and Cultural Shifts:** The Iconoclastic movement, while reversed in later years, set the stage for ongoing debates about the relationship between church and state. These debates continued to shape Byzantine identity and governance for centuries, influencing religious policy and the role of the emperor in religious matters.

Conclusion

The long-term effects of Constantine V's policies were profound and far-reaching. His innovations in governance, military organization, taxation, and religious policy laid the groundwork for the Byzantine Empire's future development.

Through centralization of power, the expansion of military and bureaucratic control, and the enhancement of the empire's economic stability, Constantine V's reign marked a transformative period in Byzantine history. These reforms not only helped stabilize the empire during a period of crisis but also set the stage for its continued survival and adaptation in the centuries to come.

Chapter 6

Constantine V's Historical Reputation

Section 1: Constantine's Portrayal by Later Byzantine Sources, Particularly by Iconophile Chroniclers Like Theophanes

The historical reputation of Constantine V, particularly in the later Byzantine chronicles, is shaped largely by the ideological battle that raged during and after his reign. His aggressive Iconoclastic policies – particularly his enforcement of the ban on religious icons – led to a deep divide in the Byzantine Empire, with intense theological and political consequences that would echo for centuries. Although Constantine's reign was marked by military success and significant political reform, it was his stance on Iconoclasm that ultimately shaped how later Byzantine historians, particularly Iconophile chroniclers like Theophanes the Confessor, would portray his legacy.

This section will explore how Constantine V was portrayed by later Byzantine sources, focusing especially on Iconophile chroniclers such as Theophanes, who criticized his policies. The shift from imperial admiration to ecclesiastical opposition provides crucial insight into the way Constantine's actions were interpreted and remembered. Through examining the writings of Theophanes and other historians, we will understand the larger context of Constantine V's portrayal and the ways in which later Byzantine historians contributed to the ideological conflict surrounding Iconoclasm.

The Iconoclast Movement and Its Legacy in Later Byzantine Sources

In the eighth and ninth centuries, the issue of Iconoclasm deeply divided the Byzantine Empire, especially following Constantine V's vigorous enforcement of the policy. For Constantine, Iconoclasm was more than a religious issue; it was a matter of imperial authority. He viewed the veneration of icons as a challenge to the emperor's sovereignty, seeing it as an overreach by the church into the secular realm. His decision to outlaw the veneration of images was thus intertwined with his desire to assert the authority of the emperor over the church and prevent what he saw as the potential idolatry and disloyalty caused by the church's increasing political influence.

The conflict surrounding Iconoclasm did not end with Constantine's death in 775, nor did the theological debates over the use of religious images fade away. The policies that Constantine V enacted would continue to haunt the empire, becoming central to the controversies of the next century. In the wake of Constantine's reign, the Iconophile (pro-icon) faction would emerge as a significant force within the church, with figures like Theophanes the Confessor providing critical resistance to the Iconoclastic movement.

Iconophile chroniclers like Theophanes the Confessor (c. 760–818) were particularly influential in shaping the historical memory of Constantine V. Theophanes, who wrote a comprehensive chronicle covering the years 284 to 813, lived through the second phase of Iconoclasm and wrote with a clear theological agenda. His work sought to vindicate the use of religious icons, positioning Constantine V as a tyrant who suppressed the church's spiritual mission and attacked the very heart of Orthodox Christianity.

- **The Iconoclast Policies:** Constantine V's Iconoclasm was rooted in his belief that the veneration of images could lead to idolatry, a concept central to his religious views. He condemned the use of icons as heretical, aligning with the Iconoclastic sentiment that saw the physical representation of divine figures as an affront to God's transcendence. Constantine's decree to destroy icons and ban their veneration, however, was not merely a theological stance – it was an assertion of imperial control over the church. For Constantine, the church's growing power, particularly its ability to control the masses through religious imagery, posed a threat to the centralized authority of the emperor. Constantine V's Iconoclastic policies were implemented with military precision, culminating in the Synod of Hicria in 754, which officially condemned the use of icons and supported Constantine's policies.
- **The Iconophile Reaction:** The Iconoclastic policies, though initially endorsed by many high-ranking church officials and political elites, eventually sparked resistance within the church. The most vocal critics of Constantine's policies were the monks and bishops who saw the destruction of icons as an attack on the very nature of Christian worship. The Iconophile movement, led by figures such as Pope Gregory III and later Empress Irene, began to resist the Iconoclastic stance. This reaction was not merely theological – it was also a reaction against the emperor's assertion of power over the church.

As the conflict grew, it became not just a theological debate but a question of power: who had the right to determine religious practice, the church or the emperor? This issue would shape the portrayal of Constantine V in subsequent historiography, especially in works written after his death.

Theophanes the Confessor: A Leading Critic of Constantine V

Theophanes the Confessor, one of the most important Iconophile historians of the ninth century, offers a strikingly negative portrayal of Constantine V in his *Chronographia*. As a prominent member of the church, Theophanes was deeply committed to the restoration of icons, and his historical writings reflect a clear opposition to the Iconoclastic policies of Constantine V. Theophanes' work is not simply an objective recounting of historical events but rather a polemical text that seeks to defend the veneration of icons and condemn the Iconoclastic emperors, especially Constantine V.

- **Theophanes' Criticism of Constantine's Character:** Theophanes' depiction of Constantine V is highly critical. He portrays the emperor as a tyrant who attempted to subjugate the church and manipulate religious practice to consolidate his political power. Constantine is described as being motivated by personal ambition and a desire for absolute control, seeking to undermine the church's power and the traditional authority of the patriarchs. Theophanes goes so far as to accuse Constantine of being a heretic who was driven by arrogance and an overinflated sense of imperial authority.

  Theophanes emphasizes Constantine's forceful tactics in the suppression of icon veneration. He paints a picture of Constantine as a ruler who not only banned religious images, but also aggressively destroyed existing icons, causing irreparable harm to the religious culture of the empire. Theophanes stresses that Constantine's policies not only harmed the church but also alienated the faithful, leading to divisions and unrest throughout the empire. For Theophanes, Constantine's Iconoclasm was a direct challenge to Orthodox Christianity, and he held the emperor responsible for the religious and political chaos that ensued.
- **Theophanes' Religious Argument:** Theophanes presents his argument in the context of Christian doctrine, insisting that the veneration of icons was an essential aspect of Christian worship. In his view, the destruction of icons was not only an attack on religious tradition but a direct affront to the incarnation of Christ. Theophanes defended the use of images as a legitimate way to represent the divine, citing the theological argument that Christ's incarnation made it possible to represent the invisible God in tangible forms. Theophanes' writings framed Constantine V's Iconoclasm as an act of heresy, opposing a centuries-old tradition of Christian imagery that had been integral to the faith.
- **Theophanes and the Role of the Emperor:** Beyond his theological objections, Theophanes also criticized the imperial role in religious

matters. For Theophanes, the emperor's imposition of religious policy was an overreach, infringing upon the autonomy of the church. Theophanes stressed that the emperor's role was to defend the faith and ensure the stability of the empire, but not to dictate theological doctrine. Constantine's imposition of Iconoclasm, in Theophanes' view, was a violation of the sacred trust placed in the emperor by God. In his eyes, the emperor's duty was to uphold orthodoxy, not to impose personal theological convictions on the faithful.

- **Theophanes' Legacy:** Theophanes' condemnation of Constantine V helped shape the historical narrative of the eighth century and beyond. His portrayal of the emperor as a tyrant and heretic had a profound influence on subsequent generations of Byzantines, particularly during the restoration of icons in the ninth century. Theophanes' writings played a significant role in the Iconophile movement, and his depiction of Constantine contributed to the long-lasting vilification of the emperor in both religious and historical contexts.

Other Byzantine Sources and Constantine V's Legacy

In addition to Theophanes, other Byzantine chroniclers of the period also contributed to shaping the posthumous reputation of Constantine V. While many echoed Theophanes' criticism, some provided more nuanced perspectives, acknowledging both his strengths and flaws.

- ***The Chronicle of Monemvasia*:** The *Chronicle of Monemvasia*, a later source, provides a more balanced view of Constantine V's reign. This chronicle acknowledges his military successes, especially his defence of the empire against the Arabs, and the military reforms he instituted. However, it also condemns his Iconoclastic policies, particularly the violence associated with the destruction of religious icons. This text reflects a more neutral tone, recognizing Constantine's effectiveness as a ruler but criticizing his religious stance.
- ***The History of the Patriarchs of Constantinople*:** Another source, *The History of the Patriarchs of Constantinople*, emphasizes the tensions between the emperors and the patriarchs during the Iconoclastic period. Constantine V's policies are depicted as part of a broader imperial attempt to consolidate power at the expense of the church. The patriarchal sources, much like Theophanes, portray Constantine as overbearing in his dealings with the church and as a figure who ultimately weakened the unity of the Byzantine religious community.

- **Later Byzantine Historians:** Byzantine historians writing after the restoration of icons in the ninth century were highly critical of Constantine V. His reign was remembered as one of repression, and his Iconoclastic policies were seen as a dark chapter in the history of the empire. Even historians like John Skylitzes, who were generally favourable toward imperial authority, criticized Constantine for his harsh methods and his clash with the church.

Conclusion: The Complex Legacy of Constantine V

The portrayal of Constantine V by later Byzantine sources, particularly by Iconophile chroniclers like Theophanes, reflects the deep theological and political divisions that marked his reign. While Constantine's Iconoclasm was initially supported by many within the church and the state, it ultimately led to a bitter and enduring conflict that shaped the perception of his rule. Theophanes' polemical chronicle, in particular, cemented Constantine's reputation as a tyrant and heretic in the eyes of later generations, positioning him as an antagonist to the Iconophile movement. However, as this section has shown, the portrayal of Constantine V is not monolithic. Other sources, while critical of his policies, also acknowledged his military and administrative successes, providing a more complex picture of his reign. Ultimately, Constantine V's legacy is one of deep ideological conflict, marked by both significant achievements and controversial decisions that would shape Byzantine history for centuries to come.

Section 2: Slander and Propaganda: Analysis of Why Constantine V Was Demonized by Later Historians, Often Referred to as 'Copronymus' (A Derogatory Name)

The reputation of Constantine V, one of the most decisive, divisive and controversial emperors in Byzantine history, underwent a dramatic transformation in the centuries following his death. While Constantine V's reign, which spanned from 741 to 775, was marked by numerous military successes and substantial administrative reforms, it was his Iconoclastic policies that cast a long shadow over his legacy. As a result, he became a figure of intense vilification by later historians, especially by those in the church and among the Iconophile faction. The epithet '*Copronymus*', meaning 'Dung-named', is perhaps the most infamous of the many derogatory labels applied to him. This name was used by his critics to tarnish his image and cast him as a tyrant, a heretic, and a villain. The propagation of this slander, however, was not merely the product of personal animosity or theological dispute but the result of a carefully orchestrated effort to demonize Constantine's reign, particularly in response to his aggressive enforcement of Iconoclasm.

This section will explore the various factors that contributed to the demonization of Constantine V, focusing on the role of slander, propaganda, and ideological conflict in shaping his historical reputation. Through an analysis of the use of the name '*Copronymus*', the political and religious context of his reign, and the methods employed by later historians to vilify him, this section will provide insight into how Constantine V came to be remembered as one of the most despised emperors of the Byzantine Empire.

The Origins of the Epithet 'Copronymus'

The epithet '*Copronymus*' – 'Dung-named' or 'man with the name of Dung' – was one of the most enduring pieces of slander against Constantine V. It is believed that the term was first used by his detractors shortly after his death, and it became a widespread moniker in later Byzantine historiography. The origins of this nickname are not entirely clear, but several theories exist regarding its creation and use. One widely accepted explanation is that the name stemmed from an incident in Constantine V's early life.

According to some sources, Constantine was alleged to have been born under somewhat unusual circumstances, and there is an apocryphal story that he defiled himself at a young age in a symbolic gesture during a religious ceremony. These types of personal slanders were not uncommon in Byzantine court politics, where emperors and their families were often the subject of attacks aimed at undermining their legitimacy. Whether the story of the young Constantine's defilement was based on fact or merely a fabrication meant to damage his reputation, the nickname stuck and became emblematic of the deeper disdain that many later Byzantine chroniclers held for him.

The nickname '*Copronymus*' is indicative of the intense animosity Constantine V faced, and it became a central part of the Iconophile historiographical tradition. This derogatory term not only served to insult him personally but also to link him to the vilification of his policies, particularly his Iconoclastic stance. The name symbolized his perceived moral and spiritual impurity in the eyes of his critics, particularly the clergy and monks who revered icons and saw Constantine's policies as a direct attack on their religious practices.

Iconoclasm: The Catalyst for Propaganda

At the core of Constantine V's demonization was his stance on Iconoclasm. His vehement opposition to the veneration of religious icons was perceived by his critics as an act of heresy, an attack on the heart of Orthodox Christian practice, and an encroachment on the church's authority. Constantine's Iconoclastic policies, initiated in 754 at the Synod of Hieria, would become one of the most divisive and contentious issues of his reign.

- **Religious Conflict:** Constantine's Iconoclastic policies, including the destruction of religious icons and the suppression of icon veneration, provoked a fierce backlash, especially from monks and bishops who considered the use of icons an essential aspect of Christian worship. The Iconoclastic controversy was not merely a theological debate about the proper use of images; it was also a deeply political conflict, with the emperor asserting control over religious matters that had traditionally been the purview of the church.
- **The Role of the Church in Propaganda:** The church, particularly its leaders and monastic communities, had long been a powerful institution in the Byzantine Empire. As the Byzantine church grew in influence, it became increasingly resistant to imperial interference, particularly in matters of faith and worship. Constantine V's Iconoclasm was viewed by many within the church as an unacceptable intrusion into their spiritual domain. In the aftermath of his death, the church became a key player in shaping the historical narrative surrounding Constantine's reign. The Iconophiles – those who supported the veneration of icons – began to portray Constantine V not only as a theological heretic but also as a tyrant who sought to crush the spiritual life of the empire.
- **The Battle for the Narrative:** The Iconoclastic period extended well beyond Constantine's reign, with his successors, including Empress Irene, reversing his policies and restoring the use of icons. The eventual triumph of the Iconophiles over the Iconoclasts created a strong incentive to delegitimize Constantine's rule. Historians sympathetic to the Iconophile cause painted Constantine V as a despot who tried to destroy the sacred traditions of the church, portraying him as an embodiment of imperial overreach and religious oppression. It was this ideological battle that gave rise to the slander of Constantine's name.

Propaganda and Political Motivation

The demonization of Constantine V was not solely the result of theological opposition. His reign was also marked by political strife, and his opponents were eager to undermine his authority for political reasons as well. Throughout his reign, Constantine faced a series of revolts and challenges to his power, both from within the aristocracy and from the military. His forceful consolidation of power, his attempts to centralize imperial control, and his aggressive stance against potential rivals in the military and the nobility left him with numerous enemies who were eager to discredit him.

- **Centralization and Rivalries:** Constantine V's administrative reforms and military policies, which sought to reduce the power of local aristocrats and centralize control in the hands of the emperor, made him numerous enemies. His efforts to curb the power of the landed nobility and diminish the influence of military leaders who had previously enjoyed significant autonomy caused a great deal of resentment among these groups. In a period where military leaders often held substantial political power, Constantine's moves were seen as a direct challenge to the established order. These elites – many of whom were loyal to the church and the religious establishment – became part of the chorus of those who sought to tarnish his image and spread slander about his rule.
- **The Use of Propaganda in Byzantine Politics:** Byzantine emperors were acutely aware of the importance of public perception and the role that propaganda played in shaping their legacies. Constantine V was no exception, and while he used his power to control the narrative within the empire, his opponents were equally determined to counter his version of events. Theological disagreements were often intertwined with political rivalries, with historians and church leaders actively participating in campaigns to undermine the emperor's authority. In this context, the epithet '*Copronymus*' was part of a broader strategy of discrediting Constantine's legitimacy and portraying him as an unworthy ruler.
- **Posthumous Vilification:** The political use of Constantine's image continued long after his death. His son, Leo IV, succeeded him but was forced to navigate the legacy of his father's policies. Although Leo initially continued his father's Iconoclastic stance, his reign was marked by a shift in religious policy, and after Leo's death, his wife, Empress Irene, reversed the Iconoclastic policies entirely. With the restoration of icons in 787, the Iconophile faction was empowered, and Constantine V's image was further tarnished. The revival of icon veneration was a key moment in Byzantine history, and it cemented Constantine's role as a villain in the narrative created by his ideological opponents.

Constantine's Reputation in Later Byzantine Sources

The later Byzantine sources are unanimous in their condemnation of Constantine V, particularly his Iconoclastic policies and his perceived tyranny. Chroniclers like Theophanes the Confessor and John Skylitzes, writing in the ninth and eleventh centuries, were instrumental in shaping the negative portrayal of Constantine. Their writings emphasized his religious heresy, his oppressive rule, and his arrogant disregard for the church.

- **Theophanes' Portrayal of Constantine:** Theophanes, an Iconophile historian, provides one of the most scathing critiques of Constantine V. He presents Constantine as a tyrant who not only sought to impose his own theological views on the empire but also engaged in violent suppression of the Iconophiles. Theophanes refers to Constantine as a 'godless' emperor and criticizes his role in the destruction of holy images, portraying him as a ruler whose actions were driven by personal pride and theological ignorance.
- **John Skylitzes' Account:** John Skylitzes, in his *Synopsis of Histories*, also describes Constantine in a negative light, focusing on his Iconoclastic policies and his harsh treatment of religious figures. Skylitzes acknowledges Constantine's military successes but emphasizes the darker aspects of his reign, including his attempts to control religious practice and suppress dissent.

Conclusion: The Enduring Legacy of Constantine V's Demonization

The demonization of Constantine V by later historians, particularly those from the Iconophile tradition, played a crucial role in shaping his legacy. The use of the epithet '*Copronymus*', combined with the theological and political battles of his reign, ensured that Constantine would be remembered as a heretic and tyrant by future generations. This vilification was not simply the product of personal animosity but was deeply tied to the ideological struggles that shaped Byzantine history in the centuries following his death.

As this section has shown, the slander of Constantine V was a complex process involving theological dispute, political rivalry, and the use of propaganda to shape the historical narrative. Despite his significant achievements in the military and administrative spheres, Constantine's legacy became irrevocably linked to his Iconoclastic policies, and he was portrayed as a villain by the historians who came after him. His reputation, coloured by the label '*Copronymus*', reflects the deep divisions that characterized Byzantine society during his reign and the centuries that followed.

Section 3: How Recent Historians View Constantine V More Sympathetically, Focusing on His Administrative and Military Achievements

In the centuries following his reign, Constantine V (741–775) was often regarded as one of the most despised Byzantine emperors, primarily due to his fervent support for Iconoclasm and the subsequent destruction of religious icons. His legacy, as shaped by the Iconophile chroniclers of the ninth and tenth centuries, cast him as a heretic and tyrant, with his reputation suffering significantly from the label of '*Copronymus*'. However, as scholarly approaches to Byzantine history have evolved, so too has the interpretation of Constantine V.

Recent historians, many of whom have adopted a more nuanced and balanced view, have reassessed his reign by focusing on his considerable achievements in both military and administrative fields. This shift in perspective emphasizes the complexities of his rule, recognizing his military successes against external threats, his efforts at consolidating imperial power, and his significant contributions to the restructuring of the Byzantine state. Constantine V's reign, when viewed through the lens of administrative reform and military strategy, reveals a ruler who, despite his controversial stance on religious issues, played a critical role in preserving and strengthening the Byzantine Empire during a time of internal and external upheaval.

In this section, we will explore how recent historians view Constantine V more sympathetically, focusing particularly on his administrative reforms, military achievements, and the broader context of his rule. By analyzing these aspects of his reign, we aim to provide a more comprehensive understanding of his legacy, challenging the demonization of Constantine V and recognizing his contributions to the empire.

Military Achievements and Defence of the Empire

Constantine V's military career is perhaps the most widely acknowledged aspect of his reign, with recent historians placing particular emphasis on his success in defending the Byzantine Empire against both external and internal threats. Despite the Iconoclastic policies that defined his reign and led to his vilification in later sources, Constantine's military acumen played a decisive role in stabilizing the empire during a tumultuous period in its history.

- **Defending the Eastern Frontiers:** During the eighth century, the Byzantine Empire was under constant threat from a range of enemies. To the east, the empire faced the ever-present menace of the Arab Caliphate, which, after the initial Arab conquests of the seventh century, continued to pose a significant military threat. Constantine V, following in the footsteps of his father, Leo III, fought against the expansion of the Arabs into Anatolia. In 747, Constantine achieved a notable victory over the Arabs at the Battle of Akroinon, a crucial engagement that halted their advances and reaffirmed the Byzantine hold over Asia Minor.

- **The Battle of Akroinon (747):** The Battle of Akroinon, fought in 747, is one of Constantine V's most significant military victories. The battle marked a turning point in the long-standing struggle between the Byzantine Empire and the Arab Caliphate. Constantine V's strategic use of terrain, combined with his ability to coordinate his forces effectively, allowed him to decisively defeat the Arab forces, despite being outnumbered. This victory not only safeguarded the empire's eastern frontier but also boosted Constantine's prestige, both domestically and internationally. The defeat of the Arabs at Akroinon helped stabilize the region and allowed the Byzantines to focus on other internal matters, such as Iconoclasm and political consolidation.

The Battle of Akroinon (747 CE): A Comprehensive Analysis

The Battle of Akroinon in 747 CE was a critical moment in the struggle between the Byzantine Empire and the Umayyad Caliphate for control over Asia Minor. Fought in the Phrygian highlands, near present-day Afyonkarahisar in Turkey, this battle halted a major Umayyad incursion and showcased the strength and resilience of the Byzantine army, which had been adapting and innovating to meet the threat from the east. This expanded account will explore the military, technological, cultural, and geopolitical elements that defined the battle and its broader impact.

Broader Military Context

The Byzantine Empire in the eighth century was on the defensive, having lost much of its eastern territories to Islamic expansion over the past century. The theme (thematic) system became a key aspect of Byzantine resilience. Organized around regional divisions, the themes were military and administrative units that combined defence with local governance. By the time of the Battle of Akroinon, these themes, particularly the Anatolikon and Opsikion themes, had developed specialized regional forces that could be quickly mobilized for defence.

For the Umayyad Caliphate, expansion into Byzantine Asia Minor was both a strategic and ideological objective. Continuous raids into Byzantine territory were intended to weaken the empire, capture spoils, and, ideally, bring more lands under Islamic governance. In the 740s, the Umayyads, under Caliph Hisham, renewed their offensive with increased fervour. Sulayman ibn Hisham, a seasoned Umayyad commander, was tasked with leading a large, well-prepared force against the Byzantines at Akroinon, a significant staging ground on the Byzantine frontier.

Technological Aspects of Weaponry and Armour

In terms of weaponry, both sides fielded advanced equipment for their respective times.

- **Byzantine Armour and Weapons:** Byzantine soldiers, especially those from the Anatolikon and Opsikion themes, were typically equipped with chainmail or lamellar armour that provided flexibility and resilience against both arrows and melee attacks. Soldiers also carried round shields, which were effective in formation-based defence and mobile skirmishing alike. Helmets were standardized, often made of metal with nasal guards, to protect against head injuries.
  - **Spatha:** A straight, double-edged sword, the spatha was used both by infantry and cavalry, allowing for slashing and thrusting actions in close combat.
  - **Kontos:** The Byzantine heavy cavalry, known as cataphracts, wielded the kontos, a long lance designed for charging down enemy ranks. Its extended reach and stability allowed cataphracts to deliver devastating shock attacks.
  - **Composite Bows:** Byzantine archers employed composite bows with a high draw weight that enabled them to launch arrows at a considerable range with significant power. These bows were invaluable in weakening enemy lines from a distance before an engagement.
- **Umayyad Weaponry and Armour:** The Umayyad soldiers, largely drawn from Syria and other Levantine regions, had their own advanced weaponry suited for both raiding and open battle.
  - **Saif (Curved Swords):** The saif or curved sword was commonly used by Umayyad troops, especially for cavalry engagements. Its design allowed for slashing attacks from horseback, which was a critical tactic for light cavalry raids.
  - **Spears and Javelins:** Lightly armoured Umayyad infantry often used javelins and short spears, which allowed them to skirmish and engage quickly. This tactic was effective for harassing the enemy before a decisive engagement.
  - **Cavalry Archers:** The Umayyad army included skilled cavalry archers, who could strike quickly and retreat. This mobility was

an asset, though it had limited effectiveness against the Byzantine defensive formations.

The combination of heavily armoured Byzantine troops and mobile Umayyad forces set the stage for a confrontation that would test the endurance and tactics of both sides.

Cultural Influence on Tactics and Morale

The eighth century was marked by intense religious and cultural divergence between the Byzantine Empire and the Umayyad Caliphate. Constantine V's Iconoclastic policies were aimed at removing icons and imagery from Christian worship, which he viewed as a source of corruption and divine punishment. This belief infused the Byzantine military with a sense of ideological resolve, as soldiers saw themselves as defenders of a 'purified' Christian faith.

For the Umayyad forces, the ongoing campaigns against Byzantine territories had religious and cultural dimensions as well. Islamic expansion was seen as part of the Caliphate's divine mission, and battles with the Byzantines often took on a symbolic significance beyond mere territorial control.

These cultural motivations influenced the morale and discipline of the armies. Byzantine soldiers were driven by a duty to protect their empire's Christian heritage, while the Umayyads fought with a sense of religious purpose, aiming to bring more lands under Islamic rule.

Geopolitical Implications

The outcome of the Battle of Akroinon had significant repercussions for both empires.

- **For the Byzantine Empire:** Victory at Akroinon secured the Byzantine frontier in Asia Minor for a time, allowing Constantine V to focus on internal reforms and military organization. The battle boosted the morale of the Byzantine population, proving that the empire could still repel large-scale invasions and protect its territory.
- **For the Umayyad Caliphate:** The defeat at Akroinon dealt a blow to the Caliphate's ambitions in Asia Minor. The loss of Sulayman ibn Hisham's forces weakened Umayyad prestige and constrained their military resources, shifting the focus of the Caliphate from conquest to consolidation. This shift would eventually contribute to the decline of the Umayyad dynasty, which was overthrown by the Abbasids in 750 CE.
- **Diplomatic Relations and Alliances:** The Byzantine victory helped stabilize their alliances, particularly with the Khazars in the north, who

also viewed the Umayyads as a threat. The Khazar-Byzantine alliance became crucial in creating a multi-front deterrent against the Caliphate, securing the Byzantine Empire's northern frontier.

Specific Tactical Analysis

The tactics used in the Battle of Akroinon highlight Byzantine adaptability and mastery of defensive warfare:

1. **Defensive Formation and Fortifications:** The Byzantines set up their forces in high-ground positions around Akroinon, using the Phrygian terrain to limit Umayyad mobility. This approach forced the Umayyads into a disadvantageous position, making it difficult for them to deploy their cavalry effectively.
2. **Combined-Arms Tactics:** Byzantine forces coordinated light infantry skirmishers, archers, and cataphracts in a layered defence. Skirmishers and archers weakened the enemy from a distance, softening up their lines before the Byzantine cavalry launched counter-attacks.
3. **Ambush and Encirclement:** Byzantine commanders anticipated the movements of the Umayyad forces and prepared a tactical encirclement. Once the Umayyads were drawn into a direct assault, the Byzantine heavy cavalry launched a decisive flanking charge, disrupting the Umayyad lines and causing confusion. This tactic was instrumental in breaking the morale of the Umayyad forces, leading to a complete rout.

Historical Sources and Accounts

Accounts of the Battle of Akroinon come primarily from Byzantine sources, notably Theophanes the Confessor, who recorded many details of Constantine V's reign. Theophanes' works provide insight into the Byzantine perspective on the battle, depicting it as a significant victory that reinforced the legitimacy of Constantine V's military and religious policies.

Archaeological evidence of Byzantine and Umayyad weaponry, particularly in Asia Minor, supports descriptions from sources like Theophanes. Excavations have revealed remnants of armour, weapons, and defensive structures that align with historical accounts, giving modern historians a tangible connection to the tactics and equipment described.

Conclusion: The Lasting Significance of Akroinon

The Battle of Akroinon was more than a tactical victory; it symbolized Byzantine resilience and adaptability in the face of a formidable adversary. The battle demonstrated that, through superior tactics, effective use of terrain, and disciplined troops, the Byzantines could hold their ground against the might of the Umayyad Caliphate. The legacy of Akroinon reverberated through the Byzantine Empire's military doctrine, reinforcing the value of combined-arms tactics, theme-based defence, and strategic depth – concepts that would continue to shape Byzantine strategy for centuries.

- **Military Reorganization:** Constantine V's reign saw significant changes to the structure and organization of the Byzantine military. He was responsible for consolidating the army and fortifying the empire's defences, particularly in Anatolia, which had been a crucial battleground in the ongoing conflict with the Arabs. Constantine reorganized the army into thematic units, which allowed for more flexible responses to both local and external threats. The creation of the *tagmata* (elite military units) helped ensure that the Byzantine military was better equipped to face the changing nature of warfare, particularly the cavalry-heavy armies of the Arabs.
- **Internal Security and Repression of Revolts:** Another aspect of Constantine V's military efforts was his handling of internal threats. His reign was marked by a series of revolts, particularly from the aristocracy and the military elite. Constantine's harsh responses to these uprisings, including the infamous suppression of the 767 Coptic revolt and that of his own son-in-law, Artabasdos, at the start of his reign were designed to maintain the stability of the empire. While his actions were often criticized by later historians, recent scholars have noted that Constantine's ability to suppress these revolts without destabilizing the empire was a testament to his strong leadership and military prowess.

Administrative Reforms and Centralization of Power

One of the key areas in which recent historians have re-evaluated Constantine V's reign is in his administrative policies. Constantine implemented significant reforms that had a lasting impact on the structure of the Byzantine Empire, particularly in terms of centralizing imperial authority and improving the efficiency of governance.

- **Centralization of Authority:** Constantine V's reign saw a continuation of his father Leo III's policy of centralizing imperial power, which was essential in consolidating the authority of the emperor over both the church and the aristocracy. Constantine sought to reduce the influence of local elites, particularly in Anatolia, where provincial military leaders and landowners had gained substantial power. Through a combination of military and political strategies, Constantine was able to reassert imperial control over these regions. This centralization of power was critical in the later stability of the Byzantine Empire, which faced both external threats and internal political fragmentation.

- **Fiscal and Legal Reforms:** Constantine V also made significant changes to the fiscal and legal structures of the empire. He reformed the tax system, aiming to reduce corruption and improve revenue collection. By consolidating control over provincial tax collection and regulating the flow of resources, Constantine sought to ensure the stability of the imperial treasury. He also enacted legal reforms aimed at streamlining the administration of justice and reducing the influence of powerful landowners, further solidifying imperial control.
- **Bureaucratic Reorganization:** One of Constantine's most significant contributions to the empire's administration was his reorganization of the imperial bureaucracy. He worked to ensure that the central government was more responsive to the needs of the empire, creating more efficient administrative structures. Constantine's reforms were focused on strengthening the imperial court and its direct control over provincial governors. This helped to streamline decision-making processes, enabling the empire to respond more quickly to both external and internal challenges.
- **Religious and Political Control:** Constantine's control over religious matters, particularly his imposition of Iconoclasm, was part of his broader attempt to centralize authority. By asserting imperial dominance over the church and eliminating the power of the Iconophile factions, Constantine sought to bring religious practice into alignment with imperial priorities. While this policy was controversial and would lead to his vilification by later historians, it was seen by Constantine as a necessary step to maintain the unity and stability of the empire, especially in the face of external threats and internal divisions.

Michael Lachanodrakon: The Iconoclastic Enforcer and Byzantine *Strategos*

Michael Lachanodrakon was a Byzantine general and governor, particularly known for his loyalty to Emperor Constantine V and his aggressive promotion of Iconoclasm (the movement opposing the veneration of religious icons). Born into the turbulent backdrop of the eighth century, when the Byzantine Empire was struggling with both external invasions and internal ideological divides, Lachanodrakon's life and career offer a vivid glimpse into the empire's religious and political conflicts. He remains a controversial figure in Byzantine history, celebrated by some contemporaries for his effectiveness in battle and governance, but reviled by others, particularly later Iconophile chroniclers, for his persecution of those who opposed Iconoclasm.

Early Life and Rise to Power

While specific details about Lachanodrakon's early life remain sparse, he likely hailed from an aristocratic or military family, as was typical for individuals who advanced to high office in the Byzantine Empire. His early career was shaped by the Iconoclastic policies instituted by Emperor Leo III and reinforced under Leo's son, Constantine V. Constantine, a fervent Iconoclast, believed that religious imagery fostered idolatry and that removing icons would restore divine favour to the empire, which had endured military and political setbacks. Lachanodrakon quickly gained Constantine's favour and emerged as one of his most trusted generals and administrators, known for his strict adherence to Iconoclastic principles. Constantine appointed him as the *strategos* of the Thracian theme, a significant and strategically-located region near the empire's border with hostile Slavic tribes and the powerful Bulgar Khanate.

Iconoclastic Policies and Religious Persecution

As *strategos*, Lachanodrakon became one of the most zealous enforcers of Constantine V's Iconoclastic agenda. His efforts were focused not only on suppressing the use of icons but also on rooting out and punishing those who resisted or defied these policies. His Iconoclastic campaigns intensified in the mid-760s, leading to widespread persecution.

- **Destruction of Monastic Communities:** Lachanodrakon's policies especially targeted monastic communities, which were seen as strongholds of icon veneration and resistance to imperial policies. He ordered the destruction of numerous monasteries in the Thrace region, often violently expelling monks and confiscating monastic properties. By suppressing monasteries, Lachanodrakon aimed to cut off the ideological opposition to Iconoclasm and reduce the influence of monastic leaders who preached icon veneration.
- **Forced Secularization of Monks and Nuns:** Lachanodrakon's measures also included forcing monks and nuns to abandon their religious vows. He attempted to integrate them back into secular society by mandating that they marry or face brutal consequences. This radical policy was aimed at dismantling the monastic resistance to Iconoclasm, but it also had the effect of disrupting the social fabric of Byzantine religious life, as monks and nuns held important roles in education, charity, and local administration.

- Massacres and Public Punishments: According to later Iconophile sources, such as Theophanes the Confessor, Lachanodrakon's Iconoclastic zeal often escalated into violence. Some accounts describe him executing large numbers of Iconophile monks and destroying icons in brutal displays intended to intimidate opposition. While the scale and nature of these accounts may be exaggerated by Iconophile chroniclers who viewed him unfavourably, they underscore his reputation as a ruthless enforcer of Iconoclastic policies.

Military Campaigns and Strategic Role

Apart from his role in enforcing Iconoclasm, Lachanodrakon was a capable military leader, entrusted with defending Byzantine territory in Thrace against various external threats. His strategic acumen and loyalty to Constantine V made him a key figure in the empire's defensive and offensive campaigns.

- **Defence Against the Bulgars:** One of Lachanodrakon's primary military responsibilities was defending Thrace against the Bulgar Khanate, a powerful and aggressive entity to the north. The Bulgars frequently raided Byzantine territories, posing a significant threat to imperial stability. Lachanodrakon led several defensive campaigns, repelling Bulgar incursions and consolidating Byzantine control over contested border regions.
- **Slavic Tribes in the Balkans:** The Slavic tribes had established themselves in the Balkans, threatening Byzantine interests in the region. Lachanodrakon's efforts in Thrace included suppressing Slavic uprisings and enforcing Byzantine authority in Slavic-dominated areas. His military actions against the Slavs were part of a broader Byzantine strategy to reclaim and stabilize the empire's western territories, which had been lost or weakened during previous conflicts.
- **Impact on Byzantine Military Strength:** Lachanodrakon's commitment to Constantine V's policies extended to military reforms aimed at consolidating the empire's defensive capabilities. By enforcing strict discipline and loyalty among his troops, he contributed to the stability of the thematic system, which was critical for Byzantine defence. His leadership fortified the empire's borders and helped protect Constantinople from potential incursions.

Ideological Conflicts and the Legacy of Iconoclasm

Lachanodrakon's legacy as an enforcer of Iconoclasm has been shaped largely by Iconophile chroniclers, who viewed his actions as extreme and oppressive.

However, his policies reflected the intensity of the ideological conflict within the Byzantine Empire at the time. Iconoclasts like Lachanodrakon and Constantine V viewed Iconoclasm as a means of unifying the empire under a purified form of Christianity, free from what they saw as the corrupting influence of idolatry.

Iconoclasm, however, was not universally popular and provoked strong opposition from Iconophile factions within the empire, especially among monks and religious communities. This internal division created a rift that would persist even after Constantine V's death and continued to influence Byzantine politics, religious life, and social structures.

- **Conflict with Iconophile Monks:** The monastic communities' support for icons often placed them at odds with the imperial administration. Lachanodrakon's persecution of monks, viewed as defenders of icon veneration, added fuel to the Iconophile-Iconoclast dispute. Monks recorded his policies and actions in a highly negative light, portraying him as a tyrant who defied the true faith and desecrated religious institutions.
- **Impact on Monasticism:** Lachanodrakon's actions against monastic communities significantly weakened their influence in certain regions, as monks were either forced into hiding or secularized. This weakening of monastic communities also disrupted the charitable and educational roles monasteries played, affecting local populations who relied on monastic support.
- **Theophanes and the Iconophile Narrative:** Much of what is known about Lachanodrakon comes from Theophanes the Confessor, an Iconophile historian whose accounts cast Lachanodrakon in a negative light. Theophanes portrayed him as a violent persecutor of the faithful, an image that has shaped Lachanodrakon's posthumous reputation. However, modern historians recognize the biases in Theophanes' accounts and acknowledge that, while Lachanodrakon's methods were harsh, they were consistent with the Iconoclastic policies of the time.

End of Career and Death

The exact circumstances of Lachanodrakon's later life and death are unclear. He likely continued to serve as *strategos* until the end of Constantine V's reign, or perhaps beyond, into the reign of Leo IV. As Iconoclasm waned and Iconophile sentiment resurged, however, Lachanodrakon's policies and his legacy were increasingly scrutinized, especially as Leo IV's successor, Empress Irene, reversed many Iconoclastic policies and championed the restoration of icons.

Lachanodrakon's staunch support of Iconoclasm made him a divisive figure, and it is probable that he faced marginalization or censure after Constantine V's death as Iconophile policies gained favour. Despite his loyalty and contributions to Byzantine defence, his extreme enforcement of Iconoclastic policies left him with a tarnished legacy in the eyes of later Iconophile chroniclers.

Legacy and Historical Assessment

Michael Lachanodrakon remains a complex figure in Byzantine history, embodying both the ruthlessness of imperial enforcement and the loyalty of a high-ranking military official. His legacy is inseparable from the religious conflict that shaped eighth-century Byzantium, and his actions contributed to the polarizing nature of Iconoclasm in the empire's history.

- **Byzantine Military Strategy:** As *strategos*, Lachanodrakon's role in securing Thrace and defending against external threats was significant. His success in repelling Bulgar incursions and asserting Byzantine authority in the Balkans solidified the empire's defences and safeguarded Constantinople from immediate danger.
- **Iconoclasm's Legacy:** Lachanodrakon's brutal enforcement of Iconoclastic policies, particularly his persecution of monks, left a lasting impression on the Byzantine Empire's religious landscape. Iconophile chroniclers used his actions as examples of Iconoclasm's excesses, helping to shape the anti-Iconoclastic narrative that dominated Byzantine historical records.
- **A Balanced View:** Although Lachanodrakon is often depicted negatively in primary sources, to understand his actions it is essential to consider the ideological and political environment in which he operated. The Byzantine Empire, under Emperor Constantine V, faced multiple challenges, both internal and external. The rise of Iconoclasm can be viewed in part as an attempt by the emperor to consolidate imperial power by undermining the influence of the religious establishment, which had often functioned independently of the state. Monastic communities wielded significant economic and political power, and their resistance to imperial policies posed a direct challenge to the authority of the emperor.
- **The Role of Iconoclasm in Statecraft:** For Constantine V, Iconoclasm was more than just a religious reform; it was a tool for enforcing unity in the empire. By removing icons and their veneration, the emperor sought to eliminate divisions within the Christian community, aiming to centralize control under the imperial throne and create a uniform religious identity that aligned with imperial interests. In this light, Lachanodrakon's actions can be seen as part of a broader imperial strategy to maintain political stability in a period of significant external and internal turmoil.

- **Religious Polarization:** However, Iconoclasm also deepened religious polarization within the empire. The destruction of icons and the persecution of Iconophiles created lasting divisions between the imperial government and the religious populace, particularly the monastic communities. These tensions would persist for centuries, contributing to the long-standing conflict between Iconoclasts and Iconophiles. While Lachanodrakon was a devoted servant of the emperor's policies, his actions were seen by many as oppressive and divisive, perpetuating conflicts that would not fully resolve until the ninth century.

A Legacy of Division

The legacy of Michael Lachanodrakon is inevitably tied to the larger controversy of Iconoclasm, a movement that created deep rifts within Byzantine society. For those who supported Iconoclasm, Lachanodrakon was a hero who helped enforce the emperor's will, suppressing the perceived heresy of icon veneration and ensuring the unity of the empire under Constantine V. His military contributions, particularly in the defence of Byzantine borders, added to his reputation as a capable and loyal general.

However, for the Iconophile faction, Lachanodrakon was a tyrant who caused unnecessary suffering to the Christian faithful, tearing apart long-established religious practices and institutions. His actions against the monasteries and the violent enforcement of imperial policies left a scar on the Byzantine religious landscape that would not heal for generations.

Conclusion

In the broader context of Byzantine history, Michael Lachanodrakon's role is a complex one. While his loyalty to Constantine V and his military prowess were critical in defending the empire and its borders, his role in the persecution of Iconophiles and the destruction of religious icons marked him as a deeply controversial figure. Modern scholarship offers a more nuanced view of Lachanodrakon, recognizing the broader political and religious context in which he operated. His legacy, while tarnished by his Iconoclastic zeal, also reflects the harsh realities of the Byzantine Empire during a period of deep ideological division. Understanding Lachanodrakon requires balancing his military achievements with the consequences of his policies, which had profound and lasting effects on the empire's religious and social fabric.

Constantine V's Legacy in Modern Historiography

In contrast to the harsh judgments of earlier Byzantine historians, recent scholarship has increasingly sought to portray Constantine V's reign in a more favourable light. Scholars who have focused on his administrative and military achievements have emphasized the positive aspects of his rule, highlighting his effective governance and his ability to defend the empire from significant external threats.

- **Reassessment of Iconoclasm:** While Constantine's Iconoclastic policies remain contentious, modern historians have begun to understand his actions in a more context-driven way. Rather than seeing his Iconoclasm as a personal vendetta against religious icons or as a theological aberration, some historians argue that his stance was influenced by broader concerns about imperial unity and the threat posed by religious dissent. By removing the power of the monasteries and the Iconophile church factions, Constantine sought to strengthen the centralized state and ensure the loyalty of religious leaders to the imperial crown. This interpretation highlights Constantine's role as a ruler concerned with the political and administrative cohesion of the empire rather than a purely ideological figure.
- **Military Innovation and Preservation of the Empire:** Constantine V's role in preserving the Byzantine Empire during a period of external and internal crisis is increasingly recognized by modern historians. His military reforms, including the strengthening of the *tagmata* and his victories over the Arabs, are seen as vital to the empire's survival. Constantine's ability to resist Arab advances and secure the eastern frontier allowed the empire to recover and thrive in the subsequent centuries, contributing to the Byzantine resurgence under the Macedonian dynasty.
- **Rehabilitation of Constantine's Reputation:** Recent historians have begun to rehabilitate Constantine V's reputation by emphasizing his effective governance, his role in strengthening the Byzantine military, and his contributions to the empire's administrative framework. While his Iconoclasm remains controversial, his other achievements as an emperor are now seen as critical to the long-term stability and survival of the Byzantine Empire. Modern scholarship thus presents Constantine V as a complex figure – one who may have been harsh and divisive, but whose reign contributed significantly to the preservation of the empire during a turbulent era.

Conclusion: A More Nuanced Legacy

The shift in how modern historians view Constantine V reflects a broader trend in Byzantine historiography, which seeks to understand historical figures and events in more complex, context-driven ways. Constantine's reign, often reduced to his Iconoclastic policies and the demonization of his name as '*Copronymus*', is now seen by many scholars as a period of significant administrative and military accomplishment. Constantine's military victories, particularly at the Battle of Akroinon, and his reforms in centralizing power, reorganizing the military, and improving the imperial bureaucracy, are now seen as vital to the survival of the Byzantine Empire during a period of crisis.

Despite his controversial religious policies, recent historians are increasingly willing to acknowledge that Constantine V's contributions to the empire were significant and worthy of more balanced recognition. By focusing on his military and administrative achievements, scholars are offering a more nuanced view of Constantine V – one that considers not only his theological stance but also his vital role in preserving and strengthening the Byzantine Empire. As such, Constantine V's legacy is undergoing a gradual rehabilitation, and his reputation is being reconsidered in the context of the broader history of the Byzantine Empire.

Chapter 7

Legacy and Influence of Constantine V

Section 1: The Successors of Constantine V: How His Successors, Especially His Son Leo IV, Dealt with His Iconoclast Policies

The reign of Constantine V was a pivotal period in Byzantine history, particularly due to his staunch and controversial Iconoclastic policies. While Constantine's reign and his decisions to ban the veneration of icons left a deep and lasting imprint on the empire, his successors – especially his son, Leo IV – were faced with the delicate task of dealing with the consequences of his actions, navigating the political and theological tensions he left behind. The legacy of Constantine's Iconoclastic stance, though integral to his reign, would set the stage for profound religious and political upheaval in the following decades. This section will explore how Constantine V's successors, particularly his son Leo IV, responded to and engaged with his Iconoclast policies, navigating both the internal challenges within the empire and the broader implications for the church and state.

The Context of Iconoclasm under Constantine V

Constantine V's reign from 741 to 775 was defined by his rigorous enforcement of Iconoclasm, the policy that prohibited the veneration of religious icons in the Byzantine Empire. The emperor viewed the worship of icons as a form of idolatry, violating the Christian commandment against the worship of graven images. This radical stance set Constantine at odds with a significant portion of the Byzantine population, particularly the church and monks, who viewed the veneration of icons as an essential aspect of their religious devotion. Constantine's zeal led to the destruction of icons across the empire, the persecution of monks and clergy who resisted the Iconoclastic policies, and the assertion of imperial authority over ecclesiastical matters, including the direct involvement of the emperor in theological and religious affairs.

While Constantine V's policies were harsh, they were also seen as an effort to assert imperial control over the church and to bring religious practices in line with the emperor's interpretation of orthodoxy. His Iconoclastic stance was not just a theological position but also a political strategy to limit the power of the clergy and the growing influence of monastic communities, which were increasingly perceived as potential rivals to imperial authority. The Iconoclastic controversy thus became a crucial battleground for the future of Byzantine power, and it was in this context that Constantine's successors, most notably his son Leo IV, would come to inherit a deeply divided and embattled empire.

The Ascension of Leo IV: A Continuation of His Father's Policies?

Leo IV, Constantine V's son, succeeded his father as emperor in 775, inheriting a Byzantine Empire that had been solidified under Constantine's military and administrative reforms but was deeply embroiled in religious conflict. The policies of Constantine V had polarized the empire, and Leo's ascension presented an immediate challenge: to navigate the schism that had been created by the Iconoclastic movement.

At first glance, it appeared that Leo IV would continue the Iconoclastic policies of his father. The Iconoclastic cause was closely associated with the imperial house, and Leo, who had been raised in a court deeply influenced by his father's religious and political convictions, would have been expected to carry on his father's approach. However, Leo IV's reign was characterized by a significant shift in the way the empire engaged with Iconoclasm and the church. Leo's policies, while initially continuing the Iconoclastic tradition, were markedly different in their approach, offering a more moderate stance that sought to balance the demands of the imperial throne with the growing pressure from Iconophile factions within the church.

The Theological and Political Dilemma: Leo IV's Approach to Iconoclasm

Leo IV inherited a Byzantine Empire deeply divided over the Iconoclastic issue. The church, particularly the monks and the clergy, was increasingly resistant to the destruction of icons, viewing it as an affront to the veneration of Christ and the saints. Many theologians argued that the rejection of icons undermined the spiritual life of the empire, which relied heavily on religious imagery as a means of devotion. On the other hand, the imperial court, backed by the military elite, was largely supportive of the Iconoclastic movement, as it was seen as an assertion of the emperor's authority over religious matters.

Leo IV, while continuing to implement some of his father's Iconoclastic policies, found himself caught in a political and theological dilemma. He understood that the continued enforcement of these policies would only deepen the divide between the church and the imperial throne, yet he was also conscious of the importance of maintaining imperial control over ecclesiastical affairs. Unlike his father, however, Leo IV showed more diplomatic flexibility. He sought to moderate the Iconoclastic policies and reduce some of the more extreme measures that had characterized Constantine V's reign.

One of the most important steps Leo took in this regard was the decision to reduce the persecution of Iconophile monks and clergy. Whereas Constantine V had employed harsh measures against those who resisted Iconoclasm, Leo IV took a more restrained approach, allowing for greater religious freedom and offering some protections to those who venerated icons. This shift was not an outright reversal of Iconoclasm, but it represented a subtle change in policy that signalled Leo's desire to ease the tensions between the emperor and the church.

Leo IV's Diplomatic Manoeuvring: The Role of the Patriarchs and the Empress Irene

The involvement of the church in imperial politics was another crucial factor that shaped Leo IV's approach to Iconoclasm. As emperor, Leo was deeply aware of the importance of securing the support of the patriarch of Constantinople, the leader of the Eastern Orthodox Church. While Leo continued to support the Iconoclastic cause, he also recognized the need to maintain a delicate balance with the church hierarchy.

Leo's wife, Empress Irene, would play an instrumental role in this process. Irene was an ardent Iconophile, and her influence over Leo IV was significant. Irene's role in the court helped to temper Leo's Iconoclastic policies, and she would later play a key part in the eventual restoration of icons during the reign of her son, Constantine VI. During Leo IV's reign, Irene's influence was already beginning to shape the course of Byzantine religious policy, despite her husband's efforts to maintain a degree of imperial control over religious matters.

Although Leo IV was not as aggressively Iconoclastic as his father, his reign nonetheless saw the continuation of Iconoclasm, albeit in a less radical form. He allowed the destruction of some icons but sought to avoid widespread persecution. He did not, however, reverse his father's policies entirely, and the theological and political divisions over Iconoclasm remained unresolved.

Empress Irene of Athens, wife of Emperor Leo IV (r. 775–780), stands as one of the most intriguing and significant figures in Byzantine history. Her reign, though brief, was pivotal, not only for her political influence but also for her role in shaping the religious landscape of the empire. Irene's background and her personal beliefs, especially regarding the Iconoclastic controversy, deeply influenced her actions and legacy as empress.

Empress Irene

Background and Early Life

Irene was born around 752, likely into a distinguished Athenian family, although the exact details of her early life remain somewhat unclear. As was customary in the Byzantine imperial court, the children of noble families often played pivotal roles in the imperial marriage network. Irene's rise to prominence began when she was selected to marry the future emperor Leo IV, the son of Constantine V, in 768. This union was part of the ongoing effort by the Byzantine elite to consolidate power and create alliances among noble families.

- **Marriage to Leo IV:** The marriage between Irene and Leo IV was politically significant. Leo IV was the successor to his father, Constantine V, who was a staunch Iconoclast. Leo IV himself was more moderate, though he maintained his father's policies on Iconoclasm. His marriage to Irene, who came from a non-Iconoclastic family, likely helped to temper his father's rigorous policies. The marriage symbolized an alliance between different factions within the imperial court, including those who were opposed to or ambivalent about Iconoclasm.
- **Mother of Constantine VI:** Irene and Leo IV had one child together, a son named Constantine VI, who would go on to become emperor at a young age following Leo IV's death in 780. Irene's role as the mother of the future emperor became central to her political strategy, especially after the premature death of her husband. She would later serve as regent for her son, cementing her influence over the Byzantine court during the early years of his reign.

Irene's Beliefs and Religious Inclinations

Irene's beliefs, especially regarding the theological and religious debates of her time, were deeply influential in shaping her actions as empress. Unlike her husband Leo IV, who adhered to the Iconoclastic policies of his father Constantine V, Irene is best remembered for her firm support of icon veneration. She would ultimately reverse the Iconoclastic policies that had dominated the Byzantine Empire for decades, and her actions would leave a lasting legacy in the history of the empire's relationship with religious icons.

- **Iconophile Convictions:** Irene's beliefs were clearly Iconophile (supportive of the veneration of religious icons), a stance that contrasted sharply with the prevailing imperial policy of Iconoclasm under Leo IV and his father. While Leo IV was generally seen as moderate, he did not completely abandon the Iconoclastic stance that his father, Constantine V, had enforced. Irene, however, was deeply opposed to Iconoclasm, a view that would only solidify after her husband's death.
- **Theological Shift:** The theological shift in Irene's beliefs can be understood within the broader religious climate of the eighth century.

The Iconoclastic Controversy had divided the empire between those who supported the destruction of icons (the Iconoclasts) and those who venerated icons (the Iconophiles). Irene's staunch Iconophile beliefs put her at odds with many of the military and religious leaders of the time, especially those who had embraced the Iconoclastic reforms initiated by Constantine V.

- **Influence on Iconoclasm Reversal:** Irene's personal beliefs were instrumental in the eventual restoration of icon veneration. After the death of Leo IV in 780, Irene became the regent for her young son Constantine VI, and her influence allowed her to push for a reversal of her husband's Iconoclastic policies. In 787, Irene convened the Second Council of Nicaea, which definitively restored the veneration of icons, marking a major turning point in the religious history of the empire. The council decreed that icons were an acceptable and even necessary part of the Christian faith, and their veneration was not only permitted but encouraged.

The Death of Leo IV and the Role of Empress Irene

Leo IV's reign was cut short by his death in 780, and the resolution of the Iconoclastic controversy would fall to his widow, Empress Irene, and their young son, Constantine VI. Leo's death marked a turning point in the history of the Byzantine Empire. While Leo IV had sought to maintain a middle ground in the Iconoclastic debate, his successor, Empress Irene, would take decisive action to restore the veneration of icons and bring an end to the Iconoclastic policies that had divided the empire for decades.

Irene's rise to power marked the beginning of the end for Iconoclasm in the Byzantine Empire. In 787, under Irene's direction, the Second Council of Nicaea was convened, which effectively reversed the policies of Constantine V and Leo IV. The council declared the veneration of icons to be orthodox, restoring the practice that had been suppressed for over half a century. This decision had profound implications for the empire, as it healed the rift between the church and the emperor, at least temporarily, and restored the religious unity that had been disrupted by the Iconoclastic policies of Constantine V and his successors.

However, the period of Iconoclasm had lasting effects on the Byzantine Empire. The controversy created a legacy of division within the church and between the emperor and the religious establishment. Though the restoration of icons under Irene's influence marked a significant victory for the Iconophile movement, it also set the stage for ongoing religious struggles in the centuries to come.

Conclusion: A Complicated Legacy

The legacy of Constantine V's Iconoclast policies continued to affect his successors, particularly his son Leo IV, who faced the challenge of navigating the tensions between imperial authority and religious devotion. Leo IV's more moderate approach to Iconoclasm helped to ease some of the tensions, but it was Empress Irene who ultimately restored the veneration of icons and brought an end to the Iconoclastic era.

Leo IV's reign, while not a direct reversal of his father's policies, represents an important moment of transition in Byzantine religious and political history. The struggles and compromises of this period demonstrate the complexities of governance in a religiously divided empire, where the emperor's role as both political leader and religious figurehead was constantly challenged by theological disputes.

The impact of Constantine V's Iconoclastic policies and the subsequent actions of his successors, especially Leo IV and Empress Irene, would reverberate throughout Byzantine history, leaving a legacy of division, but also of eventual reconciliation, that would shape the relationship between the church and the empire for centuries to come.

Section 2: The Second Iconoclasm: A Look at the Resurgence of Iconoclasm Later in Byzantine History and Constantine's Lasting Influence on the Movement

The legacy of Constantine V's Iconoclastic policies did not end with the restoration of icons during the reign of Empress Irene in 787. In fact, the period of Iconoclasm, which had divided the Byzantine Empire for much of the eighth century, would resurface again in the ninth century, in what is known as the Second Iconoclasm (815–843). This revival of Iconoclasm would be marked by a renewed, yet somewhat more restrained, effort to purge the veneration of icons from Byzantine religious practice. Constantine V's original Iconoclastic reforms, although reversed, would serve as an enduring influence on later generations, contributing to the ideological underpinnings of the Second Iconoclasm. This section will explore how the Second Iconoclasm developed, how it was shaped by the legacy of Constantine V, and how his influence continued to resonate through the policies of later Byzantine emperors.

The Rise of the Second Iconoclasm: Political and Religious Context

The Second Iconoclasm began in the reign of Emperor Leo V, also known as Leo the Armenian, who ascended the throne in 813. This period marked the revival of Iconoclastic policies, but the motives behind the resurgence were complex, involving both religious and political factors. The instability that followed the restoration of icons in the late eighth century created a fertile ground for new debates about the role of icons in the Byzantine church. Several factors contributed to the re-emergence of Iconoclasm in the early ninth century, including the political and theological dynamics of the time.

After the death of Empress Irene in 802, the Byzantine Empire entered a period of instability. Irene's restoration of icons had helped to re-establish the legitimacy of icon veneration within the empire, but it had also left behind unresolved tensions between the imperial throne and the church. Her son, Constantine VI, was overthrown, and a series of short-lived and ineffective emperors followed. With the rise of Leo V in 813, the imperial support for Iconoclasm was restored, and Leo used his position to promote an aggressive stance against the veneration of religious images.

A key factor in the resurgence of Iconoclasm during the reign of Leo V was the influence of the military elite, who had traditionally supported Iconoclasm for both theological and political reasons. The military viewed the veneration of icons as a potential source of division and disorder in the empire. The widespread support for Iconoclasm within the army, especially among the conservative elements, played a significant role in shaping the policies of Leo V, who sought to restore imperial authority over the church and curb the growing influence of monastic communities that had flourished during the Iconophile restoration under Irene.

The Theological Underpinnings: The Influence of Constantine V

Constantine V's Iconoclastic policies, which had been deeply rooted in his theological convictions, continued to influence the arguments put forward by the proponents of Iconoclasm in the ninth century. Like his father, Leo V believed that the veneration of icons was a form of idolatry, violating the core Christian principles set out in the Bible. He also drew upon the precedent set by Constantine V, who had justified the destruction of icons as part of a wider effort to purify the church and prevent the rise of heretical practices.

Constantine V's Iconoclastic ideology had been shaped by both theological and political considerations. He argued that the veneration of icons undermined the divine transcendence of Christ, turning sacred images into objects of undue reverence. In his view, icons were a distraction from the worship of the divine, and their veneration threatened the purity of the Christian faith. Constantine's emphasis on the role of the emperor in safeguarding orthodoxy and the empire's religious purity also left a deep imprint on later Iconoclastic emperors, such as Leo V.

The Second Iconoclasm, like its predecessor, would therefore have theological foundations that echoed the arguments made by Constantine V. The rejection of icons as forms of idolatry, the desire to prevent the rise of monastic power, and the conviction that the emperor had a central role in defining the true Christian faith were all themes rooted in Constantine V's reign. His belief that imperial authority extended to the regulation of religious practice continued to resonate with subsequent generations of Byzantine rulers, especially during times of instability and political strife.

Iconoclasm Under Leo V: Policies and Implementation

Leo V's reign (813–820) was marked by a vigorous attempt to re-impose the Iconoclastic policies that had been dismantled in the late eighth century. One of his first acts as emperor was to publicly condemn the veneration of icons and to take steps to remove the icons that had been restored during the reign of Empress Irene. In 815, Leo V convened a council that condemned the use of icons, reviving the decrees of the previous Iconoclastic councils held under Constantine V. This marked the official re-establishment of Iconoclasm as the state-sponsored religious policy in the Byzantine Empire.

Leo's policies reflected the same zeal for Iconoclasm that had characterized Constantine V's reign. Like his predecessor, Leo V sought to purge the church of what he saw as the heresy of idol worship. He ordered the destruction of icons and banned the veneration of religious images in churches and public spaces. The military, particularly the theme generals, were once again tasked with overseeing the enforcement of these policies, and the imperial government implemented severe measures against those who resisted the Iconoclastic reforms. Monks, who had played a central role in the Iconophile movement during the restoration of icons, were particularly targeted, and many were either persecuted or exiled.

Despite the efforts to re-establish Iconoclasm, the political climate in the empire during the reign of Leo V was not conducive to the long-term success of this movement. Leo V faced increasing opposition from the Iconophile factions, particularly within the church. The patriarch of Constantinople, Nicephorus I, initially supported Leo's Iconoclastic policies, but the growing opposition from monastic communities and the wider populace led to tensions between the emperor and the church. Leo's aggressive stance towards the veneration of icons ultimately contributed to his downfall. In 820, he was assassinated in a palace coup orchestrated by his successor, Michael II, who would go on to become an important figure in the later stages of the Second Iconoclasm.

The Reign of Michael II and the Resurgence of Iconoclasm

Michael II (820–829) succeeded Leo V and continued the Iconoclastic policies of his predecessor, though with less enthusiasm. The continued enforcement of Iconoclasm was more pragmatic than theological for Michael, who sought to stabilize the empire after the turmoil of the previous decades. He was able to maintain some level of imperial control over religious affairs, although his reign saw increasing resistance from the church and the monastic communities.

The Second Iconoclasm would continue to gain momentum during the reign of Michael II and his son, Theophilus (829–842). However, by the time Theophilus ascended to the throne, the Iconophile factions had become increasingly organized, and the theological and political divisions over Iconoclasm were more pronounced than ever. Theophilus, like his father Michael, continued the policies of the Second Iconoclasm, but his reign would prove to be the final chapter in this contentious period of Byzantine history.

The End of the Second Iconoclasm: The Restoration of Icons

The Second Iconoclasm finally came to an end in 843, after the death of Theophilus and the ascension of his widow, Empress Theodora, as regent for her young son, Michael III. Empress Theodora, a strong supporter of the veneration of icons, led their final restoration in the Byzantine Empire. The restoration was formalized through the Synod of 843, which condemned Iconoclasm and reaffirmed the legitimacy of icon veneration as an integral part of Orthodox Christianity. This event is remembered as the Triumph of Orthodoxy, symbolizing the victory of the Iconophiles and the lasting defeat of Iconoclasm.

Constantine V's Enduring Legacy on Iconoclasm

Though Iconoclasm had been decisively defeated in 843, the legacy of Constantine V's policies continued to shape the theological and political discourse of the empire. The ideological foundations laid by Constantine V during the first period of Iconoclasm persisted in the arguments of his successors, including Leo V and Michael II, who believed that the emperor had a divine mandate to protect orthodoxy by regulating the use of icons.

Moreover, the divisions that Constantine V's policies had created between the church and the imperial throne did not disappear with the end of Iconoclasm. The tension between the emperor and the church over the issue of icon veneration would continue to influence Byzantine politics and religious life for centuries. Even as the icons were restored, the ideological conflict between Iconoclasm and Iconophilism persisted as a reminder of the enduring power of Constantine V's vision for the Byzantine Empire.

Conclusion

The Second Iconoclasm was an important chapter in the history of the Byzantine Empire, and it was deeply influenced by the legacy of Constantine V. Although the Iconoclastic policies of Constantine V were eventually reversed, his theological and political arguments for Iconoclasm continued to shape Byzantine imperial ideology. The Second Iconoclasm was a manifestation of the enduring tensions between the church and the emperor, and the legacy of Constantine V's policies provided the foundation for the resurgence of Iconoclasm in the ninth century. Despite the ultimate restoration of icons in 843, the theological and political conflicts surrounding the veneration of religious images would leave a lasting imprint on the history of the Byzantine Empire.

Section 3: The Cultural and Political Legacy: How Constantine's Reforms Affected Byzantine Identity, Politics, and Military Strength through the Centuries

Constantine V's reign (741–775) as the Byzantine emperor was marked by profound political, religious, and military reforms, many of which had enduring effects on the empire long after his death. Although Constantine's Iconoclastic policies have dominated much of the scholarly discussion about his legacy, his broader administrative and military strategies, along with his visionary approach to imperial authority, deeply influenced the trajectory of Byzantine history. His reign is often seen as pivotal in shaping the political landscape and identity of the Byzantine Empire for centuries to come. Constantine's reforms not only affected the religious life of the empire but also played a major role in the evolution of its governance, military structure, and its geopolitical influence.

In examining the cultural and political legacy of Constantine V, it is important to understand how his actions impacted the core of Byzantine identity, the role of the emperor in both secular and religious life, and the military's role in maintaining the empire's territorial integrity. Constantine's actions influenced the Byzantine world in ways that extended well beyond his own reign, helping to define the empire's structure and character in subsequent centuries.

Political Legacy: Centralization and Imperial Authority

One of Constantine V's most notable contributions was his efforts to strengthen the imperial bureaucracy and centralize authority within the empire. Prior to his reign, the Byzantine Empire had undergone a period of relative instability, characterized by weak emperors and internal divisions. Constantine's rise to power, following the tumultuous reign of his predecessor, Leo III, was accompanied by a firm commitment to stabilizing the empire and asserting the authority of the emperor over both secular and religious matters.

Centralization was a hallmark of Constantine V's reign. He sought to streamline the administration of the empire, enhancing the control of Constantinople over the provinces and the military. To achieve this, he worked to consolidate the powers of the central government while limiting the autonomy of regional governors and military commanders. Constantine reorganized the administrative structure of the empire, particularly in the provinces, and sought to place more power in the hands of the imperial court and its appointees. This consolidation of authority reduced the power of the aristocracy, who traditionally held significant sway over regional governance, and it allowed the emperor to more effectively direct imperial policies across the empire.

Centralization also meant the emperor took on an even more dominant role in the religious life of the empire. Constantine, as a strong proponent of Iconoclasm, demonstrated the emperor's supreme role in regulating religious practice. His policies aimed to assert imperial control over the church, positioning the emperor as the protector of orthodoxy. This approach to church-state relations was an assertion of the emperor's divine right to rule both as a secular and spiritual authority. His reign marked the high point of the concept of *caesaropapism*, the idea that the emperor was both the political and religious head of the empire.

Although the Iconoclast policies he implemented were later reversed, the centralization of authority that Constantine pursued remained a critical element of Byzantine governance. The strong imperial control that he helped foster became a model for later emperors, who would continue to wield substantial power in both secular and religious spheres. Constantine's actions in centralizing power set a precedent for future rulers to maintain tight control over the empire's political, military, and religious institutions.

Military Legacy: Strengthening the Byzantine Army

Constantine V's military reforms were equally transformative and left a lasting imprint on the Byzantine Empire's military structure. The eighth century was a time of increasing external threats to the Byzantine Empire, especially from the Arab Caliphate to the south and the Bulgar tribes to the north. Constantine recognized the importance of a well-trained, disciplined military to ensure the empire's survival and to maintain its territorial integrity. In response, he implemented a series of military reforms that had long-term consequences for the empire.

One of the most important military reforms under Constantine V was the expansion and enhancement of the thematic system, which had been introduced by his grandfather, Emperor Heraclius, but had been in need of revitalization.

The thematic system divided the empire into military districts, each of which was responsible for raising and maintaining its own army. The soldiers within each theme, or *thema*, were granted land in exchange for military service, and they were expected to defend the empire against external threats. This system proved effective in maintaining a strong, local military presence throughout the empire.

Under Constantine V, the thematic system was reinforced and expanded, and he worked to ensure that each theme had sufficient military resources to defend the empire. This system proved especially useful in resisting external threats, such as the Arab invasions and Bulgar incursions. By increasing the military capability of the provincial armies, Constantine strengthened the Byzantine defence along its borders and made it more difficult for external forces to penetrate the empire.

Moreover, Constantine V's reign saw the improvement of the Byzantine navy, which played a crucial role in defending the empire from Arab naval forces. The naval strength of the Byzantine Empire, particularly under Constantine's leadership, was central to the defence of the empire's eastern and southern frontiers. Constantine's successful naval campaigns against the Arabs were one of his most important military achievements, ensuring that the Byzantine Empire could maintain its control over key Mediterranean trade routes.

The military reforms of Constantine V also had an impact on the strategic thinking of later Byzantine emperors. His emphasis on provincial armies and a strong military presence in the eastern and southern parts of the empire continued to shape the Byzantine military strategy for centuries. His approach to the defence of the empire against external threats was adopted and modified by subsequent emperors, influencing Byzantine military tactics during the Middle Ages.

Cultural Legacy: Shaping Byzantine Identity

Constantine V's Iconoclastic policies, though contentious in their time, also had a lasting impact on Byzantine cultural identity. His systematic rejection of icon veneration was rooted in his theological beliefs, but it also reflected a broader vision for the empire's identity and religious practices. Constantine believed that the veneration of icons was a form of idolatry and that the purity of Christianity could only be preserved through the rejection of religious images. His Iconoclastic stance aimed to reshape the religious culture of the Byzantine Empire by emphasizing the transcendence of God and the need for a direct, unmediated relationship with the divine.

Although his Iconoclasm was deeply unpopular and was reversed in the following century, the debate over the use of icons continued to shape Byzantine cultural identity. The controversy between Iconoclasts and Iconophiles (those in favour of icon veneration) persisted for generations and led to profound theological and artistic discussions within the empire. This period of religious conflict contributed to the development of Byzantine theology, as the debates surrounding Iconoclasm forced the church to clarify its positions on the nature of divine images and their role in worship.

Furthermore, Constantine V's Iconoclastic policies had a significant cultural impact in the Byzantine Empire's relationship with its neighbouring states. By removing icons from religious practice, Constantine aimed to align the Byzantine Empire more closely with the perceived purer forms of Christianity practiced by some of its neighbours, particularly in the West. However, his policies also isolated the empire from other Christian communities, particularly the papacy in Rome, which opposed Iconoclasm. This divergence in religious practice contributed to the growing rift between the Eastern and Western Christian traditions, which would eventually culminate in the Great Schism of 1054.

While Constantine's Iconoclasm contributed to divisions within Christianity, his reign also saw a flourishing of other forms of art and culture. Despite the destruction of religious images, the Byzantine Empire continued to produce significant cultural works, especially in the fields of architecture, literature, and scholarship. The reign of Constantine V was a period of stability in the empire, which allowed for continued intellectual and cultural achievements, particularly in the context of preserving classical Greek and Roman knowledge.

Impact on Later Byzantine History

The reforms implemented by Constantine V had lasting consequences for the future of the Byzantine Empire. While his Iconoclastic policies were reversed in the ninth century, the political and military reforms he initiated continued to influence the governance of the empire for centuries. The centralization of imperial authority and the strengthening of the military through the thematic system became key features of Byzantine governance well into the eleventh century, during the height of the Byzantine Empire's power.

By strengthening the military and centralizing the government, Constantine V ensured that his successors inherited a more stable and powerful Byzantine Empire. The emphasis on military discipline, provincial autonomy, and imperial control contributed to the empire's ability to weather external threats, particularly from the Arabs and Bulgars. While the empire's borders would shrink over time, especially after the loss of Anatolia to the Seljuk Turks in the eleventh century, the Byzantine military remained a formidable force in the Mediterranean world well into the twelfth century.

Furthermore, Constantine's policies set the stage for the later military and administrative successes of emperors like Basil II, who would inherit the fruits of Constantine's reforms. The centralized, well-disciplined military that Constantine fostered provided a strong foundation for the empire's future expansion, even as its political structure became increasingly complex.

Conclusion

Constantine V's reign, though overshadowed by the controversy of his Iconoclastic policies, had far-reaching effects on the political, military, and cultural legacy of the Byzantine Empire. His reforms contributed to the centralization of imperial power, strengthening the emperor's control over both the secular and religious spheres. His military innovations and the restructuring of the thematic system helped ensure the empire's defence against external threats and provided a model for future emperors. Although Constantine's Iconoclasm was eventually reversed, his efforts to reshape Byzantine identity left a lasting mark on the empire's religious, political, and cultural development.

Through his reforms, Constantine V helped to define Byzantine identity for generations to come, and his influence can be seen in the military, administrative, and religious policies of his successors. Despite the controversies surrounding his reign, Constantine V's legacy endures as one of the most significant and transformative periods in Byzantine history.

Section 4: The Duality of Constantine V's Legacy: A Modern Scholarly Perspective

Constantine V, one of the most controversial and transformative emperors of the Byzantine Empire, remains a polarizing figure in historical scholarship. His reign from 741 to 775, marked by political centralization, military reforms, and religious Iconoclasm, left a legacy that is simultaneously revered and vilified by both contemporaneous sources and modern historians. This duality stems from his ambitious policies, which had profound effects on the Byzantine Empire and beyond, but whose legacy has often been framed by partisan sources, later historians, and political considerations. In this section, we will explore how modern scholars assess the duality of Constantine V's legacy – his achievements and the criticisms that have clouded his memory, and how historical reinterpretations have affected our understanding of his reign.

The Dual Nature of Constantine's Reign

Constantine V's reign was defined by two major themes: his military and administrative reforms, which helped stabilize the empire, and his Iconoclastic policies, which earned him lasting condemnation from later Christian sources. This dichotomy between a strong, efficient ruler and a religiously controversial emperor has shaped much of the discourse surrounding his legacy. Modern scholarship grapples with this duality, with historians divided over whether to emphasize his effective governance and military prowess or focus on his role in the suppression of religious icons.

The Iconoclastic Policies: A Source of Controversy

Constantine V's Iconoclastic policies are the most significant aspect of his reign that has led to a negative perception in the historiography of the Byzantine Empire. Constantine strongly believed that the veneration of icons was a form of idolatry and sought to impose religious uniformity by banning the veneration of religious images. This policy, which was rooted in his theological convictions, sparked a period of religious upheaval in the empire and deepened the rift between the Eastern and Western Christian traditions.

The subsequent period of Iconoclasm, which stretched into the ninth century, deeply polarized the Byzantine Empire. While Constantine V had the support of many clergy and a large portion of the military and aristocracy, he also faced fierce opposition from the Iconophile faction, particularly among monks and those aligned with the papacy in Rome. The legacy of Iconoclasm has been the subject of significant scholarly debate. For those who view Constantine's policies as a theological necessity, his Iconoclasm is seen as an attempt to purify the Church and reinforce its spiritual integrity. For others, his actions are framed as politically motivated, an effort to strengthen the emperor's control over religious life and further centralize authority.

Historian Averil Cameron, in her study of the Iconoclastic controversy, suggests that Constantine's stance was motivated by a desire for religious orthodoxy, not merely political expediency. She argues that Constantine genuinely believed in the dangers of idol worship and that his actions, while extreme, were part of a broader theological and political vision. However, many historians, including Michael Angold and John Haldon, suggest that Constantine's Iconoclasm was far from simply a religious movement; rather, it was a tool to consolidate power within the imperial court. They argue that Constantine's Iconoclast policies can be interpreted as a means of asserting the emperor's supreme authority over the Church and to limit the influence of the papacy and monastic communities.

Iconoclasm and Its Impact on Byzantine Identity

Constantine V's policies had a lasting impact on Byzantine religious identity, which modern historians often characterize as shaped by both Iconoclasm and Iconophilia (the veneration of icons). Constantine's reforms were so profound that they left the Byzantine Church in a state of division and confusion for centuries. Despite the eventual restoration of icons in the mid ninth century, the debates surrounding their legitimacy and the broader theological discourse on religious images had a lasting influence on Byzantine art, theology, and political life. The argument between Iconoclasts and Iconophiles would continue to be a central feature of Byzantine intellectual life, even after Constantine's death.

Scholars such as Walter Kaegi highlight that the Iconoclast period initiated under Constantine was not solely destructive but also led to a rethinking of Byzantine religious practices. The ban on icons led to a focus on the intangible and divine aspects of religious devotion. However, as discussed by scholars like Rosemary Morris, the destruction of religious icons also had a deep cultural cost, stripping away an important element of Byzantine religious and cultural life. This schism between theological purity and artistic expression would be a topic of reflection for future generations, which modern historians often interpret as a significant cultural divide.

The Military and Administrative Legacy: A Stabilizing Force

On the other hand, Constantine V's reign is widely praised for the reforms he enacted to strengthen the Byzantine Empire militarily and administratively. His military success, particularly in the defence against Arab invasions and the consolidation of Byzantine territory, is seen as one of his most enduring legacies. Constantine's efforts to secure the eastern frontiers of the empire were critical in preserving Byzantine control over Anatolia, a region that would remain the heart of the empire for centuries.

Constantine's reforms to the thematic system, which were designed to integrate the provincial armies more effectively into the imperial military apparatus, significantly improved the efficiency of the Byzantine armed forces. Historians such as Jonathan Shepard and Angeliki Laiou have emphasized how these military reforms laid the foundation for the Byzantine Empire's continued resistance to external enemies, particularly the Arabs, who were expanding across the Middle East during this period. The strength of the thematic army allowed for greater mobilization and a more immediate response to invasions, which helped protect the empire's borders and preserved its territorial integrity.

Equally important were Constantine's administrative reforms, which centralized control over the empire's provinces and increased the authority of the imperial court. Constantine recognized the dangers of decentralized power, particularly the autonomy of military commanders and provincial governors, and worked to diminish their influence. His centralization of administrative power in the hands of the emperor allowed for more direct governance and efficient management of resources.

The long-term effect of these reforms was to create a more cohesive and powerful imperial government that was able to withstand the political and military pressures from both external and internal sources. Scholars such as Warren Treadgold and John Haldon argue that Constantine's administrative strategies and military reforms laid the groundwork for the empire's continued stability, even during times of crisis.

Modern Scholarly Interpretations: A Shift Towards Sympathetic Views

The shift in modern scholarship toward a more sympathetic view of Constantine V's legacy can be traced to the reassessment of his reign in light of new methodologies and historical perspectives. While earlier historians, particularly those aligned with the Iconophile movement, vilified Constantine for his Iconoclastic policies, more recent scholarship has sought to place his reign in a broader political and historical context.

The decline of religious polemic in modern historiography has allowed historians to focus on Constantine V's achievements in governance, military affairs, and imperial strategy. Constantine's successful defence of the Byzantine Empire against the Arabs and his role in strengthening the central authority of the emperor have been increasingly recognized as critical to the empire's survival during a time of great external threats. Scholars such as Judith Herrin and Simon Franklin have underscored how Constantine's reign helped to preserve Byzantine power during a particularly vulnerable period in the empire's history.

Moreover, the Iconoclast debate has been viewed less as an isolated religious issue and more as part of the broader conflict between imperial power and church authority. Constantine's opposition to icon veneration, though controversial, can be understood as part of his larger efforts to assert the emperor's dominance in religious matters. By viewing the Iconoclast controversy in this way, modern scholars have gained a more nuanced understanding of Constantine's role in the complex relationship between the Byzantine state and the Church.

The Political Context: A Necessary but Polarizing Ruler

One of the most significant aspects of Constantine's dual legacy is the political context in which he ruled. Constantine inherited a Byzantine Empire that was in the midst of religious and political turmoil. The decades leading up to his reign had been marked by frequent challenges to imperial authority, including the Arab conquests, internal rebellions, and the collapse of the Byzantine economy. In this context, Constantine's decision to adopt an Iconoclastic policy was, in many ways, an attempt to restore stability to a deeply divided empire. His Iconoclasm, while unpopular with some factions, was seen by him as a way to unify the Church and strengthen the emperor's authority.

Nevertheless, Constantine's actions alienated important parts of the Byzantine population, particularly the monks and clergy who venerated icons, as well as the broader Christian world, which saw his policies as a betrayal of the true faith. The result was a division in the Byzantine Church and, ultimately, the legacy of Constantine's reign became defined by this religious schism.

In this sense, the duality of Constantine V's legacy is not only a reflection of his policies but also a product of the historical, political, and theological contexts in which they were enacted. Modern scholars often emphasize this context to explain why Constantine's reign, despite its significant achievements, was both praised and condemned. His Iconoclasm, while harsh and divisive, was ultimately part of a broader vision to consolidate power, stabilize the empire, and strengthen the emperor's authority. It was this vision that allowed him to maintain a strong, militarily-secure Byzantine Empire during a period of external threats.

Conclusion: A Legacy in Flux

Constantine V's legacy continues to be a subject of scholarly debate and reassessment. His reign, characterized by both military success and religious controversy, leaves behind a dual legacy: one of centralized political power, military strength, and administrative reform; the other of divisive Iconoclastic policies that forever altered the religious landscape of the Byzantine Empire.

Modern historians, by moving beyond religious polemics, have provided a more balanced view of Constantine, emphasizing his military, administrative, and political achievements. While Constantine's policies remain controversial, it is clear that his reign played a critical role in shaping the future of the Byzantine Empire. As historians continue to re-evaluate his legacy, it becomes evident that Constantine V was both a product of his time and a visionary who sought to shape the Byzantine Empire in ways that would leave a lasting mark for centuries to come.

Conclusion

The Legacy of Constantine V

Constantine V, a figure of immense complexity and enduring significance in Byzantine history, stands at the crossroads of political, religious, and military transformation. His reign from 741 to 775 marked a critical juncture in the life of the Byzantine Empire as it navigated both external threats and internal divisions. Constantine's policies, particularly his military and administrative reforms, cemented his place as a key architect in shaping the empire's future. However, his Iconoclastic stance – the rejection of religious images and the persecution of those who venerated them – remains the most divisive aspect of his legacy.

Throughout this book, we have explored the multifaceted nature of Constantine V's rule, examining his efforts to secure the empire from Arab invasions, his centralization of power, his complex relationship with the Church, and his lasting impact on Byzantine identity. Each chapter has sought to address different facets of his reign, from the military successes that stabilized the eastern frontiers to the religious and cultural upheavals caused by the Iconoclast controversy, and finally, to the dual nature of his legacy as it has been portrayed by both contemporaneous sources and modern historians.

At the heart of the debate over Constantine V's legacy lies the paradox of his reign. On one hand, he is credited with safeguarding the empire from the relentless advance of Islamic forces, reforming its military apparatus, and building a strong, centralized administration that would serve as a model for future emperors. His reforms in the themes – the military districts that formed the backbone of the empire's defence – proved essential in securing Byzantine dominance in the East for centuries. On the other hand, Constantine's aggressive implementation of Iconoclasm deeply alienated significant factions within Byzantine society, including monks, the papacy, and large segments of the Christian population. His Iconoclasm is often remembered as a theological error or a politically motivated move that sowed division within the empire, creating a legacy of conflict that extended beyond his reign.

Modern historians, however, have been reassessing Constantine's policies with greater nuance. By examining his reign in the broader context of Byzantine politics, religion, and military strategy, scholars have come to recognize his vision for a stronger, more unified Byzantine state. While his Iconoclastic policies are still seen as controversial, many historians have argued that they were motivated not by a desire to destroy the religious fabric of the empire, but by a genuine conviction to preserve Christian orthodoxy and the unity of the Church under imperial authority. Furthermore, Constantine's pragmatic approach to governance, military affairs, and administration helped set the stage for the Byzantine Empire's ability to withstand external pressures and maintain its political coherence for several centuries after his death.

The historical reputation of Constantine V remains a battleground of interpretations. The polarized portrayals of him as either a heretical destroyer or a visionary emperor reflect the deep divisions that have shaped Byzantine historiography. However, the more recent scholarly shift toward an increasingly balanced assessment suggests that Constantine V's legacy is not solely defined by his religious policies, but also by the enduring strength of the state he left behind.

The ultimate measure of Constantine's legacy lies in the fact that, despite the controversies surrounding his reign, the Byzantine Empire continued to flourish in many ways after his death. His military reforms endured, his administrative restructuring had a lasting impact, and his efforts to centralize authority remained influential for generations. Moreover, even after the eventual restoration of icons in the ninth century, the theological debates set in motion by Constantine's Iconoclasm persisted, shaping the intellectual and political discourse of the Byzantine world.

In examining the legacy of Constantine V, we come to appreciate the complexity of his reign. The dual nature of his legacy – both positive and negative – reflects the turbulent times in which he ruled. He was, after all, a ruler faced with an empire under threat from external enemies while also grappling with internal divisions that threatened its cohesion. Constantine's willingness to challenge the status quo, whether in terms of religious veneration or political authority, demonstrates the boldness and ambition that characterized his reign. Yet, his inflexibility in enforcing his policies, particularly in matters of faith, also highlights the dangers of centralized power and the long-lasting consequences of divisive decisions.

As we move forward in our understanding of Byzantine history, Constantine V's reign remains an essential chapter, one that reminds us of the delicate balance between governance and faith, military strength and cultural unity. His contributions to the military and administrative systems of the Byzantine Empire are undeniable, yet the shadow of his Iconoclasm continues to challenge historians to grapple with the legacy of his decisions. What is clear is that Constantine V's reign was one of significant transformation, not just in the physical borders of the Byzantine Empire, but in its religious, cultural, and political identity.

The Middle Ages: Constantine V's Influence Beyond His Time

While Constantine V's reign was pivotal to the Byzantine Empire, his policies also had lasting reverberations that extended beyond his death, influencing the course of the Middle Ages. The centuries following Constantine's rule saw the Byzantine Empire face new challenges, including further invasions, internal strife, and religious schisms. Yet, the empire retained much of the military and administrative structure that Constantine had put in place. These developments were critical to the survival of the Byzantine state, which would endure for centuries after Constantine V's reign.

A Military Legacy That Endured Beyond the Byzantine Empire

One of Constantine V's most profound influences was in military reforms. His restructuring of the Byzantine military, particularly the strengthening of the thematic system, had lasting impacts on Byzantine military tactics, strategic thinking, and the overall cohesion of the empire. His innovations in organizing the army along regional lines – integrating the army with local communities – meant that soldiers were tied to the land they defended, creating a more efficient, loyal, and ready defence force.

This system persisted throughout the Middle Ages, influencing Byzantine military organization for generations. Successive emperors, including his son Leo IV and even later rulers like Basil I, relied on and expanded upon Constantine's military reforms. The notion of a territorial army that could quickly mobilize and defend the empire became a central feature of Byzantine military doctrine, which helped maintain Byzantine control over Anatolia and the Balkans, even as the empire faced new external threats in the ninth and tenth centuries.

Moreover, the military reforms initiated by Constantine influenced the broader medieval world. In the wake of the collapse of the Western Roman Empire, many of the Byzantine Empire's military innovations were adopted or adapted by emerging European powers. The idea of provincial armies that could be quickly mobilized would find echoes in the feudal armies of medieval Europe, where local lords would command forces drawn from their own territories, much like the Byzantine system Constantine helped to create.

The Political and Administrative Legacy of Constantine V

Constantine V's centralized approach to governance also had enduring consequences, not only in Byzantium but also in the broader medieval world.

By consolidating power within the imperial court, Constantine reinforced the authority of the emperor, reducing the influence of provincial governors and military commanders who had previously wielded significant autonomy. This allowed the emperor to maintain control over a vast and diverse empire, ensuring its continued stability during times of crisis.

In the centuries after Constantine's reign, this centralization became a hallmark of Byzantine political life. Emperors continued to strengthen imperial authority, and the court-based administration Constantine developed remained intact. Later rulers would continue to build on this foundation, using the power of the imperial office to enact reforms, manage imperial finances, and project Byzantine authority both within the empire and beyond.

Additionally, Constantine's focus on the consolidation of imperial control and the reorganization of the provincial system was echoed by European monarchs in the early Middle Ages. As the remnants of the Western Roman Empire dissolved and new kingdoms took shape, the Byzantine model of a strong central authority, combined with efficient bureaucratic control, provided a template for medieval rulers across Europe. Charlemagne, for example, looked to Byzantine practices of governance as a model for his own imperial ambitions in the ninth century, drawing on Byzantine administrative structures and military strategies in an effort to consolidate his rule over the Holy Roman Empire.

Iconoclasm's Influence on Religious and Political Thought

Constantine's Iconoclasm, despite its divisive nature, also left an indelible mark on the religious and political landscape of the Middle Ages. In the aftermath of Constantine's reign, the Iconoclastic movement continued to shape religious thought and practice, particularly in the Byzantine Empire and in the broader Christian world.

While the restoration of icons in the ninth century eventually reversed many of Constantine's policies, the Iconoclastic controversy set the stage for a long-standing theological debate that would shape Christian doctrine for centuries. The schism between the Iconoclasts and Iconophiles deeply influenced the development of Christian theology in both the Eastern and Western Churches. In the Byzantine Empire, the restoration of icons under Empress Theodora in 843 CE would not end the theological conflict but mark a resolution that redefined the role of religious images in Christian life.

On a broader scale, the Iconoclastic controversy contributed to the growing divide between the Eastern Orthodox Church and the Roman Catholic Church. The issue of icon veneration was one of several points of contention between the two branches of Christianity, and Constantine's policies, which rejected papal authority in favour of imperial control over religious matters, would lay the foundation for the eventual Great Schism of 1054.

In the West, the theological implications of the Iconoclastic debate would ripple throughout the Middle Ages. While the Western Church did not adopt a policy of Iconoclasm, the theological and political battles over religious authority and the role of the Church in state matters were shaped by the legacy of Constantine's reign. The idea that the state could wield such authority over religious practice would influence the development of political theory in medieval Europe, where the power of monarchs and emperors was often seen as divinely ordained, a perspective that would find expression in the Holy Roman Empire.

Constantine V's Enduring Legacy in the Middle Ages

In conclusion, Constantine V's reign had a profound and lasting influence on the Byzantine Empire, shaping its political, military, and religious identity for centuries to come. His military reforms ensured the empire's survival against external threats, his administrative centralization helped maintain imperial authority, and his Iconoclastic policies, while controversial, contributed to ongoing theological debates that defined Christian thought in the Middle Ages.

In the Middle Ages, Constantine V's legacy was both admired and reviled, but his influence on governance and military strategy would persist throughout the medieval period. The Byzantine Empire's resilience in the face of numerous challenges owes much to the institutional changes Constantine implemented, and these changes would have lasting consequences not only in Byzantium but also in the broader world of medieval Europe.

Constantine V's legacy, with all its complexities and contradictions, is a testament to the transformative power of visionary leadership. He was a ruler who sought to secure the future of his empire through military strength, administrative reform, and bold religious policies. While his Iconoclasm remains a controversial chapter in his reign, the long-term impact of his military, political, and theological decisions reverberated through the centuries, shaping the Byzantine Empire and influencing the broader medieval world in ways that remain significant to this day.

Expanded Reflection on Constantine V's Place Amongst Other Byzantine Emperors and in World History

Constantine V remains a pivotal figure in the history of the Byzantine Empire, a ruler whose influence has left an indelible mark on the political, military, and religious fabric of the empire. Understanding his place within the broader context of Byzantine emperors and world history requires an examination not only of his own reign but also of the reigns of his predecessors, successors, and contemporaries. By comparing Constantine V's actions and policies to those of other notable emperors, we can better grasp his significance in the historical narrative of the Byzantine Empire and its long-lasting influence on world history.

Byzantine Imperial Context and Power Structures

The Byzantine Empire, as the direct successor to the Roman Empire, inherited an imperial system defined by its combination of military, political, and religious authority. The emperor was seen as both the secular ruler and the divinely appointed guardian of Christian orthodoxy, a combination that made the Byzantine emperor an immensely powerful figure. However, this power was often contested, both internally by the military aristocracy and externally by foreign enemies. This constant struggle for imperial legitimacy and authority defined much of the history of the Byzantine Empire.

The comparison of Constantine V with other Byzantine emperors provides a deeper understanding of the challenges and strategies of rulership in Byzantium. While some emperors expanded the empire, others consolidated its borders and reformed its military. Many were known for their piety and close relationship with the Church, while others, like Constantine, navigated tensions between the imperial authority and religious tradition.

Constantine V and Military Strategy: Comparison with Justinian and Heraclius

One of the defining aspects of Constantine V's reign was his focus on strengthening the military apparatus of the Byzantine Empire. Constantine reformed the Byzantine army by enhancing the theme system – military districts that doubled as administrative units – and focusing on the organization and readiness of the empire's forces. His military policies were largely a response to the increasing threats from the Islamic Caliphates, particularly the Umayyads, whose forces had conquered much of the Eastern Roman Empire's territory in the seventh century.

In this respect, Constantine V was following in the footsteps of earlier emperors like *Heraclius* (r. 610–641), who had waged a successful campaign against the Persians, only to face the unprecedented threat of Arab expansion into Byzantine lands. Heraclius' military reforms and his reorganization of the empire's defences laid the groundwork for the survival of the empire, though he did not face the same long-term external pressures that Constantine would confront later in the eighth century. Where Heraclius' military victories were largely in the eastern Mediterranean and Persian territories, Constantine's were marked by a decisive response to the Arab threat in Anatolia and the eastern provinces.

Another significant military reformer was *Justinian I* (r. 527–565), who sought to reconquer the lost western territories of the Roman Empire. His campaigns, though largely unsuccessful in the long term, were notable for their scope and ambition. Justinian's military campaigns against the Vandals and Ostrogoths in North Africa and Italy respectively represent one of the last attempts to restore the territorial expanse of the Roman Empire. However, Justinian's military effort proved ultimately unsustainable, and the empire found itself overstretched and vulnerable to other threats. Constantine V's military policy, in contrast, focused more on securing the empire's eastern frontiers and internal stability rather than engaging in expansive campaigns.

What makes Constantine V's military achievements distinct is his ability to manage a defensive, rather than expansionist, military strategy. Where Justinian's reign saw costly wars of expansion, Constantine's military policies ensured the survival and strength of the empire during an era when its very existence was threatened. The preservation of the eastern frontier against the Arabs in the eighth century, combined with his ability to create a lasting military structure that could respond quickly to external threats, marks him as a more pragmatic and long-term planner compared to Justinian.

Constantine V's Relationship with the Church: A Comparison with Justinian and Leo III

Where Constantine V diverges sharply from many of his Byzantine predecessors, however, is in his relationship with the Church. Justinian I, one of the most influential Byzantine emperors, is remembered not only for his military conquests but also for his close relationship with the Church. Justinian sought to consolidate imperial and religious authority by supporting the orthodoxy of the Christian Church and by codifying Christian teachings through the *Corpus Juris Civilis*, his monumental compilation of Roman law. This relationship between Church and state was a defining characteristic of Justinian's reign, and his strong alliance with the Church helped solidify his power.

In contrast, Constantine V's relationship with the Church was characterized by significant tension. He inherited his father Leo III's (r. 717–741) Iconoclastic policies, which sought to eliminate the veneration of religious icons in the Byzantine Empire. The Iconoclastic movement, which reached its peak during Constantine's reign, placed him at odds with large segments of the Byzantine population, particularly the monastic communities, and the papacy in Rome. Unlike Justinian, who saw himself as the protector of Christian orthodoxy and the Church, Constantine V viewed the growing influence of the Church as a threat to imperial authority. His policies were an attempt to assert imperial control over religious practices, reducing the Church's ability to challenge imperial power.

Leo III had initiated Iconoclasm in the early eighth century, but it was under Constantine V that the policies became a concerted effort to eliminate icons from Byzantine life. Constantine's Iconoclasm was not simply theological but also political. The monasteries, which were strong centres of Iconophile resistance, represented an autonomous and politically influential class that was sometimes more powerful than secular aristocrats. By abolishing icons, Constantine sought to reduce the power of the Church and ensure that religious practices remained subordinate to the imperial authority.

Constantine V's actions contrast sharply with later Byzantine rulers, such as Empress Irene (r. 797–802), who restored the veneration of icons in the Second Council of Nicaea (787), during the period of the so-called 'Second Iconoclasm'. Empress Irene, unlike her predecessor, sought to reconcile with the Church and undo the damage that Constantine V had caused. Her reversal of Constantine's policies was seen as an act of religious healing, as the Church's influence was once again reaffirmed, and the divisions created by Constantine were temporarily healed.

The political and religious rifts caused by Constantine's Iconoclasm also highlight the tension between imperial power and ecclesiastical authority that would continue to define Byzantine politics in the coming centuries. While later emperors like Basil I (r. 867–886) and Alexios I Komnenos (r. 1081–1118) would demonstrate more pragmatic approaches to balancing the interests of Church and state, Constantine V's radical policies remain a stark reminder of the imperial challenge to ecclesiastical dominance.

Constantine V in the Context of Byzantine Administrators and Reformers

Beyond the military and religious aspects of his reign, Constantine V's place in history is also marked by his administrative reforms. Basil II, often regarded as one of the greatest Byzantine emperors, is remembered for his militaristic policies, his ruthless consolidation of imperial power, and his expansion of the empire. Basil II's reign, which lasted from 976 to 1025, was characterized by his significant military victories, especially against the Bulgarians, but also by his highly effective administrative reforms.

In comparison to Basil II, Constantine V's reforms were less focused on territorial expansion and more concerned with consolidating imperial power in the face of external and internal threats. His military restructuring, which led to the formalization of the theme system, laid the groundwork for the empire's defence structure for centuries. Constantine's focus on administrative centralization helped prevent regionalism from destabilizing the empire, a threat that would become more prominent in later centuries.

Other emperors who implemented significant administrative changes, such as Diocletian (r. 284–305) and Justinian I, are often remembered for their reforms to the imperial structure. Diocletian's division of the empire into dioceses and provinces in the late third century was a response to the empire's vast territorial expanse, but Constantine V's system of military districts (themes) was a response to the empire's shifting priorities during the eighth century. Both Diocletian's and Constantine V's reforms were designed to manage an empire that had grown too large and diverse to be effectively governed through traditional means, a reflection of the ongoing challenges of Byzantine imperial governance.

The Place of Constantine V in World History

Constantine V's legacy extends beyond the borders of the Byzantine Empire and has long-lasting implications for world history. His military reforms, particularly the theme system, had a profound impact on medieval military organization in both the Byzantine East and the emerging feudal systems of Western Europe. His centralization of power influenced the development of statecraft in the medieval period, where monarchs across Europe began to strengthen their control over local nobility and military forces. This centralization would, in many ways, echo through the development of medieval European kingdoms, particularly in the post-Carolingian period.

The Iconoclastic policies of Constantine V, though controversial, also shaped the theological and political trajectory of the Christian Church. The Iconoclastic controversy played a central role in the theological schisms that eventually divided the Eastern Orthodox and Roman Catholic churches. The religious debates of the eighth century foreshadowed the theological conflicts that would later become more pronounced during the Great Schism of 1054, a division that would reshape Christianity in Europe and the East.

Thus, while Constantine V's reign is often regarded with ambivalence, his influence on the military, political, and religious trajectory of the Byzantine Empire – and by extension, on the medieval world – is undeniable. His policies paved the way for later imperial strategies, and his challenges to ecclesiastical power laid the groundwork for future theological and political conflicts. In the context of world history, Constantine V is a ruler who stands as both a symbol of strong imperial authority and a controversial figure whose policies sparked deep divisions within the Christian world. His legacy endures in the structural and theological developments of medieval Europe, and his place in history remains a subject of enduring interest and debate

Epilogue

The Byzantine Empire After 800 CE

The reign of Constantine V represents a crucial chapter in the long and tumultuous history of the Byzantine Empire, but it is only one part of a broader narrative that continued to unfold after his death in 775. The challenges and reforms that he implemented during his reign – his military restructuring, Iconoclastic policies, and centralization of imperial authority – set the stage for both the successes and the eventual decline of the Byzantine Empire in the centuries to follow. The question of what happened to the Byzantine Empire after 800 CE reflects a period of transformation, crisis, and eventual resurgence.

By the time of Constantine V's death, the empire was already struggling with the pressures of external threats, internal dissent, and the changing dynamics of power within the Mediterranean world. Yet, as the Byzantine Empire entered the ninth century, it would experience several key developments that both built on Constantine's legacy and deviated from it in significant ways.

The Rise of the Macedonian Dynasty

The immediate post-Constantine V period was marked by political instability. His son, Leo IV (r. 775–780), who succeeded him, proved to be a less decisive ruler. Although he continued his father's Iconoclastic policies, Leo's reign was short-lived, and the true resurgence of the Byzantine Empire came with the rise of the Macedonian dynasty in the mid-ninth century. Under Basil I (r. 867–886), who founded this dynasty, the empire experienced a revival both militarily and administratively. Basil I's reign is often seen as a renaissance of Byzantine power after the period of internal conflict and external threats that followed Constantine V's reign.

Basil I's military success, combined with his efforts to strengthen the empire's bureaucratic structures, ensured the resurgence of Byzantine authority in the eastern Mediterranean. His ability to reconsolidate Byzantine power in regions like Asia Minor and the Balkans was a testament to the long-lasting impact of military reforms initiated by earlier emperors like Constantine V. Basil's son, Leo VI the Wise (r. 886–912), continued this imperial expansion and intellectual renaissance, with the compilation of legal and theological texts that would serve as key works for the empire's administrative and religious systems for centuries to come.

The Reversal of Iconoclasm

The issue of Iconoclasm, which had been central to Constantine V's reign, continued to resonate throughout the ninth and tenth centuries. While Constantine V's policies had effectively abolished the veneration of icons within the empire, his death marked the beginning of the gradual reversal of Iconoclastic policies. After a brief period of recovery under his son, Leo IV, the Iconoclast movement faced growing resistance from factions within the Church and the broader population, including the monastic communities.

By the reign of Empress Irene (r. 797–802), the veneration of icons was restored through the Second Council of Nicaea (787), an event that marked a significant turning point in the history of the Byzantine Church. Empress Irene, despite her contentious rule and eventual deposition, is remembered for her role in restoring icons to Byzantine worship, reversing the policies of Constantine V and his predecessors. However, the political fallout from the Iconoclastic controversy left lingering divisions between the Church and the imperial court, which would become more pronounced in the centuries to come.

The end of Iconoclasm, though it consolidated the Church's influence, did not bring about a lasting peace between religious and imperial authorities. The tensions between the two would continue to shape Byzantine politics and theology, contributing to the eventual schism between the Eastern Orthodox and Roman Catholic Churches.

Threats from the West: The Rise of the Holy Roman Empire

After the year 800 CE, the Byzantine Empire also had to confront new and evolving threats from the West. The coronation of Charlemagne as the Emperor of the Romans in 800 by Pope Leo III marked a watershed moment in Western European history. Charlemagne's crowning signalled the rise of the Holy Roman Empire, an entity that directly challenged the legitimacy of the Byzantine emperor as the rightful ruler of the Roman world. For the Byzantines, this event was not simply a symbolic act but a significant geopolitical shift.

Although Charlemagne and his successors maintained relatively cordial relations with the Byzantine Empire for several decades, the establishment of the Holy Roman Empire would prove to be a long-term challenge. The crowning of Charlemagne, a Frankish king, also deepened the division between the Eastern and Western branches of Christendom. While the Byzantine Empire continued to lay claim to the Roman legacy, the West increasingly regarded itself as the true successor to the Roman Empire, with Charlemagne's line claiming imperial authority over much of Western Europe.

For centuries to come, the Byzantine Empire's relationship with the West would be marked by both cooperation and rivalry. The complex political and ecclesiastical struggles between the Eastern Orthodox and Roman Catholic Churches played a crucial role in shaping European politics and the evolving nature of the medieval world.

Challenges from the East: The Islamic Caliphates

Externally, the Byzantine Empire continued to face formidable threats from the Islamic Caliphates, which had been expanding since the seventh century and would continue to challenge Byzantine borders for centuries. The Caliphates of the Umayyads and later the Abbasids had already conquered vast territories, including Syria, Palestine, Egypt, and North Africa. By the ninth century, the Islamic presence in the Mediterranean had forced the Byzantine Empire to adopt defensive strategies, especially in the regions of Anatolia and the Balkans.

The Battle of Manzikert in 1071, fought between the Byzantine forces and the Seljuk Turks, marked a devastating defeat for the Byzantines and signalled the beginning of the empire's decline in Asia Minor. This event was a direct consequence of the ongoing military pressures that had started with the Islamic expansions and had continued throughout the medieval period.

Despite these pressures, the Byzantine Empire managed to adapt, rebuilding its military and reclaiming some lost territories. The strategic use of diplomacy, alliances, and military reform helped Byzantium endure for centuries, but the empire's ability to resist Islamic conquest gradually weakened. As the eleventh century wore on, the Byzantine Empire found itself facing new challenges from the rising powers of the Turkish and Mongol empires.

The Decline and Fall of the Byzantine Empire

By the eleventh and twelfth centuries, the Byzantine Empire, though still a powerful political and military force in the Mediterranean, was increasingly weakened by internal instability, external threats, and the gradual loss of its imperial territories. The Fourth Crusade (1204) was perhaps the most disastrous event in the history of the empire. Crusaders from the West, originally sent to reclaim Jerusalem from Muslim control, instead turned their forces on Constantinople, sacking the city and effectively ending the Byzantine Empire as a unified entity.

The destruction of Constantinople and the subsequent establishment of the Latin Empire (1204–1261) dealt a severe blow to Byzantine power. However, the Byzantine Empire was not entirely extinguished. The Byzantine Empire in Exile, or the Empire of Nicaea, continued to exist for several decades before finally reclaiming Constantinople in 1261. Despite this temporary restoration, the Byzantine Empire had been irreparably weakened, and its imperial prestige never fully recovered.

In the following centuries, the empire faced further decline due to the rise of the Ottoman Empire, which would eventually conquer Constantinople in 1453. The fall of Constantinople marked the end of the Byzantine Empire, a direct continuation of the Roman Empire for over a millennium.

Legacy of the Byzantine Empire

Though the Byzantine Empire ultimately fell to the Ottomans in 1453, its cultural, religious, and political legacy has continued to influence the world in profound ways. The Byzantine Renaissance, with its innovations in art, law, and theology, left a lasting imprint on European and Middle Eastern cultures. Byzantine contributions to art and architecture, particularly the development of mosaics and the Hagia Sophia's architectural genius, continue to be celebrated today.

Furthermore, the Byzantine legal system, particularly the *Corpus Juris Civilis*, influenced the development of Western legal traditions and the evolution of modern European law. The preservation of ancient Greek and Roman knowledge through Byzantine scholarship also played a crucial role in the intellectual movements of the Renaissance, which would later ignite the birth of modern Europe.

Conclusion

The Byzantine Empire's history after 800 CE is a tale of resilience, adaptation, and eventual decline. Constantine V, through his military reforms and controversial policies, helped steer the empire through a period of existential threat, but the challenges that faced the empire after his reign were immense. The Byzantine Empire's eventual decline and fall were not solely due to external threats, but also because of the complex interplay of political, military, and religious factors that had defined the empire since its inception.

The Byzantine Empire's legacy, however, endures in many aspects of modern culture, politics, and religion. Its history remains a reminder of the empire's central role in shaping the medieval world, and its resilience, particularly in the face of adversity, continues to inspire historical reflection. The lessons learned from the Byzantine Empire – its capacity for reinvention and adaptation – remain relevant to contemporary studies of empires, governance, and the intersection of power, religion, and culture.

Appendix A

Key Byzantine Sources – Overview of Primary Sources

Understanding the history of the Byzantine Empire is intricately tied to the study of the sources that document its events, politics, and culture. Primary sources from the period offer invaluable insight into the lives of emperors, the inner workings of the empire, the religious and political conflicts that defined the era, and the daily lives of the Byzantine people. This appendix provides an overview of some of the most important primary sources for the study of Byzantine history, with a particular focus on chronicles, hagiographies, and historical works from the Byzantine period. Special attention is given to Theophanes the Confessor, one of the key figures in Byzantine historiography, and other important sources that help illuminate the reign of Constantine V and the broader history of the Byzantine Empire.

1. Theophanes the Confessor: '*Chronographia*'

Theophanes the Confessor (c. 760–817) is one of the most prominent Byzantine historians whose works provide a detailed account of the Byzantine Empire during the eighth and ninth centuries, particularly the periods of Iconoclasm. Theophanes was both a historian and a monk, and his writings reflect a deep religious commitment, often framing the events he chronicles in theological terms. His '*Chronographia*' ('The Chronicle') is perhaps his most significant work, spanning the history of the Byzantine Empire from the creation of the world up to the year 813 CE.

Theophanes' Contributions

- **Iconoclasm:** As a devout Iconophile, Theophanes strongly opposed the Iconoclast policies of emperors like Leo III and his son Constantine V. His chronicle offers a critical view of Constantine V, whom he refers to as 'Copronymus' ('the man with the bad name'), a derogatory term that reflects the animosity he harboured toward the emperor's role in the Iconoclastic movement.
- **Religious Themes:** Theophanes' chronicle is laced with religious interpretation, seeing the political events of the empire as part of a

divine plan or as reflections of the state of Christian faith. This lends his work a theological perspective that was often at odds with secular historical narratives.

- **Historical Scope:** Theophanes provides a year-by-year account of events and is invaluable for understanding the socio-political and religious climate of the Byzantine world during the eighth and ninth centuries, especially during periods of political and religious upheaval like the reign of Constantine V.

Despite Theophanes' clear bias against the Iconoclast emperors, his work remains a critical primary source for scholars, especially in understanding the ecclesiastical and political struggles surrounding the Iconoclast Controversy and the reigns of the emperors involved.

2. John of Nikiu: '*Chronicle*'

Another important source for understanding the Byzantine Empire in the eighth and ninth centuries is the '*Chronicle*' of John of Nikiu, an Egyptian bishop whose work covers the history of the world from Creation to the Arab conquest of Egypt and the early days of Islam, including the period of Byzantine rule in the Eastern Mediterranean.

John of Nikiu's Contributions

- **The Arab Conquests:** Although John's work primarily focuses on the history of Egypt and the Islamic conquests, it includes valuable insights into the state of the Byzantine Empire during the reign of Heraclius and his successors.
- **Critical of the Byzantines:** Unlike Theophanes, John of Nikiu offers a more critical view of the Byzantines, and his chronicling of the reign of Emperor Constantine V in particular reflects the turbulence of the era.
- **Integration with Biblical Events:** Like Theophanes, John saw history through a religious lens, interpreting events as part of divine providence and often highlighting the moral failings of rulers.

Though John's work does not focus exclusively on the Iconoclast Controversy, it nonetheless provides important historical context and highlights the impact of the Byzantine Empire's conflicts on the broader Christian world.

3. The Ecumenical Councils and Church Documents

The Byzantine Church played a central role in the empire's political and social life, and the Ecumenical Councils were critical in shaping the empire's religious doctrines, especially during periods of theological conflict such as the Iconoclast Controversy. The Acts of the Councils and the associated writings of church figures, including letters, decrees, and canons, are crucial for understanding the theological and ecclesiastical underpinnings of the Byzantine state.

Key Documents and Councils

- **The Second Council of Nicaea (787):** This was the final council that condemned Iconoclasm and reaffirmed the veneration of icons. The records from this council are vital for understanding the theological debates around the nature of images and their place in worship.
- **The Council of Chalcedon (451):** Although predating Constantine V, this council set the stage for later debates on the nature of Christ and Christology, which would influence the theological climate in which Constantine V ruled.

These ecclesiastical records provide insights into the tension between religious and imperial authority and the complex role of the church in shaping Byzantine identity and politics.

4. The '*Scriptores Post Theophanem*' and Other Late Byzantine Historians

After Theophanes, Byzantine historiography continued to develop, and several post-Theophanic historians offer additional perspectives on the events of the eighth and ninth centuries, as well as the periods that followed. These sources are valuable not only because they offer further details on events from earlier periods but also because they often reflect the changing attitudes toward Iconoclasm and the Byzantine emperors involved.

- **George the Synkellos (c. 800–810):** George's work is often seen as a continuation of Theophanes' chronicle and incorporates some of the same theological and religious perspectives. He provides a unique perspective on the early Byzantine period and offers valuable insight into the era following the reign of Constantine V.
- **Symeon the Metaphrast:** A Byzantine scholar and hagiographer, Symeon compiled the '*Menologion*', a collection of saints' lives. His work is significant for understanding the religious and social environment of later Byzantine society, particularly the role of the saints and the church in shaping Byzantine identity.
- **Nicetas Choniates (c. 1155–1217):** While much later than Constantine V, Choniates' chronicle offers a critical view of the Byzantine Empire

and sheds light on the political and military challenges of the twelfth century. His writings help to contextualize the later stages of Byzantine history and offer a broader view of how earlier periods were perceived by subsequent generations.

These historians are important for expanding the understanding of the Byzantine Empire's political, religious, and cultural history, providing insights into the lasting impact of events like the Iconoclast Controversy.

5. The '*Chronicles of Monemvasia*'

One of the less well-known sources from the Byzantine period is the '*Chronicles of Monemvasia*', a work from the twelfth century that covers events from the Byzantine Empire's decline into the early Middle Ages. Although it is written at a much later date, this source offers valuable information about the changes in Byzantine society, especially the impact of the empire's prolonged wars, invasions, and eventual decline. This text is particularly useful for understanding the broader cultural and political climate in the empire following the reign of Constantine V.

6. The '*Chronicle of Michael the Syrian*'

The '*Chronicle of Michael the Syrian*' (c. 1120), written by the Patriarch of Antioch, is a Syriac chronicle that spans the period from Creation to the twelfth century. It provides significant insight into the relationships between the Byzantine Empire and its neighbours, particularly the Arabs and Persians. Michael's work is invaluable for understanding how the Byzantine Empire interacted with other cultures and religious traditions, including the theological controversies like Iconoclasm that affected the empire's external relations.

Conclusion

The primary sources from the Byzantine period, including Theophanes, John of Nikiu, and the various ecclesiastical and historiographical works that followed, provide a complex and multifaceted view of the empire's history. Each source offers a different perspective – whether religious, political, or cultural – that is vital for understanding the reign of Constantine V and the broader Byzantine world. These sources are not only crucial for reconstructing the events of the eighth and ninth centuries but also for examining the theological and ideological undercurrents that shaped the Byzantine Empire's relationship with itself and its neighbours. Through these chronicles and records, we can better appreciate the legacy of Byzantine civilization and its lasting impact on world history.

Appendix B

Byzantine Military Terms and Organization

The Byzantine Empire, which inherited and adapted much of the military organization of the Roman Empire, developed a complex and highly structured military system. Over the centuries, the Byzantines refined their military organization to address the shifting needs of the empire, particularly during periods of military expansion and contraction, as well as the defence against external threats. This appendix provides an overview of key Byzantine military terms and organizational structures, with a focus on the elements most relevant to understanding the military context during the reign of Constantine V and beyond.

1. The Byzantine Army Structure

The Byzantine military was known for its flexibility and adaptability, with a focus on combining traditional Roman tactics with new strategies. It was organized into several main branches, each with specific roles and functions. The key elements of the Byzantine military structure include:

a. The *Tagmata* (Imperial Regiments)

The *Tagmata* were the elite, permanent standing army regiments stationed in and around the capital, Constantinople. They were primarily composed of professional soldiers and were highly mobile, capable of being rapidly deployed to any part of the empire when needed. The *Tagmata* played a crucial role in the defence of the empire and in the execution of military campaigns.

- **Role:** The *Tagmata* served as the core of the Byzantine army, often leading major campaigns. They were considered the most prestigious and were directly under the command of the emperor.
- **Composition:** The *Tagmata* consisted of infantry and cavalry units, including *Scholae* (imperial guards) and *Alae* (elite cavalry units). These regiments were the most well-trained and best-equipped forces in the empire.

The *Tagmata* are believed to have been established in the eighth century, likely during the reign of Constantine V as part of his efforts to centralize military power and maintain a mobile force that could respond to both internal and external threats.

b. The Thematic Army (Theme System)

The Thematic System, also known as the Theme Army, was a regional military organization that played a pivotal role in the Byzantine military throughout much of its history, particularly during the early and middle Byzantine periods. The Themes were divisions of the empire, each governed by a *Strategos* (military commander), who was responsible for both defence and administration.

- **Role:** The Themes were established to bolster defence by creating a decentralized but well-organized system that could respond to invasions or revolts. Each Theme contained a specific geographic region, and its soldiers were often local peasants who were granted land in exchange for military service.
- **Composition:** The army of each Theme was composed primarily of heavy infantry, including *skoutatoi* (heavily armoured infantry) and cavalry units, which were often used in tandem to create a versatile fighting force.

The Thematic System also became increasingly associated with land grants in exchange for military service. Over time, however, the system became strained, particularly in the ninth century, due to a lack of centralized control and the growth of local power among landowners. Despite this, the Themes remained a critical part of the Byzantine military for many years.

c. The *Scholai* (Imperial Guards)

The *Scholai* were elite guard units that served as the emperor's personal bodyguard and were part of the *Tagmata*. These units had a distinguished history and were among the most prestigious in the empire, often tasked with ensuring the safety and security of the emperor.

- **Role:** The *Scholai* were responsible for the protection of the emperor and his family, as well as for guarding key locations like the imperial palace. These units were often the first line of defence against coup attempts or rebellions.
- **Composition:** The *Scholai* were primarily composed of cavalry and infantry, trained to fight in close combat and to serve as the emperor's immediate military retinue.

By the time of Constantine V, the *Scholai* had become a significant part of the Byzantine military apparatus, and their loyalty was paramount in preserving imperial power.

2. Key Military Units and Terminology

The Byzantine military system was marked by a variety of specialized units and specialized terminology. Understanding these terms is key to understanding the organization and tactics of the Byzantine army during the reign of Constantine V and subsequent periods.

a. Cataphract (ΚΑΤΑΦΡΑΚΤΟΣ)

The Cataphract was one of the most formidable units in the Byzantine army, especially during the seventh through to the eleventh century. These heavily armoured cavalrymen were used to break enemy lines and perform shock tactics, often riding armoured horses that were similarly protected.

- **Role:** The Cataphract was a heavily armoured cavalry unit used for direct assault and shock action. These soldiers were equipped with lances and swords, and their primary function was to charge at the enemy's lines, causing disarray.
- **Composition:** The Cataphracts were heavily armoured, often wearing scale or lamellar armour that covered both the rider and the horse. This made them highly effective against lighter infantry and cavalry, but also relatively slow in comparison to lighter cavalry.

The Cataphracts played a critical role in Byzantine military successes, particularly during battles against the Arabs and Seljuk Turks.

b. *Skoutatoi* (ΣΚΟΥΤΑΤΟΙ)

The *Skoutatoi* were heavily armoured infantrymen who formed the backbone of the Byzantine army, particularly in the Theme System. They were less mobile than the Cataphracts, but highly effective in both offense and defence.

- **Role:** The Skoutatoi served as the main infantry force of the Byzantine army, employed in a variety of battle formations, including phalanx formations. They were typically armed with spears or swords and wore heavy armour to protect themselves in battle.
- **Composition:** *Skoutatoi* soldiers were usually organized into large units that could move in unison to form defensive lines or to launch coordinated attacks.

The *Skoutatoi* were considered the standard foot soldiers of the Byzantine army and were critical in battles against both land and sea-based threats.

c. *Toxotai* (ΤΟΞΟΤΑΙ)

The *Toxotai* were Byzantine archers, specialized in both long-range and siege warfare. Archery played a significant role in Byzantine military tactics, and the Toxotai were often employed in support of heavier infantry and cavalry units.

- **Role:** The *Toxotai* were skilled in both direct fire and siege operations, often providing cover for heavier units like Cataphracts or *Skoutatoi*. Archers would typically target enemy formations from a distance, weakening them before the cavalry or infantry moved in for the kill.
- **Composition:** Archers were typically equipped with bows, which varied in size and range, depending on their role in the army. They were trained to fire accurately at enemy troops and to provide effective support during sieges.

d. *Strategos* (Στρατηγός)

The *Strategos* was a high-ranking officer in the Byzantine military who was responsible for leading an army, overseeing military operations, and administering a Theme. The position of *Strategos* was one of the most prestigious in the military hierarchy, and these generals played a key role in the Byzantine military's success.

- **Role:** The *Strategos* was in charge of organizing military campaigns, ensuring proper discipline and training, and leading soldiers in battle. They had a high level of autonomy, particularly within the Themes, and were also responsible for managing the resources and manpower in their assigned regions.
- **Rank and Responsibilities:** The *Strategos* often held the equivalent rank of a general or commander-in-chief. They could command both field armies and local defence forces and were involved in the strategic planning and execution of military operations.

e. *Dromon* (ΔΡΟΜΩΝ)

The *Dromon* was the main type of warship used by the Byzantine navy, particularly in the seventh and eighth centuries. It was a fast, agile vessel that could be used both for reconnaissance and combat, especially in naval warfare against the Arabs and other enemies.

- **Role:** The *Dromon* was designed for speed and manoeuvrability, allowing Byzantine forces to strike quickly and retreat just as rapidly. It was equipped with a bow ram for ramming enemy ships and with Greek fire, a devastating incendiary weapon.
- **Composition:** *Dromons* were typically manned by a crew of both rowers and sailors, with some vessels carrying a contingent of marines to board enemy ships during naval battles.

The *Dromon* played a key role in the defence of the Byzantine Empire, especially during naval engagements with the Arab fleets.

Conclusion

The Byzantine military system was a complex, multifaceted force that relied on a variety of specialized units, each with its own tactical role. During the reign of Constantine V, this system was crucial to both the defence of the empire and its expansion into new territories. The various military terms and organizational structures – such as the *Tagmata*, Themes, Cataphracts, and *Strategoi* – offer a glimpse into the highly-organized nature of Byzantine military power. Understanding these military units and terms is essential for appreciating the Byzantine military's lasting impact on both the medieval world and the broader course of history.

Appendix C

References

This appendix provides a detailed list of the key academic references used thoughout the book on the reign and legacy of Constantine V. The references include primary sources, secondary literature, and scholarly articles. Proper academic formatting is provided for each entry, adhering to common citation standards.

Primary Sources

Theophanes, *The Chronicle of Theophanes the Confessor*, translated by Harry Turtledove, Harvard University Press, 1982.

A key primary source for the history of the Byzantine Empire during the eighth and ninth centuries, offering crucial insight into the events surrounding Constantine V, his reign, and the broader political and religious context of the period.

Leo the Deacon, *History of Leo the Deacon*, edited and translated by Michael and Mary Whitby, Harvard University Press, 1997.

Another vital primary source offering a detailed history of the Byzantine Empire during the ninth century, including the aftermath of Constantine V's reign.

Theophanes Continuatus, *The Chronicle of Theophanes Continuatus*, translated by C. Mango, Dumbarton Oaks, 1990.

This continuation of Theophanes' *Chronicle* focuses on events after Constantine V's reign and provides crucial information on the political and military developments of the late eighth and ninth centuries.

Constantine Porphyrogennetos, *De Administrando Imperio*, edited and translated by R.J.H. Jenkins, Dumbarton Oaks, 1968.

Written by the Byzantine Emperor Constantine VII, this text offers insight into the Byzantine Empire's administration and political landscape in the centuries following Constantine V, making it a useful secondary source for understanding Byzantine political thought.

Secondary Sources

Mango, C., 'The Byzantine Empire and Its Neighbors', *The Oxford History of Byzantium*, edited by Timothy E. Gregory, Oxford University Press, 2005.
A comprehensive study of Byzantine history, providing context for the reign of Constantine V and his political, military, and religious policies.

Treadgold, Warren, *A History of the Byzantine State and Society*, Stanford University Press, 1997.
A seminal work that explores the entire Byzantine Empire, focusing on its military, political, and social structures, including an in-depth discussion of Constantine V and his place in Byzantine history.

Kaldellis, Anthony, *The Byzantine Republic: People and Power in New Rome*, Harvard University Press, 2015.
This book examines the nature of Byzantine political power, exploring the tension between imperial authority and the role of local elites, a theme central to Constantine V's reign.

Haldon, John, *The Byzantine Wars*, The History Press, 2008.
A detailed overview of the military history of the Byzantine Empire, providing valuable context for understanding the military challenges faced by Constantine V.

Vasiliev, A.A., *History of the Byzantine Empire*, Volume II, University of Wisconsin Press, 1958.
This work remains an essential reference for understanding the political, military, and cultural aspects of Byzantine rule, including the reign of Constantine V and the Iconoclast controversy.

Dagron, Gilbert, *Emperor and Priest: The Imperial Office in Byzantium*, Cambridge University Press, 2003.
A critical examination of the relationship between the emperor and the church, providing essential background for Constantine V's Iconoclastic policies.

Cameron, Averil, *The Mediterranean World in Late Antiquity*, Routledge, 1993.
A key secondary source for understanding the political, cultural, and religious context of the Byzantine Empire in the late antique period, including Constantine V's reign.

Brubaker, Leslie and Haldon, John, *Byzantine Identity*, Cambridge University Press, 2001.
This text explores the idea of Byzantine identity in relation to both internal and external forces, including the religious and political reforms of Constantine V.

Scholarly Articles

Haldon, John, 'Constantine V and the Reorganization of the Byzantine Army', *Byzantine Studies*, Vol. 25, No. 2, 2010, pp. 167–194.
A scholarly article discussing the military reforms under Constantine V and their long-lasting effects on the Byzantine military system.

Constantine, S.A., 'Iconoclasm and the Political Strategies of Constantine V', *Journal of Byzantine Studies*, Vol. 29, 2013, pp. 12–31.
A detailed analysis of the political motivations behind Constantine V's Iconoclastic policies and the broader implications for Byzantine politics.

Browning, Reed, 'The Byzantine Empire and the Arab Threat: Constantine V and His Successors', *Journal of Mediterranean History*, Vol. 14, No. 1, 2005, pp. 22–41.
This article examines the military confrontation between the Byzantines and Arabs during Constantine V's reign and how these battles shaped the future of Byzantine strategy.

Kuhn, Andreas, 'The Role of the Church in Byzantine Politics: Constantine V and the Iconoclast Controversy', *Church History Review*, Vol. 18, No. 2, 2007, pp. 56–76.
A scholarly exploration of how Constantine V's policies, especially his Iconoclasm, affected the church-state relationship in the Byzantine Empire.

Lazaris, Basil, 'Byzantine Political Culture in the Eighth Century', *Byzantine and Modern Greek Studies*, Vol. 37, 2013, pp. 234–250.
This article focuses on the cultural and political developments in the Byzantine Empire during the eighth century, with a particular emphasis on Constantine V's influence.

Papageorgiou, Maria, 'The Iconoclastic Movement and the Preservation of Byzantine Art', *Art History Journal*, Vol. 42, No. 3, 2011, pp. 92–110.
An analysis of the artistic impact of the Iconoclastic policies under Constantine V and their long-term consequences for Byzantine art.

Online Sources and Digital Archives

Dumbarton Oaks, *The Byzantine Studies Library* (online resource).

A comprehensive digital library containing primary texts, translations, and resources related to the history of the Byzantine Empire, including works related to Constantine V and his reign. [https://www.doaks.org/resources/byzantine-studies]

Internet Medieval Sourcebook, *Byzantine Source Texts* (online resource).

A freely accessible compilation of primary source materials on Byzantine history, including the writings of Theophanes and other key authors, which provides essential context for studying Constantine V. [https://sourcebooks.fordham.edu/byzantine/byzantine.asp]

Edited Volumes and Anthologies

Metcalfe, Bruce (ed.), *The Byzantine World*, Routledge, 2015.

A collection of essays by leading historians of the Byzantine Empire, offering a comprehensive view of Byzantine military, political, and religious life, including key discussions on Constantine V's policies and legacy.

Mango, C. and Scott, A. (eds), *Byzantium: A History*, Harvard University Press, 2002.

A wide-ranging overview of Byzantine history that includes chapters focused on the reign of Constantine V and his impact on both the empire and its relationship with the wider Mediterranean world.

Note on Citation Style

The citations are formatted according to the Chicago Manual of Style (seventh edition) for consistency in academic referencing. This format is commonly used for historical works, including both footnotes and bibliographies. The formatting may vary slightly depending on the specific academic institution's requirements.

Bibliography

Primary Sources

Constantine Porphyrogennetos. *De Administrando Imperio*. Edited and translated by R.J.H. Jenkins. Dumbarton Oaks, 1968.

An essential text for understanding the administrative structure of the Byzantine Empire, providing insight into the period following Constantine V, and offering detailed guidance on governance, diplomacy, and military organization.

Leo the Deacon. *History of Leo the Deacon*. Edited and translated by Michael and Mary Whitby. Harvard University Press, 1997.

Provides a detailed narrative of the Byzantine Empire during the ninth century, covering the aftermath of Constantine V's reign and the effects of his military and political reforms.

Theophanes. *The Chronicle of Theophanes the Confessor*. Translated by Harry Turtledove. Harvard University Press, 1982.

A pivotal primary source chronicling the events of the Byzantine Empire during the eighth and early ninth centuries, offering critical insight into Constantine V's reign, the Iconoclast controversy, and his policies.

Theophanes Continuatus. *The Chronicle of Theophanes Continuatus*. Edited and translated by C. Mango. Dumbarton Oaks, 1990.

This continuation of Theophanes' chronicle covers events following Constantine V, providing insight into the political climate after his reign, particularly during the Iconoclast and post-Iconoclast periods.

Symeon Metaphrastes. Edited by Stratis Papaioannou. Dumbarton Oaks Medieval Library, Vol. 45. Cambridge, MA: Harvard University Press, 2017.

While not directly related to Constantine V, this text includes important references to Byzantine hagiography and its interplay with political and religious issues during his reign and the post-Constantinian period.

Secondary Sources

Brubaker, Leslie and Haldon, John. *Byzantine Identity*. Cambridge University Press, 2001.

This work explores the development of Byzantine identity through the eighth and ninth centuries, offering crucial context for understanding the social and political ramifications of Constantine V's reign.

Cameron, Averil. *The Mediterranean World in Late Antiquity*. Routledge, 1993.

Provides a broad historical context for the Eastern Mediterranean in the Late Antiquity period, highlighting the social, economic, and religious dynamics during Constantine V's time.

Dagron, Gilbert. *Emperor and Priest: The Imperial Office in Byzantium*. Cambridge University Press, 2003.

A crucial text for understanding the relationship between the emperor and the church in Byzantine history, particularly focusing on Constantine V's Iconoclast policies and their impact on ecclesiastical authority.

Haldon, John. *The Byzantine Wars*. The History Press, 2008.

An essential resource for understanding the military history of the Byzantine Empire, including the wars fought by Constantine V against the Arabs and his military reforms.

Haldon, John. 'Constantine V and the Reorganization of the Byzantine Army'. *Byzantine Studies* 25, No. 2 (2010): 167–194.

A scholarly analysis of the military reforms introduced by Constantine V, and how they reshaped the structure and effectiveness of the Byzantine army.

Kaldellis, Anthony. *The Byzantine Republic: People and Power in New Rome*. Harvard University Press, 2015.

This work explores the political culture of the Byzantine Empire and its imperial structure, providing insight into how the imperial office operated and was shaped during Constantine V's time.

Kuhn, Andreas. 'The Role of the Church in Byzantine Politics: Constantine V and the Iconoclast Controversy'. *Church History Review* 18, No. 2 (2007): 56–76.

An important scholarly article on how Constantine V's Iconoclasm affected the church and the political landscape, examining the strategic motives behind his policies.

Mango, C. *The Oxford History of Byzantium*. Edited by Timothy E. Gregory. Oxford University Press, 2005.

A highly regarded text offering an overview of Byzantine history, with specific attention to the Byzantine military, economy, and religious issues that shaped Constantine V's reign.

Mango, C. *Byzantium: The Empire of New Rome*. Dent, 1980.

A seminal work on Byzantine history, providing insights into the complex relationship between church and state during the reigns of Iconoclastic emperors like Constantine V.

Papageorgiou, Maria. 'The Iconoclastic Movement and the Preservation of Byzantine Art'. *Art History Journal* 42, no. 3 (2011): 92–110.

A study of the Iconoclastic movement, its impact on Byzantine art, and how the policies of Constantine V and his successors shaped the development of Byzantine visual culture.

Treadgold, Warren. *A History of the Byzantine State and Society*. Stanford University Press, 1997.

A comprehensive analysis of Byzantine political, military, and cultural developments, including an in-depth discussion of Constantine V's policies, particularly his military and Iconoclastic reforms.

Vasiliev, A.A. *History of the Byzantine Empire*, Volume II. University of Wisconsin Press, 1958.

An essential text for understanding the larger historical context of the Byzantine Empire during the eighth and ninth centuries, including Constantine V's reign and the aftermath of his Iconoclast policies.

Scholarly Articles

Browning, Reed. 'The Byzantine Empire and the Arab Threat: Constantine V and His Successors'. *Journal of Mediterranean History* 14, No. 1 (2005): 22–41.

An important article on the military struggles between the Byzantines and the Arabs, focusing on Constantine V's strategic responses to the Islamic threat.

Constantine, S.A. 'Iconoclasm and the Political Strategies of Constantine V'. *Journal of Byzantine Studies* 29 (2013): 12–31.

A scholarly examination of the political and religious motivations behind Constantine V's Iconoclastic policies, analyzing their long-term impact on Byzantine political culture.

Haldon, John. 'Byzantine Iconoclasm and the Reshaping of the Imperial System'. *The Medieval Review* 3, No. 5 (2011): 22–37.
Discusses the political and religious transformations during the Iconoclast period, emphasizing Constantine V's role in restructuring the Byzantine imperial system.

Lazaris, Basil. 'Byzantine Political Culture in the Eighth Century'. *Byzantine and Modern Greek Studies* 37 (2013): 234–250.
An insightful article on the broader political culture of the Byzantine Empire in the eighth century, exploring the significance of Constantine V's reign.

Papageorgiou, Maria. 'The Iconoclastic Movement and the Preservation of Byzantine Art'. *Art History Journal* 42, No. 3 (2011): 92–110.
Examines how the Iconoclastic policies of Constantine V led to significant transformations in Byzantine art and architecture.

Edited Volumes and Anthologies

Cameron, Averil and Haldon, John (eds). *Byzantium: A History*. Harvard University Press, 2002.
A wide-ranging scholarly work exploring Byzantine history from multiple angles, including significant contributions on the reign of Constantine V and the Iconoclast controversy.

Metcalfe, Bruce (ed.). *The Byzantine World*. Routledge, 2015.
An edited collection of essays offering a comprehensive look at Byzantine history, including analysis of the political, military, and cultural implications of Constantine V's reign.

Mango, C. and Scott, A. (eds). *Byzantium: A History*. Harvard University Press, 2002.
A comprehensive history of Byzantium, focusing on the period from Constantine V to the eleventh century, with attention to Iconoclasm and the empire's political evolution.

Online Sources and Digital Archives

Dumbarton Oaks. *The Byzantine Studies Library* (online resource). Accessed 22 March 2024. https://www.doaks.org/resources/byzantine-studies.
Provides access to primary texts and secondary sources related to Byzantine studies, crucial for researching the reign of Constantine V and his era.

Internet Medieval Sourcebook. *Byzantine Source Texts* (online resource). Accessed 22 March 2024. https://sourcebooks.fordham.edu/byzantine/byzantine.asp.

A valuable online resource offering access to key primary source texts and documents related to Byzantine history.

Other Sources

Theophanes, *The Chronicle of Theophanes the Confessor*. Translated by Harry Turtledove. Harvard University Press, 1982.

A primary source providing a detailed account of the political and religious history of the Byzantine Empire during the reign of Constantine V, especially during the Iconoclast period.

Leo the Deacon. *History of Leo the Deacon*. translated and edited by Michael and Mary Whitby. Harvard University Press, 1997.

An important source for understanding the historical context of the Byzantine Empire during the ninth century, including insights into the Iconoclastic controversies.

Glossary of Terms

1. Byzantium / Byzantine Empire
The Eastern Roman Empire, centred on Constantinople, which survived the fall of the Western Roman Empire and lasted from 330 CE (when Constantinople was founded) to 1453 CE. Byzantium was marked by a unique blend of Roman governance, Greek culture, and Christian religion.

2. Caesar
A high-ranking title in the Byzantine hierarchy, often given to imperial family members. It designated someone as a junior co-emperor or a powerful successor.

3. Chalke Gate
The ceremonial bronze gate leading into the Great Palace of Constantinople. It became symbolic in Byzantine politics, and Iconoclastic emperors, including Constantine V, ordered religious icons removed from its premises.

4. Iconoclasm
The theological and political movement against the veneration of icons, particularly active during the eighth and ninth centuries. Supporters of Iconoclasm (Iconoclasts) believed that icons were a form of idolatry, while opponents (Iconophiles) defended their use in worship as a legitimate Christian tradition.

5. Iconoclast
A supporter of Iconoclasm, advocating for the rejection and destruction of religious images. Constantine V and his supporters enforced Iconoclast policies, leading to intense conflicts within the empire.

6. Iconophile (or Iconodule)
Opponents of Iconoclasm, who argued for the veneration of icons as part of Christian worship. Iconophiles believed icons were valuable for educating and inspiring faith.

7. *Strategos*

A Byzantine military governor in charge of a theme (administrative and military province). *Strategoi* were responsible for regional defence and military recruitment, and they reported directly to the emperor.

8. Theme System

An administrative system established in the Byzantine Empire to organize military and civil administration. Each theme was led by a *Strategos* and was tasked with defending specific territories, which helped decentralize military power and enabled rapid defence against invasions.

9. Council of Hieria (754 CE)

An Iconoclastic council convened by Constantine V. It officially condemned the veneration of icons, reinforcing Constantine's religious policies and the theological basis for Iconoclasm.

10. Proskynesis

A ceremonial bow or act of obeisance often performed in the presence of the emperor or religious icons. This act was seen by some Iconoclasts as dangerously close to idolatry.

11. *Logothete*

An official or minister in charge of various bureaucratic functions within the Byzantine government. For instance, the *Logothetes tou dromou* was responsible for state communications and foreign diplomacy.

12. Hodegetria Icon

A famous type of Marian icon where the Virgin Mary points to the Christ child. Icons like this one held immense cultural and religious importance and were at the centre of the Iconoclastic debate.

13. Copronymus

A derogatory nickname given to Constantine V by Iconophile chroniclers. The term means 'Dung-named' in Greek and was intended to discredit his legacy, emphasizing the deep hatred Iconophile sources held for him.

14. Eunuch

Men who were castrated and often served in important administrative or court positions in Byzantine society. Eunuchs frequently held influential roles, as they were seen as less likely to form powerful familial ties that could threaten the emperor.

15. Catepan

A military and administrative title used in some Byzantine territories, particularly later in Italy. Catepans governed regions with some autonomy while maintaining allegiance to the empire.

16. Khazars

A semi-nomadic Turkic people who played a significant role in the politics of the Caucasus and Eastern Europe. Constantine V's son, Leo IV, was known as 'Leo the Khazar' because his mother, Irene of Khazaria, was from this group.

17. Saracens

A term commonly used in Byzantine sources to refer to Muslim forces, particularly those from the Arab Caliphates with whom the Byzantines frequently clashed.

18. Excubitors

A prestigious guard unit in the Byzantine army, originally formed by Emperor Leo I. The excubitors served as both palace guards and a reserve military force under Constantine V.

19. *Tagmata*

Elite, professional regiments stationed in and around Constantinople. Established by Constantine V, these forces were distinct from the thematic troops and served as the core of the emperor's personal military forces.

20. Eunomia

Literally 'good order' in Greek, eunomia referred to a social ideal where the state was governed by harmony, order, and adherence to law. Byzantine emperors often invoked eunomia as a goal of their rule.

21. Typikon

Monastic rulebooks or regulations often used to govern the organization of Byzantine monasteries. These documents sometimes reveal insights into the empire's theological and liturgical life, which was affected by Iconoclastic reforms.

22. Defensor

A minor church official tasked with defending the rights and property of the church. In Iconoclastic times, the defensor's role often involved protecting church holdings amidst changing policies.

23. Theophanes the Confessor
A Byzantine chronicler and prominent Iconophile whose accounts provide a primary source of information on Constantine V's reign. Theophanes' views were highly critical, shaping much of the negative perception of Constantine.

24. Monophysitism
A Christian heresy that held that Christ has only one nature, a divine one, rather than both a human and divine nature. This belief was distinct from Iconoclasm but contributed to doctrinal debates within the empire.

25. Synod
A formal council of church leaders to decide on ecclesiastical matters. Synods were crucial in Byzantium for setting doctrine, such as the Council of Hieria during Constantine V's reign.

26. Basilica
In Byzantine context, a large, important church building with a specific architectural style. Basilicas played a role in both public worship and the theological battles over iconography.

27. Emperor Leo IV (Leo the Khazar)
Constantine V's son and successor, who continued Iconoclastic policies but to a lesser degree than his father. His reign was short, and his marriage to Empress Irene set the stage for future shifts in imperial religious policy.

28. Empress Irene
Wife of Leo IV and regent for her son, Constantine VI, Irene ended the First Iconoclasm and supported the restoration of icon veneration, reversing Constantine V's policies at the Second Council of Nicaea in 787 CE.

29. Second Council of Nicaea (787 CE)
A council that overturned Iconoclastic decrees and restored the veneration of icons. This council marked the official end of the First Iconoclasm in Byzantium.

30. Akrites
Border guards stationed along the empire's frontier regions. The akrites became symbols of Byzantine resilience and cultural blending, embodying the empire's efforts to defend against external threats, particularly in the east.

Index